MODELLING FIGURES
for cake toppers

JACK
18

Julie Rogerson

MODELLING FIGURES
for cake toppers

THE CROWOOD PRESS

First published in 2022 by
The Crowood Press Ltd
Ramsbury, Marlborough
Wiltshire SN8 2HR

enquiries@crowood.com
www.crowood.com

British Library Cataloguing-in-Publication Data
A catalogue record for this book is available from the British Library.

ISBN 978 0 7198 4009 8

Cover design: Sergey Tsvetkov

Acknowledgements

As a self-confessed book lover, it is an absolute privilege to be in a position to be writing my own book, and I have a few people to acknowledge and thank, as they have certainly been instrumental in getting me to this point. I am going to start with my family, as they are my whole world.

The most influential person in my life growing up was most definitely my late mum, Joan Rogerson, and I like to think I have inherited some of her stubborn nature and strong determination, which have definitely helped me in more recent years with starting and running my own business. It is with such sadness to think that although she was instrumental in my love of baking, she knew nothing of my adventures through cake decorating, which have led me to this point. But I do like to think that she would have been very proud of what I have achieved.

It seems natural to move on to thanking my dad, Jim Rogerson, next. An absolute rock of a man, always there for me, no matter what, and a very big part of my life. Such a family man, you couldn't want for a better dad, and he has helped me through the bad times as well as the good. I hope I have made you proud, Dad.

Huge shoutout to my partner, Mark Wilde, who has taught me that I need to take chances and opportunities when they present themselves. 'We only get one shot at life, it is not a rehearsal!' is one of his favourite things to say to me (whilst I am being constantly indecisive), as well as 'If you want to, just do it'. He has certainly helped me to believe in myself, and I really owe him so much for bringing out the best in me. I should also take this opportunity to thank Mark for some of the photography in this book (as well as for a few of my other projects).

I think perhaps my greatest achievements to date have been my three fabulous children (in age order – no favouritism): Andrew Towse, Rachel Towse and Jack Towse. They have brought me so much joy, and now they are older, they are so supportive in my chosen path. I love their enthusiasm for my seemingly never-ending parade of 'Look what I have made!' cakes and cake toppers – as well as for eating the cake offcuts, of course. I am so proud of you all.

To Suzi Witt I owe a huge gratitude, for mentoring and coaching me to believe I can and will succeed in whatever I put my mind to, and to know that I am never too old to do something new. You inspire me to be the best version of myself every day, to which I am very grateful: thank you.

I must also thank Melanie Underwood for being the first person to give me the opportunity to have one of my cake-decorating tutorials published in *Cake International* magazine, back in 2017. She gave me the confidence to believe I could do it, and it has also been a pleasure working with her on several projects over the past few years at the Cake International Show.

To the staff at *Cake Decoration and Sugarcraft* magazine, for whom I still write cake-decorating tutorials. Leeanne Cooper (former editor) and Joanne Garwell, you have both been amazing to work with: thank you for your support.

Finally, I would like to thank the amazing team at The Crowood Press Ltd for getting this book off the ground, from concept and into print.

Graphic design and typesetting by Peggy & Co. Design
Printed and bound in India by Parksons Graphics

Contents

······

Introduction

As a cake decorator, whatever your skill level, and regardless of whether you make cakes as a hobby for family occasions or as a business owner, selling your creations to customers, you will probably have been asked to make a figure to be used as a cake topper at some point. Trust me, if you haven't yet, it won't be long, so prepare yourself!

Whether you are looking to create a figure to resemble the recipient of the cake, a cartoon-styled figure for a children's birthday cake, or even just a generic figure to compliment the theme, being able to create a person to put on a cake is most definitely a useful skill to have.

When you first start making models, particularly figures, it can be a daunting prospect, though I totally understand, I've been there too. Perhaps you have already tried without much success, or maybe you keep putting it off, as the thought just terrifies you?

What equipment do you need? There is such an array to choose from – how do you know what to buy, and maybe more importantly, what *not* to buy? Then there is the question of pastes: what is the difference between sugar paste and the other more specialist types of paste on the market? Which should you use? Why did your paste crack when you tried to model with it, or sag when you tried to stand it up?

Figures make very popular choices for cake toppers, especially when they are made to resemble the recipient of the cake, along with their favourite things.

◀ One of my absolute favourite figures that I have created to date was this pirate mermaid figurine for a display table at the Cake International Show in 2018. She was modelled entirely from modelling paste and modelling chocolate, with an internal armature. The table of pirate-themed exhibits was awarded first place in our category at the show, for a collective display by a group of international cake artists.

One of my very first figure models, which started me off on a journey of learning and discovery. I remember being so proud of it at the time, and had no idea where this new venture would take me.

I certainly remember thinking all of these things (and more besides) when I first started modelling figures back in my early days of cake decorating. I had many failed attempts, not really knowing where to go for help, as well as finding so many conflicting answers to my questions during my online searches. So I started to experiment, buying different pastes to test, seeing what worked and what didn't. I bought lots of different tools and gadgets, many of which were relegated to the back of a drawer when I found they didn't give me the results they had promised and that I wanted to achieve! But through this search, I narrowed it down to what I actually found worked.

The results of these trials, as well as years of practising and honing my modelling skills, are what you will find in this book, without having to go through the long experimental stages yourself. I will be sharing all my secrets, hints and tips with you, to save you money and shortcut your way to making fabulous figures. I will show you the basic set of tools that I use for all my models, as well as a few extras that are useful to have for more advanced modelling techniques. You will also find useful information about the different types of pastes available, and which is best to use for the different types of modelling.

This book will take you on a journey through figure modelling, beginning with creating the simpler styles of sitting and lying figures. These are the perfect starting point for those new to modelling, or if you just want to perfect your skills before advancing.

We will then move up a level, looking at how to make figures stand up on cakes, as well as introducing the techniques for adding some simple clothing to your models and more intricate facial details.

Finally we will explore figures with more complicated internal support armatures. These are fabulous for making sturdy figures in a variety of poses, especially useful for sporting and adventure-themed cakes. I will also show you how to fully dress a figure, including how to create your own templates. Through detailed instructions and full colour step-by-step photographs, I will guide you through everything you need to know, to start creating your own amazing cake toppers, which will delight and amaze your family, friends and customers alike.

For each model in the book there is also a finished cake design, giving you ideas and inspiration on how to use your models on a cake – but I am sure you will be able to come up with lots of your own ideas too.

So what are you waiting for? Let's get started…

Standing figures, often used as wedding-cake toppers, can also be used for a wide variety of other occasions.

A standing figure with internal armature support lends itself well to a whole range of sporting and action-themed cake designs.

Sitting or lying down figures make great cake toppers, are simple to create and a perfect introduction to modelling figures.

CHAPTER 1

Equipment Used for Figure Modelling

There is a huge range and choice of equipment and tools available on the market for modelling with edible pastes, and it can sometimes be hard to know what you actually need, particularly if you are new to cake decorating and sugar crafting. Start with a few basic tools, some of which you will probably already have, and then build up your tool box from there, depending on the types of model you want to make. In this chapter you will find the basics you need to start with, and also some more specialized tools that you may wish to use as you progress.

BASIC EQUIPMENT

The following tools would be a good starting point for your modelling tool kit as a beginner. You can then build on this kit with more specialized tools as you progress, and improve your skill set in this genre of cake decorating.

Non-stick workboard: Although not absolutely essential, a non-stick workboard gives you a really good surface to work on, and is easily cleaned. Place a non-slip mat underneath to stop it sliding around on your surface.

Sharp knife/scalpel: Both of these are useful to have, as they serve different purposes. You can use a small, sharp kitchen knife for cutting larger pieces of paste, whilst the scalpel is perfect for making small, precise cuts. Instead of a scalpel, you could use a small, sharp craft knife instead – just remember to keep it to use for your modelling work only.

Scissors: Ideally you would benefit from having two different pairs of scissors: general kitchen-style scissors for cutting your internal supports and templates, as well as a small sharp pair of scissors for making precise cuts in your paste.

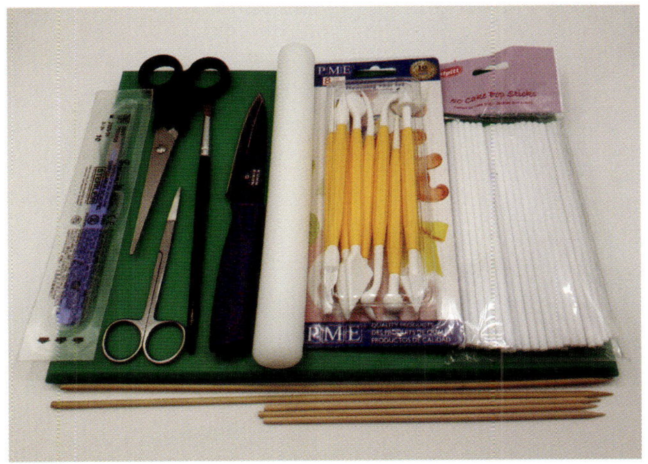

My suggested basic set of equipment that you will need in order to get started with modelling figures.

◀ There is a wide range of equipment that can be used for modelling work.

Paintbrushes: You will need to have a few different shapes and sizes of paintbrush, both for using with water or edible glue for sticking paste, as well as for dusting your models with edible dusts. New, clean make-up brushes are also suitable for using with your models. Soft, fluffy brushes are good for dusting cheeks, whereas thinner, flat brushes are good for dusting eyelids and lips. Very fine, precise brushes are good for adding thin lines of water to adhere eyelashes or eyebrows to faces. Make sure that any brushes you use have not been used for anything other than food-safe purposes. Keep a separate set, just for use with your modelling work.

Small rolling pin: A small, non-stick rolling pin is a 'must have' tool for rolling small pieces of paste, for example for clothing. As a cake decorator, you will most likely already have one of these anyway.

Internal supports: For small, basic models, you will still need some internal support, particularly for keeping the head in place. Whilst you can use dried spaghetti strands for support, it isn't always strong enough for heads, as they are too heavy for the thin pasta to cope with. I am speaking from experience here, after losing a few heads back in my early days of modelling! Instead, you could use cake pop sticks, as they are strong, food safe, and easy to cut to size with scissors. An alternative would be to use thin wooden skewers, as these are also food safe. These can be used for taller, standing figures, as the cake pop sticks are too short. Just be careful when cutting the skewers, as they can splinter.

Be sure always to tell the recipient about any internal supports that have been used within the figures you have made. I would never recommend that the models or figures I make should be eaten, but some people will do so anyway. However, they will need to be aware to dismantle the figure and remove any inedible supports before consuming.

Basic set of modelling tools: Modelling tools come in a wide range of sizes, shapes and materials, sold either in packs or individually. If you are new to modelling you would be best to choose a basic set of tools, such as the PME set in the photograph. This set contains a good selection of modelling tools you will need to get started with, and you can then add other individual tools as you need them. More detail about the different types of modelling tools, and what they are used for, will be given later in this chapter.

OTHER PIECES OF EQUIPMENT YOU MAY FIND USEFUL

Other equipment that you may want to add to your starter kit.

Metal ruler: Use to measure paste or to help you cut straight lines (for example for items of clothing/trims).

Pizza roller cutter: You may find it easier to cut strips of paste using a pizza roller cutter (either with or without the aid of a metal ruler).

Stitching tool: Roll along the paste to add a stitched detail effect for clothing. This small detail can add to the realism of your models, and is so simple to do.

Small plastic cutting wheel: This is a double-ended tool with two different sized cutting wheels. It is especially useful when using a non-stick workboard, to avoid scratching the surface, which you would do with a metal knife/cutter.

Small cake card/polystyrene cake dummy: You may find it easier to construct models and figures separately from the cake on a cake card or polystyrene dummy, adding them to the cake when they are complete. This helps to avoid accidentally damaging your cake whilst working on the figure. It also means you can make your figure in advance, ready to just transfer to the cake when required. The cake card is good when making sitting or lying figures for the top of cakes, whereas the dummy would be more useful for figures that will be sitting on the edge of a cake, as well as for standing figures.

Cornflour pouch: Sometimes when working with modelling paste or modelling chocolate, the paste can become a little sticky, especially if you have warm hands. Dabbing your hands with a little cornflour is very useful, to prevent the paste from sticking to you. You can also use a cornflour pouch to dust your work surface. You can buy different styles of cornflour pouches, or you can easily make your own.

Make Your Own Cornflour Pouch

To make your own cornflour pouch, use a square piece of muslin or cheesecloth (the style used for straining fruits in jam or wine making). Add some cornflour in the centre, then gather up the edges, securing with a piece of ribbon. You could store it in an empty cupcake case, or you could use a small plastic container.

How to make your own cornflour pouch.

MODELLING TOOLS

As mentioned earlier in this chapter, there is a wide variety of modelling tools available to buy, in addition to the basic modelling tool set. These include tools made from different materials, as well as specific tools to do a particular job, or to be used for a specialized technique. In this section I will introduce you to a few alternatives to the basic modelling tools, and explain how they differ.

Dresden Tool

This is quite possibly the tool that is most often used by cake decorators. It can be used for a wide variety of purposes, both for cake decorating and making models or figures. When making figures, it can be used for:

- texturing hair details
- marking detail on hands
- drawing and opening up details such as the mouth
- making creases for joints (elbow and knee)
- marking crease lines in clothing
- smoothing paste together
- creating and defining facial features

In the basic PME tool set, the Dresden tool is a double-ended tool made from plastic, with a narrow, pointy end and a wider, spoon-like end. However, there are other different styles of this tool available, depending on the manufacturer, and also other variants made from hard silicone or metal. Each does a broadly similar job, but personal preference can be a deciding factor as to which you choose. You may wish to have more than one style of Dresden tool to use for different texturing effects.

A wide array of modelling tool types and styles.

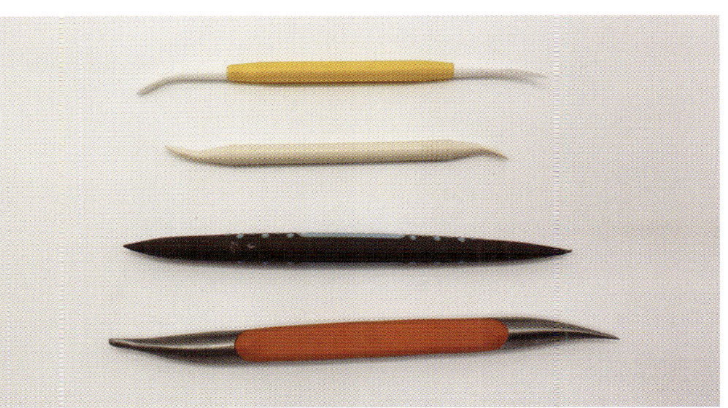

Different types/styles of the Dresden modelling tool.

Ball Tool

Again, this is a very popular type of modelling tool that is often used across a whole range of cake-decorating, flower-making and modelling projects. When modelling figures, the ball tool is used primarily to indent or hollow out paste (for example when creating eye sockets or sleeves in clothing, and when adding a neck into the body of simple figures). However, it is also useful for smoothing and blending pastes together.

The plastic ball tools can have a seam running around the centre, whereas the metal ball tools are generally seamless. This seam can cause issues with some decorating techniques, such as flower making, but on the whole it is not too much of a problem for figure making.

It is always a good idea to have at least two or three different sizes available to use, and they often come in sets of assorted sizes. The double-ended ball tools usually have a small and a large end, such as the one from the PME set, which are useful for when you are starting out. The metal ball tools are often bought as a set of double-ended tools with varying sizes, which are ideal for using on modelling projects.

Another type of ball tool that I use for figure making is the very tiny nail art-style ball tool. The fine point on these is ideal for marking in nostrils, and also for painting on a dot of white paint for highlights in eyes.

Silicone-Tipped Modelling Tools

Silicone-tipped modelling tools are particularly useful for more advanced figure making, in particular for making more detailed faces. The hard-tipped, pointy tools are good for making nostrils, drawing eye outlines and marking mouth openings.

The softer-tipped tools are excellent for smoothing, blending and drawing softer lines on the face, as well as defining the lips and nose. Although these can be also be done with a Dresden tool, you need to be more careful not to leave hard lines behind on the paste. The softer silicone-tipped tools can be used very gently on the paste, for more subtle definition.

Other Modelling Tools/Tool Sets

You can also find lots of other modelling tools out there, with new sets being released on a regular basis, as new variations and techniques for modelling are developed. These tools range in price, are made from different materials, and include different-shaped tips. They can be multi-functional, used for a variety of techniques for both general cake-decorating projects and model/figure making. As skills and new techniques are developed over the years, there will always be new products to look at and consider using, to improve your results.

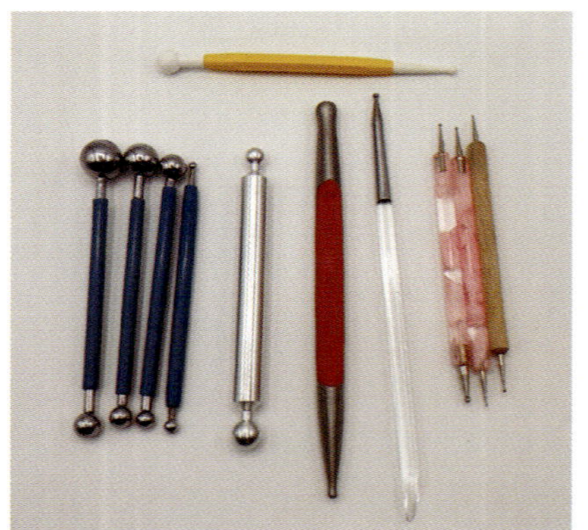

A selection of ball tools.

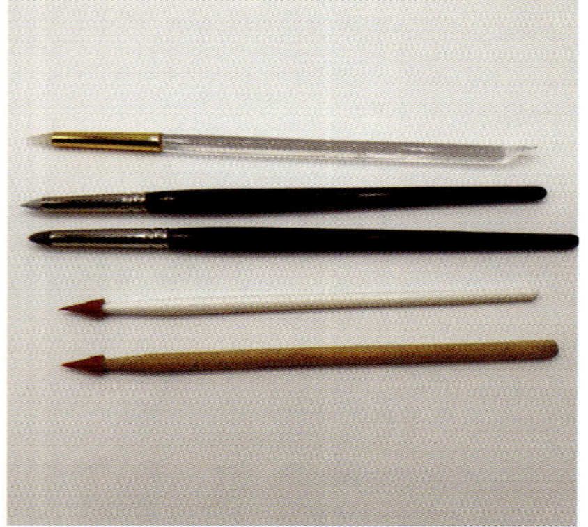

A range of silicone-tipped modelling tools.

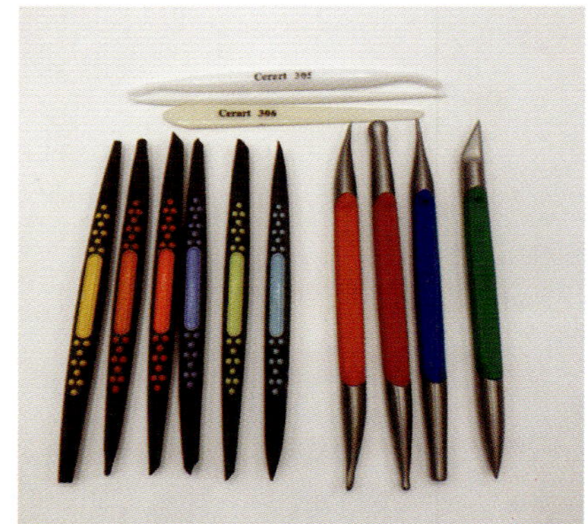

Other modelling tools and tool sets.

EQUIPMENT TO CREATE TEXTURE AND EMBELLISHMENTS WHEN DRESSING YOUR FIGURES

There is a wide range of products designed for cake decorating, which can also be used for adding more details, and creating embellishments for your figures. Here is a selection of products that you may want to consider using. Some you may already have, but may not have thought about using in this way.

Creating texture: Either textured impression mats (silicone or flexible plastic) or textured rolling pins can be used to add texture to your paste; this is particularly useful when making clothing for your figure.

Creating embellishments: Silicone moulds can be used to easily create detailed embellishments such as bows or flowers. Geometric and flower-shape cutters are really useful for creating necklines, collars and sleeves for clothing. Very tiny shaped cutters can also be used to imprint a pattern on to clothing.

TOOLS AND EQUIPMENT FOR MAKING INTERNAL ARMATURES

For larger figures, or for figures that require gravity-defying features or poses, you will need to create an internal armature to support the paste. There are a variety of ways to do this, but the equipment and tools that I use in this book are as follows.

Floral/florist wire and tape: Florist wire is referred to by a number gauge. The numbers refer to the thickness of the wire: the larger the number, the thinner the wire. Florist wires tend to range between the thickest 16-gauge down to 32-gauge, which are the finest wires. I use two different gauges within the same armature, 16-gauge and 18-gauge. These are strong enough to support the paste, but flexible enough to bend into the desired shape position, either by hand or with the help of pliers. The wires are held together with floral tape. I tend to use full width, white tape. When using the tape, you need to stretch it gently to release the adhesive, before wrapping it round the wires.

Pliers: Because of the thickness of the wires, especially when taped together in pairs, you will need pliers to cut through them. The pliers can also be used for bending the wires to shape if it is too difficult to do this by hand.

Polystyrene cake dummy: The ends of the wires in the internal armature are inserted into the polystyrene, to keep it stable whilst you work on it. It also leaves both of your hands free for the modelling process, whilst adding the paste to the structure.

Hollow cake dowels: These are used to insert the ends of the wires into, before putting them into the cake. Because the wires and tape are not food safe, they must not come into contact with the cake. You could also use flower picks, but I find the dowels better, because they can easily be cut to the correct length. Sometimes the flower picks are too short to give enough stability to the figure when it is added to your cake.

Equipment for creating texture for clothing.

Equipment that can be used to create details and embellishments for your figures.

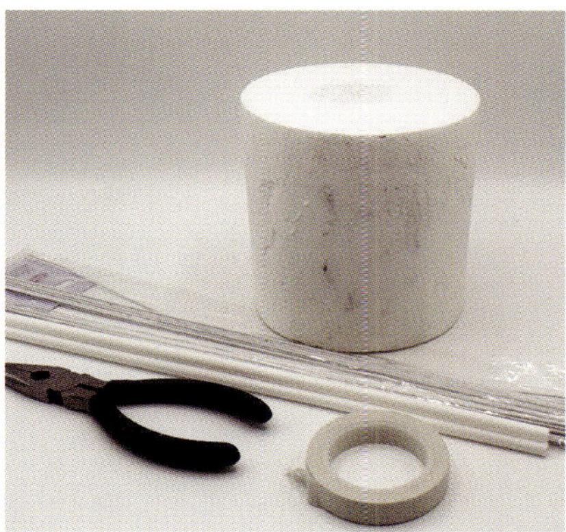

Tools and equipment to use when creating internal armatures for your figures.

CHAPTER 2

Materials Used for Figure Modelling

The paste that you choose to use for your modelling projects depends on the size, style and complexity of the piece you are trying to make, as well as your own personal preference.

TYPES OF PASTE TO USE

Sugar Paste (Fondant)

Sugar paste (fondant) is widely used as a covering for decorated cakes, and is available in white, or there is a large range of pre-coloured pastes. Although sugar paste (fondant) is quite soft, you can use it for small pieces of simple modelling. Simply mix it with a little Tylose powder (or CMC) to enable the paste to dry firm. The ratio to use is ¼ teaspoon of powder mixed with 250g of sugar paste. For smaller quantities of paste, just sprinkle a pinch of powder on to the paste and knead to mix through.

Advantages:

- Sugar paste (fondant) tends to be a cheaper option.
- It is more widely available – you can just use your regular brand that you buy for covering cakes.
- Available in white, as well as in a wide range of colours and shades.
- Can be coloured with gel/paste colours.

Disadvantages:

- The paste is soft, so you may need to allow the piece to dry in stages to avoid the model 'sagging'.
- The paste is likely to dry out quite quickly, which can cause cracking.
- You cannot re-work details, as the paste will have dried.

You could also use a 50:50 mix of sugar paste (fondant) with flower paste (gum paste) to make a firmer paste for modelling with, in a similar way to adding the Tylose or CMC powders.

Different types of paste that can be used for modelling work.

Tylose (or CMC) powder can be added to sugar paste (fondant) for simple modelling work.

Flower Paste (Gum Paste)

Flower paste is not particularly advisable to use for making full models, although you can use it for smaller items, such as accessories for figures, that you wish to dry very firm. You can also use it for making clothing to dress your figure, as it can be rolled very thinly, and dries quickly so it holds its shape. It can also be added to sugar paste (fondant) to create a simple modelling paste, using a 50:50 mix.

Advantages:

- Flower paste (gum paste) can be rolled very thinly for clothing and holds its shape.
- Great for modelling small items and accessories that need to dry hard.
- Can be coloured with gel/paste colours.

Disadvantages:

- The paste dries very quickly, which can cause cracking, so you need to work fast.
- You cannot re-work details, as the paste will have dried.
- When rolled thinly, the paste dries very brittle, so needs to be handled carefully.

Modelling Paste

For figure modelling you would definitely be advised to use specialist modelling paste, particularly for the more detailed areas, such as heads and limbs. These modelling pastes smooth and blend together more easily, due to the addition of cocoa butter to the paste. They also harden without drying, so remain malleable for longer periods, which enables you to go back and adjust/refine details as you work.

Modelling pastes are mostly commonly available in white, which you can colour as required (*see* the colouring paste section on page 20). They are often available to buy in different sized packs, depending on the brand, which makes them suitable for those who don't do much modelling, through to professional cake makers who make a lot of models.

Some brands also offer a range of pre-coloured modelling pastes, which are particularly useful for achieving consistent colours, such as for colours you use quite often. They are also ideal for stronger/darker shades, such as red and black, which are difficult to colour yourself. These pre-coloured pastes can be mixed together to achieve different colours and tones, and can also be added to white paste to make paler shades.

Advantages:

- Very good for fine detail work.
- The paste blends well where it joins, giving seams that are barely noticeable.
- Supports itself and stays in shape, so you can work on a model from start to finish, without waiting for parts to dry or firm up.
- Some brands are available in a number of different colours.
- White paste can be coloured with gel/paste colours.
- It can be rolled very thinly – ideal for clothing on figures.

Disadvantages:

- It is not as widely available in retail outlets – mostly from online cake supply companies.
- It is a little more expensive than sugar paste.

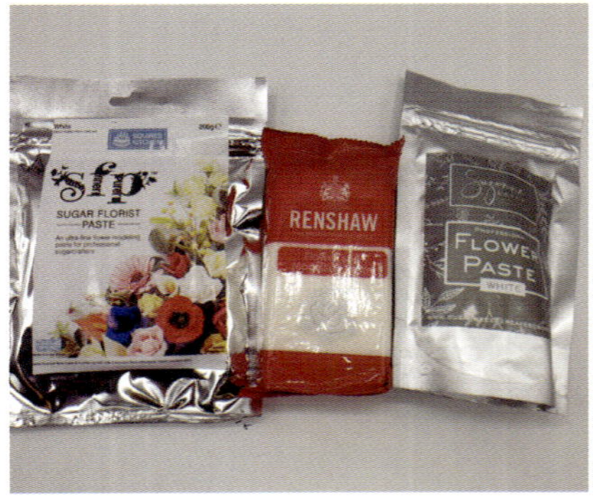

Flower paste, or gum paste as it is also known, dries very quickly, so is not often used for modelling, except for small pieces.

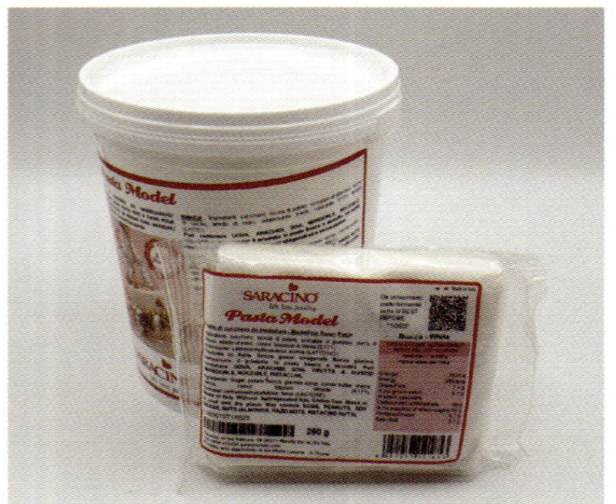

Commercially available white modelling paste is my recommendation to use for modelling, particularly for figures.

Commercially available pre-coloured modelling pastes are great to use, as you don't need to add any other products to colour them.

- It can be quite firm to start with, so may need quite a bit of kneading to soften it.
- It can soften too much whilst working, particularly if you have warm hands, or if you overwork the paste.

There are a number of commercially made modelling pastes available, and I would highly recommend you try different brands to find the one that works best for you. Some pastes are firmer than others, and different brands will have varying ratios of sugar to cocoa butter. If you do find that the paste becomes too soft as you work due to the cocoa butter content, just leave it for a few minutes until it firms back up enough for you to continue.

Throughout the projects in this book I use Saracino modelling paste (Pasta Model), as it is my preferred brand to use and works well for me. I have tried others that are also good, but this is just my personal preference. The commercial modelling pastes can be quite firm when first taken out of the packet, but once you have kneaded them, they soften into a more pliable consistency.

Modelling and Sculpting Chocolate

Although it is used to achieve a similar effect, modelling chocolate is very different to modelling paste in that it is essentially chocolate, with added syrups to soften it. The higher ratio of chocolate/cocoa butter makes it more susceptible to heat or warm hands. You can make modelling chocolate yourself, or buy commercially produced products.

Modelling chocolate and sculpting chocolate can also be used for modelling figures.

Sculpting chocolate contains more sugar than cocoa butter, so is a little easier to work with for some people. As with the modelling paste, these products tend to be very hard when first removed from the packaging, but soon soften as you knead them, and are then very pliable to work with.

Advantages:

- Very good for fine detail work.
- The paste blends extremely well where it joins, giving seams that are barely noticeable.
- Supports itself and stays in shape, so you can work on a model from start to finish without having to wait for parts to dry/firm up.
- Some brands are available in a number of different colours.
- White paste can be coloured with gel/paste colours.

Disadvantages:

- It is not as widely available in retail outlets – mostly from online cake supply companies.
- It is a little more expensive than sugar paste.
- It can be quite firm to start with, so may need quite a bit of kneading to soften.
- It can soften too much whilst working, particularly if you have warm hands, or if you overwork the paste.

As mentioned earlier, it is good to try out a few different pastes, to see which you prefer to work with, as we are all different and have our own preferences.

COLOURING YOUR MODELLING PASTE

Colouring White Modelling Paste

When colouring white paste it is important to use a concentrated gel or paste colouring. The more colour that is added to the paste, the more it will affect its consistency. Using these concentrated colours will allow you to achieve a good strength of colour whilst only adding a small amount of the product. Start by adding a very small amount of colour to your white paste – it is easier to add more colour to achieve your desired shade than it is to lighten it if you have added too much.

These colourings come in a very wide range of colours and shades, but if you have a basic set of colours you can still mix different shades by using two or more colours – for example, using red and yellow to make orange.

If you wish to achieve a very strong or dark colour (such as red or black), it would always be best to buy pre-coloured paste, as it is difficult to colour these yourself without compromising the consistency of your paste.

Making Different Colours with Pre-Coloured Paste

If you have a selection of different pre-coloured pastes you can use them to achieve a whole spectrum of colours. You can add white to pre-coloured paste to lighten the colour (tint), black to darken the colour (shade), or mix two colours together to create a different colour altogether. For example, in the photograph you will see how adding black, white or yellow will change the original green, pre-coloured paste.

By mixing pre-coloured pastes together you don't risk changing the consistency by introducing additional products, such as gel/paste colours. This is particularly useful when trying to achieve darker shades.

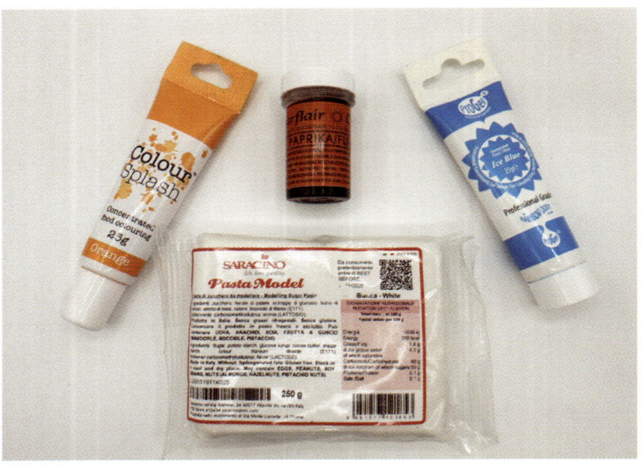

Colouring your white paste.

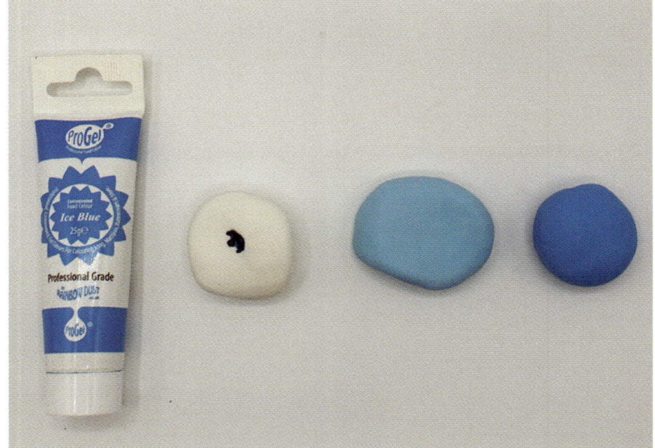

Use more or less of the concentrated colour to adjust the intensity of the colour for your paste.

Creating different tints, shades and colours with your pre-coloured paste.

Creating Different Skin Tones

When using the pre-coloured skin-tone paste you can adjust this colour by adding either gel/paste colours or brown pre-coloured paste. Varying the amount that you add will change the resulting shade.

Adding a tiny amount of paprika/skin-tone concentrated paste colour gives you more of a peachy-coloured paste.

Adding varying amounts of pre-coloured brown paste to the skin-tone paste will give you a range of skin-tone colours. In the photograph the following amounts of brown paste were added to 5g of pre-coloured skin-tone paste: 0.25g, 0.5g, 1g, 2g, 5g, 10g.

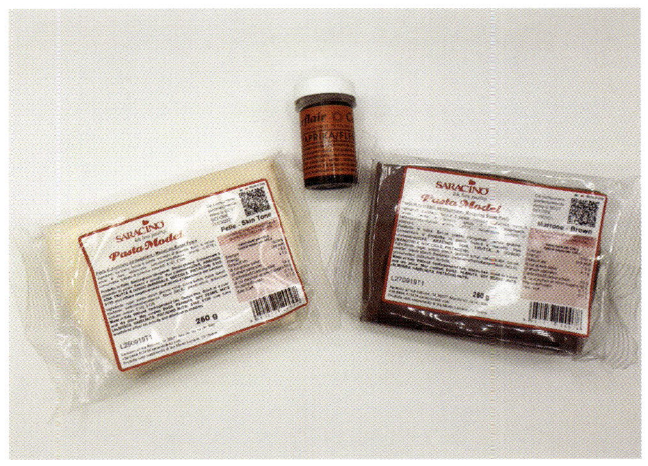
Creating different skin tones using pre-coloured paste.

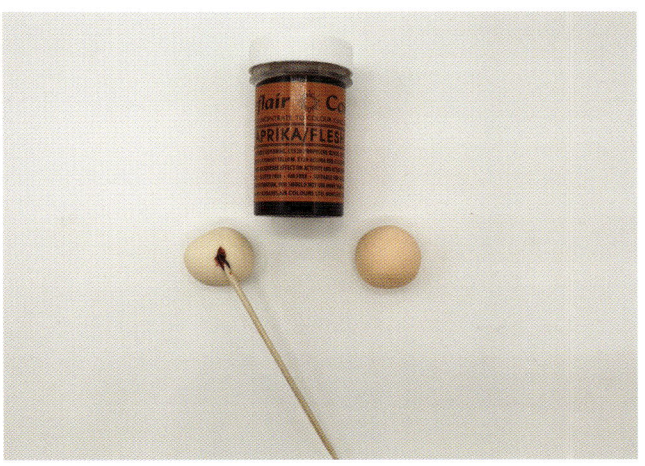
Adding concentrated paste colour.

Adding pre-coloured brown paste.

OTHER MATERIALS YOU MAY FIND USEFUL FOR FIGURE MODELLING

As well as the modelling pastes, there is a variety of other materials that you may find you will need to use whilst making your models.

Edible Glue

Water is often good enough for sticking paste together when modelling, but sometimes, especially with larger pieces, you may want to use edible glue for extra strength. You can buy commercially produced edible glue, but it is very easy (and much cheaper) to make your own, using Tylose powder and water.

Making Your Own Edible Glue

Making your own edible glue is quick and easy to do. Add a pinch of Tylose or CMC Powder to two tablespoons of cooled, boiled water, and allow to stand for a few minutes. Stir together with a clean paintbrush, or fork to combine fully. The edible glue should be of a pouring, syrup consistency. If it is too thick, add a tiny amount of water at a time until the correct consistency is achieved. Edible glue can be stored in an airtight container for approximately one week, or for up to three weeks in the fridge.

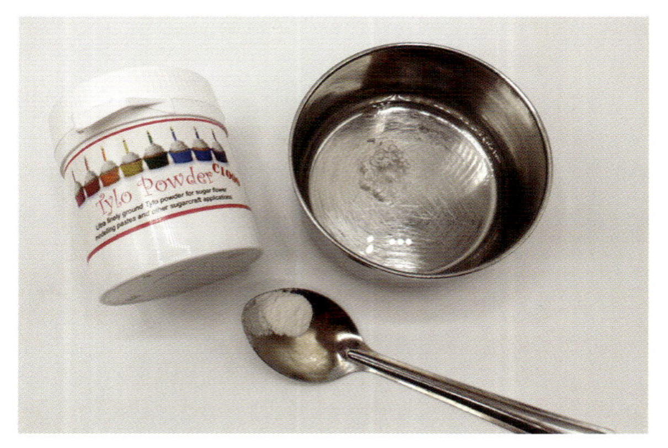

A range of other materials you may need to use whilst modelling figures.

Dried Spaghetti Strands

You can use small pieces of dried spaghetti for internal support in your figures, particularly for joining limbs to the body. They are considered as edible supports, but be sure to inform whoever is receiving the figure, so they can be removed if they intend to eat the model. I tend to use a stronger support for heads, but if you wish to use dried spaghetti, it would be advisable to use two or three strands together for additional strength, to support the weight of the head.

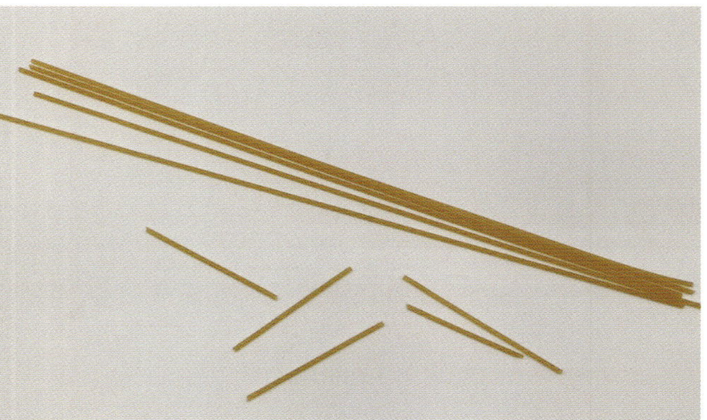

Use dried spaghetti to add support if this is needed.

Black Sugar Pearls

These small black sugar pearls are available to buy in various sizes, and make really easy eyes for simple figures. I tend to use either 4mm or 7mm black sugar pearls, depending on the size of the model. Alternatively you can, of course, use small pieces of black paste rolled into balls instead.

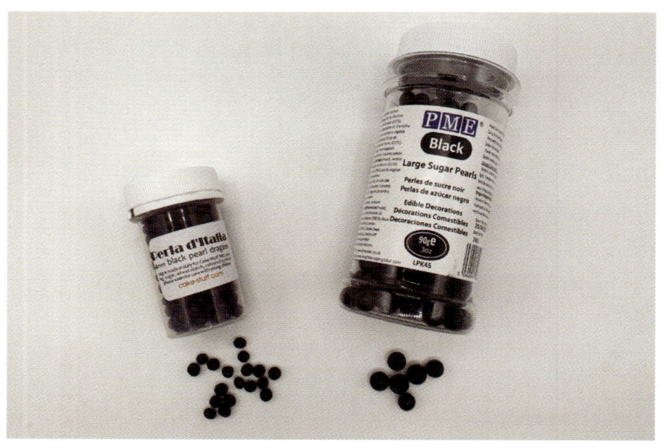

Black sugar pearls can be used for eyes in very simple styled models.

Confectioner's Glaze

Confectioner's glaze can be applied to modelling paste to give a shiny effect. For example, it is really effective when added to shoes, to give a polished look. Apply two to three thin coats, allowing them to dry in between.

Some of the smaller bottles of confectioner's glaze come with a brush in the lid, but if you use a separate paintbrush, be sure to clean it with a glaze cleaner when you have finished. You can also get spray glaze in an aerosol can, but this is more useful for using on larger areas, rather than figures.

Confectioner's glaze is good for adding shine to features of your model.

Edible Marker Pens

These pens come in an array of colours, and are great for adding fine detail to your figures. They are particularly useful for drawing on eyebrows and adding highlights to eyes, although they do have many other uses, too.

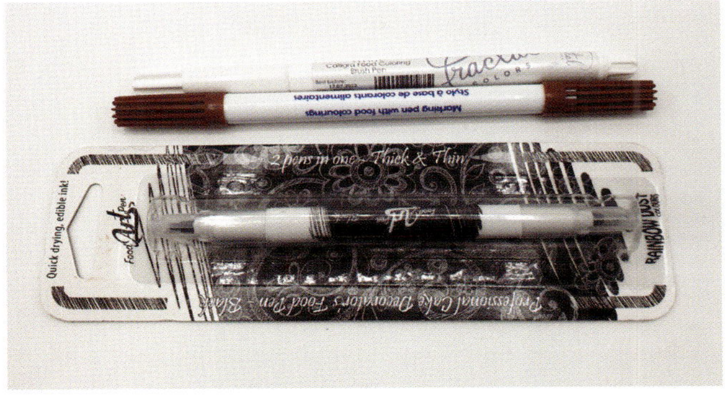

Edible marker pens are great for adding fine details to your figures.

Edible Paints

Edible paints can be used to create extra details for your models. You can use them on clothing for patterns, for facial details, or even for metallic accents on buckles. Ready-made edible paints are available from a variety of different brands, in both matt and metallic finishes. These are convenient, as they are the correct consistency to be used straight from the bottle. You can make your own edible paints by mixing rejuvenator fluid or dipping solution with edible dusts. You can also mix dusts with a clear alcohol, such as Vodka, although these do not dry as quickly.

Petal Dusts

Edible petal dusts (often used in sugar-flower making) can be applied to your models with a dry brush, to add colour to cheeks and lips. They can also be used to add more detailed make-up if desired; they can be mixed with white vegetable fat (such as Trex) to make a lipstick for adding extra colour to lips.

It is useful to have a selection of pinks available, as well as other neutral colours. A variety of different brands are available, each offering a good range of colours and shades to choose from. Darker colours of dust can be mixed with a little cornflour to achieve a slightly lighter shade. This can be particularly useful when adding a slight blush to cheeks.

Peta dusts are useful for adding colour to cheeks and lips, as well as for eye make-up.

Edible paints are readily available to buy ready made, in small bottles, in a wide selection of matt or metallic colours. It is also possible to make them yourself, using petal dusts mixed with either rejuvenator fluic, dipping solution or clear alcohol.

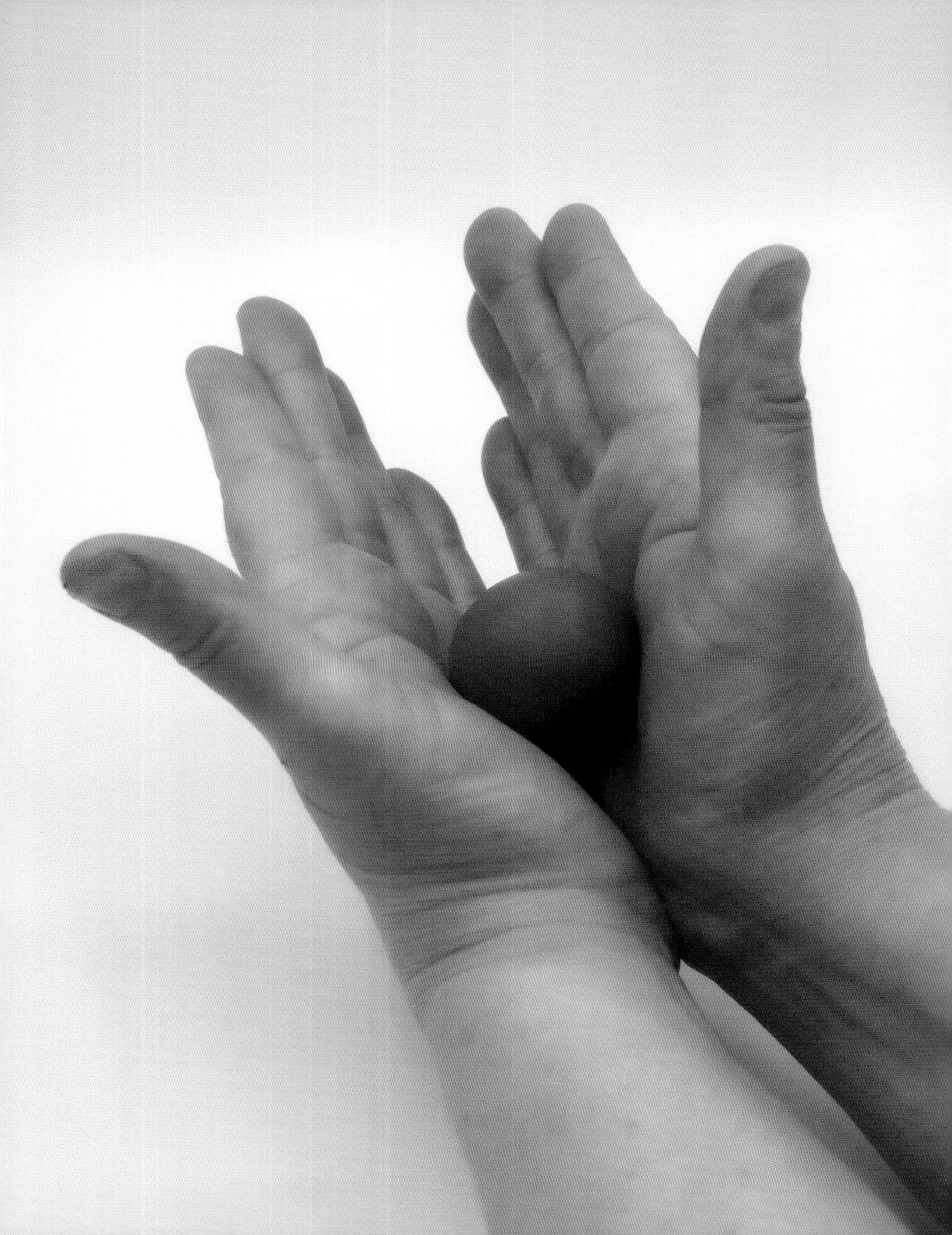

CHAPTER 3

Basic Shapes and Proportions Used for Figure Modelling

SHAPES

During the modelling process, regardless of whether you are making figures or other models, each piece tends to start off as one of four basic shapes. These basic shapes are then altered and refined by shaping them further with your hands or tools, transforming them into different parts of the body and/or other items.

Ball Shape

All shapes in modelling start off as a ball. They will vary in size, depending on what you are creating, but will always start out being rolled into a ball. After kneading your paste to soften it, roll it around between the palms of your hands in a circular motion. As well as creating the shape, this movement, in addition to the warmth of your hands, will help to smooth the surface of your paste, removing cracks or creases. You may find that you still have a few small, fine creases, but these can easily be placed to the bottom of the shape, so they remain hidden from view.

Once you have a smooth ball shape, you can either then go on to shape it into one of the following other basic shapes, or use it as it is, depending on the item you are working on. For example, when creating figures, ball shapes can be used as heads if you are working with a more cartoon-style character, or a small child/baby figure.

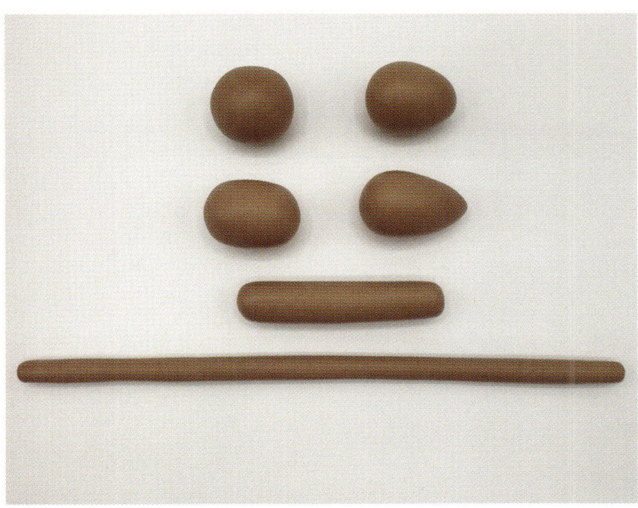

The basic shapes needed for modelling figures.

Everything in modelling starts with a ball shape.

Egg or Cone Shape

Starting with a smooth, ball-shaped piece of paste, cup your hands together to make a V-shape and gently roll the ball backwards and forwards in your hands. This will start to elongate the ball at one end. By varying the positioning of your hands, as well as the pressure you apply to the paste, you can create a pointed cone or a more rounded egg shape, depending on the result you want to achieve.

You can also make the shape on a workboard, by positioning your hand at a 45-degree angle to the ball of paste, and just rolling your palm backwards and forwards across the top of one half of the ball. The cone shape can be further elongated into a teardrop or carrot shape if required, by continuing to roll the pointed end longer and thinner.

When creating figures, cone or egg shapes can be used for making bodies, ears or hair, for example.

Oval Shape

An oval shape is made by rolling a smooth ball-shaped piece of paste gently backwards and forwards, either between your hands (held in a straight position) or on your workboard. You don't need to apply much pressure to make an oval: you need to keep it still rounded, otherwise it will turn into more of a sausage or rope shape.

When creating figures, ovals can be used for heads, noses (for simple faces), ears or bodies.

Making a ball into an egg or cone shape.

Making a ball into an oval shape.

Sausage or Rope Shape

You can continue to shape an oval piece of paste into a sausage or rope shape, varying the length and thickness of the shape to suit the purpose. Just keep rolling the shape back and forth on the workboard with your hand, or you may prefer to use a smoother if you struggle to get an even shape. As the shape elongates (for example, as for a rope), you will need to use both hands or two smoothers to ensure a consistent thickness to the shape.

When creating figures, these shapes are often used for arms and legs. Tiny strands can be rolled for using as eyebrows or eyelashes, narrowing one end slightly to a point.

If you want to roll out a thin rectangle of paste, perhaps to use as a trim on clothing for your figure, roll your paste into a sausage or rope shape first, then roll it out as a rectangle with your rolling pin.

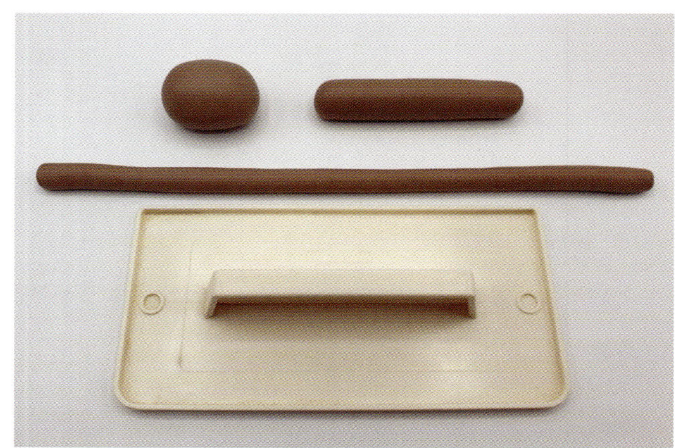

Making a ball into a sausage or rope shape.

PROPORTIONS

When modelling figures, it is particularly important to pay attention to the proportions of bodies and faces, as this can make a huge difference in the finished look of your model. Getting the proportions wrong – for example, making the body too short, or putting the eyes in the wrong position on the face – will make your figure look odd. A few simple adjustments to the sizing and placement will really improve the look of your figures.

Figure Proportions

As people, we all vary greatly in height and body shape, but as a rough guide to keeping the proportions of your figure more realistic, you can use the guides given here. These are very basic and generalized measurements that are often used when drawing figures, but apply equally well to modelling and sculpting figures. They work by using the size of the head as a measurement against the rest of the body.

These guides are useful for making generic figures, but if you are modelling your figure on an actual person, it will be helpful to get a full-length photo of them to use as an additional check. Proportions vary according to whether you are making an adult, a child or a baby, so I have separated them out in the guides.

Adult Proportions

An adult figure, on average, tends to be measured as approximately seven-and-a-half to eight heads high, as shown in the diagram – the difference being that using the eight-head example will give the figure slightly longer legs. Some key measurements, using this guide, are as follows:

- Three heads down from the top of the figure is the navel (belly button), which aligns with the elbow.
- Four heads down aligns with the pubic bone/hip joint area.
- Six heads down aligns with the knees.

Child Proportions

When modelling the figure of a child you will need to consider their approximate age, as their proportions change as they get older, with their heads becoming smaller in relation to the rest of their body. For example, the illustration shows the proportions for a child between five and six years of age, whose total height is approximately five heads. Some key measurements, using this guide, are as follows:

- Two heads down from the top of the figure is the elbow joint.
- Three heads down aligns with the pubic bone/hip joint area.
- Four heads down aligns with the knees.

Younger Child/Infant Proportions

The proportions for a younger child (or infant) reflect their much larger head in relation to the rest of their body. In this example, the total height is made up of just four heads, with the following key measurement points:

- Two heads down aligns with the navel (belly button) area.
- Three heads down aligns with the knees.

These guides are useful when wishing to achieve a more realistic figure with your work. If you are looking to create a cartoon or caricature effect, these will normally have a larger head in proportion to the rest of the body.

Head and Facial Feature Proportions

The first thing to consider is that heads are not oval shaped, they are more of an egg shape, with the chin area being narrower than the forehead. In a female head the chin tends to be more pointed, whereas a male head has a more angular jawline, with a flatter chin. When it comes to creating faces for your figure models, it is important to understand the basic principles of where features are situated on a face. Getting this correct will make a real difference in the finished piece.

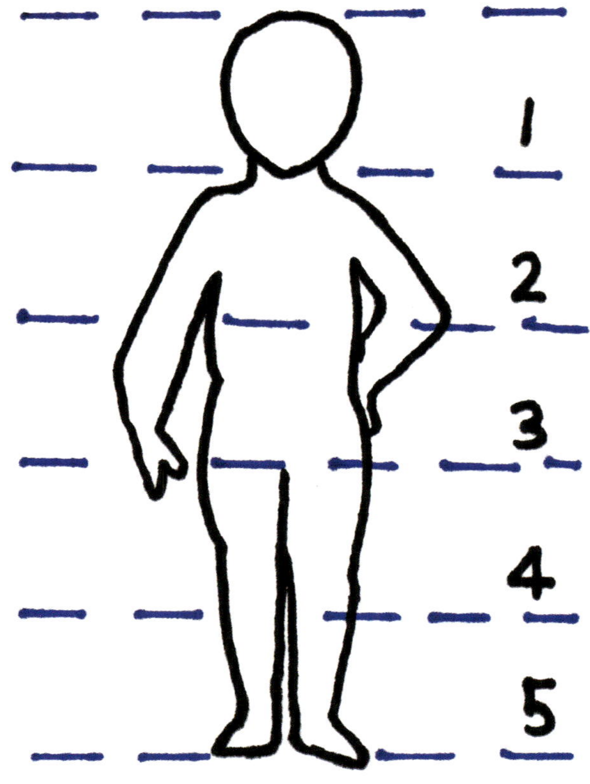

Average proportions guide for a child.

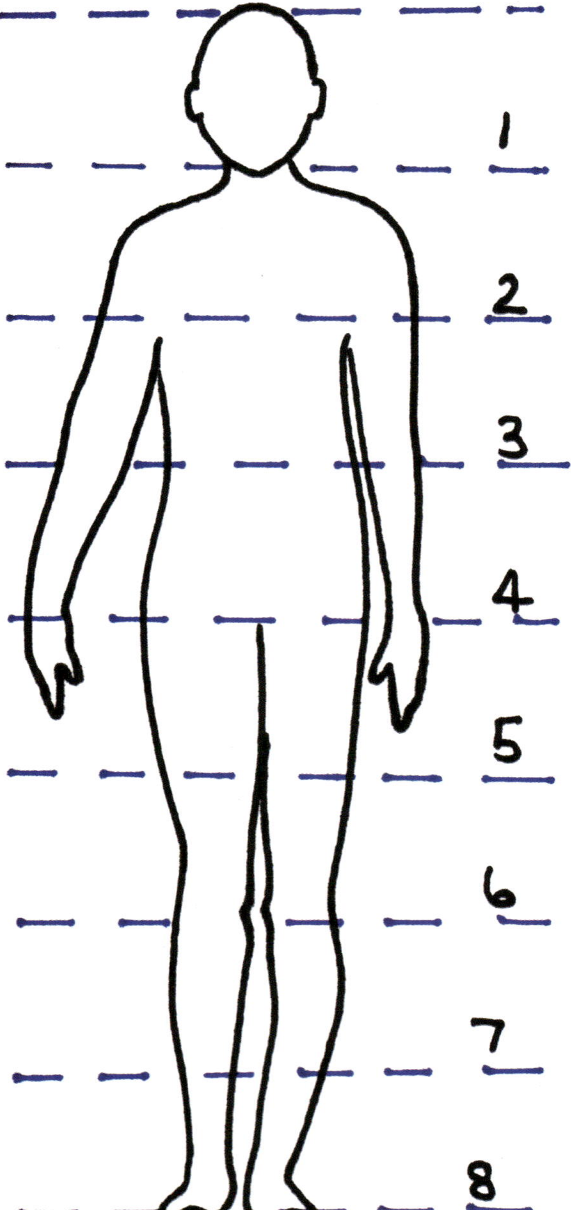

Average proportions guide for an adult figure.

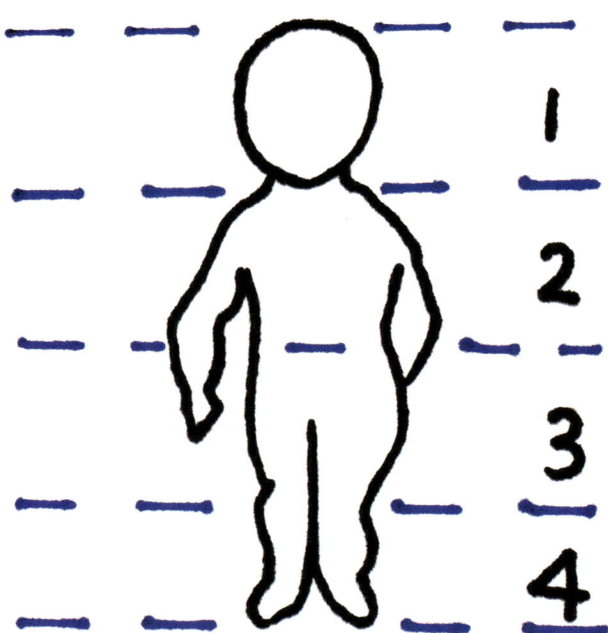

Average proportions guide for a younger child/infant.

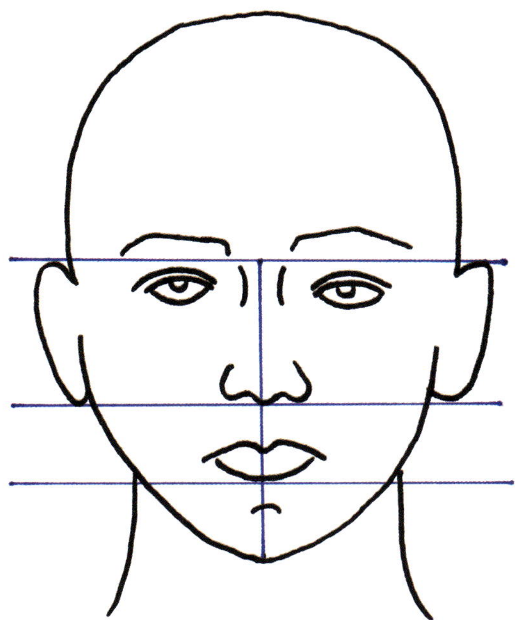

A guide to the positioning of facial features.

The diagram shows the placement of key facial features, which will help to give a more realistic look to a figure. This will vary slightly depending on the age of the subject, but in general, the following principles apply.

The eyes: Although the eyes are the highest feature on the face, they are situated just below the halfway point of the face, as measured between the top of the head and the bottom of the jaw. The most common error is placing the eyes too high up, which really does give the face a peculiar look. As a rule, the head is five eyes wide, so the gap between the eyes is about the same width as the eye itself. This is obviously very general, and will be different for individuals, but it is a good reference point to consider when figure making.

The nose: The bottom of the nose sits at the halfway point for the lower half of the face (between the eyes and the chin). The width and shape of the nose can vary greatly from person to person, so this will need to be considered, depending on the look you are going for. Male noses tend to be larger and a little more prominent, with a wider nasal base, whereas the female nose is more often small and slender, with more delicate features.

The mouth: The bottom lip sits at the halfway point between the bottom of the nose and the bottom of the chin. Giving more detailed definition to the top lip will make the face look more feminine.

The ears: Generally, the tops of the ears should be positioned slightly above the tops of the eyes, with the bottom of the ears in line with the bottom of the nose. Again, ear shapes and sizes are very different from one person to the next, so there is no hard and fast rule for this.

Other Useful Ways of Learning About Proportion

A very useful piece of equipment to have to hand is an artist's mannequin. These wooden figures can be positioned in different poses and are very useful for referring to. The small (mini) version is approximately 15cm (6in) tall, making it a good size to use when modelling cake toppers. Other useful sources of information are books and online tutorials for figure pencil drawings, as well as sculpting. They contain a lot of information and advice for proportions and poses, as well as covering different facial expressions and tips for making your faces look more masculine or feminine. Another reliable way of getting those proportions correct is to use a photograph of yourself (or the person you are replicating), scaled to the size of model you want to create. Refer to this for sizing and the placement of features whilst you make the figure.

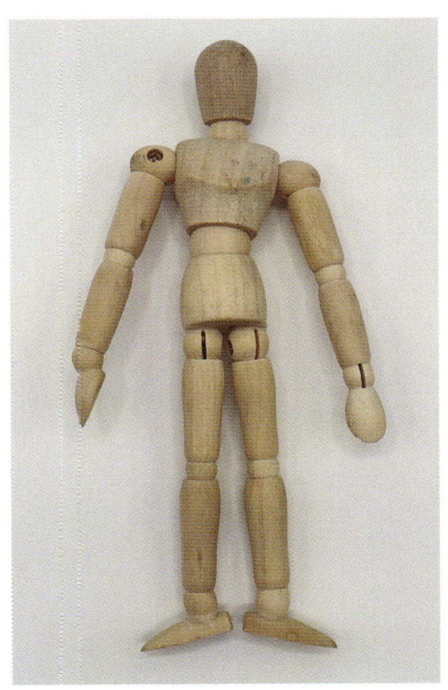

A small wooden artist's mannequin.

CHAPTER 4

Male Figure in Sitting Pose

When first starting out with modelling figures, or when making figures for use on simple cake projects, sitting or lying down figures are the best choice. These particular styles of model, when combined with fairly simple facial features, are quick to make, which is ideal when making cost-effective commercial cake toppers, for customer cakes. Their cute cartoon style is particularly well suited for children's cakes. They need minimal internal support, and are made using the basic modelling shapes, as discussed in Chapter 3 of this book.

Attaching them to your cake is simple, as the supports that are used are completely food safe, meaning they can be inserted straight into your cake. A little royal icing can be used underneath a model to keep it securely in place. Just be careful not to use too much, as it can squash out from underneath when you press it down.

These easy-to-make styles of sitting or lying-down figures make a perfect choice for those first starting out in figure modelling. They can easily be restyled with different coloured clothing, hair styles/colours and so on, to create a whole range of different characters. Add different accessories to theme with your cake to create a more detailed cake topper.

◀ This sitting footballer figure, complete with football scarf and mini football, is simple to create, and would make the perfect cake topper for any football fan's cake. It could also be made to sit over the edge of a cake, by bending his legs at the knee.

SITTING FOOTBALLER FIGURE

Using basic modelling tools and techniques, this footballer figure is very simple and quick to make, and would make a great addition to any sports-themed cake. It can easily be changed to the recipient's favourite team or club colours and kit. You could also change the football to a rugby ball or other sports-themed equipment to accessorize the figure.

This model is used as a cake topper on a 15cm (6in) round cake, covered in green sugar paste, sitting on a 25cm (10in) round, covered cake drum. The figure is secured to the cake with a small amount of royal icing, before edging the cake and cake drum with 15mm-wide ribbon.

Making the Sitting Footballer Figure

Equipment

- small rolling pin
- sharp knife
- scalpel
- ball tools (variety of sizes)
- Dresden tool
- smile tool
- metal ruler
- small, sharp scissors
- 10mm circle cutter
- number cutter (optional)
- paintbrushes for water and for dusting cheeks
- cake pop stick for supporting the head (or use a wooden skewer)

Materials

- 70g skin-tone modelling paste
- 120g white modelling paste
- 40g red modelling paste
- 40g black modelling paste
- pink petal dusts for cheeks (I used Fractal Kitty Nose Pink)
- 2 × 4mm black sugar pearls (optional)

For this sitting figure we will start by making the legs first, and then work our way up the body to finish with the head.

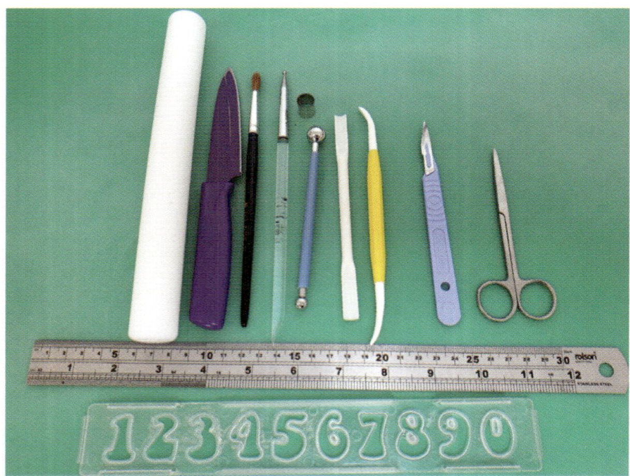

A basic tool set and general cake-decorating equipment is all that is required to make this simple sitting footballer figure, with a couple of optional extras to add further detail if you want to.

I used ready coloured Saracino modelling paste in skin tone, white, red and black to create this model. You can substitute the red and white paste for different colours to match with a specific team or club kit if you prefer.

Making the Legs

Start by rolling 20g of skin-tone coloured modelling paste into a smooth ball, then into an even-sized sausage shape, measuring approximately 12cm (4.7in) in length. Cut in half with a sharp knife, using a gentle sawing action so as not to distort the shape.

Place your little finger 1cm down from the top of each leg, and gently rock it backwards and forwards. This will create a slight indentation, which will form the knee area. Gently bend the leg at a 45-degree angle, and squeeze the top and bottom of the knee area gently between your fingers and thumbs to define the angle.

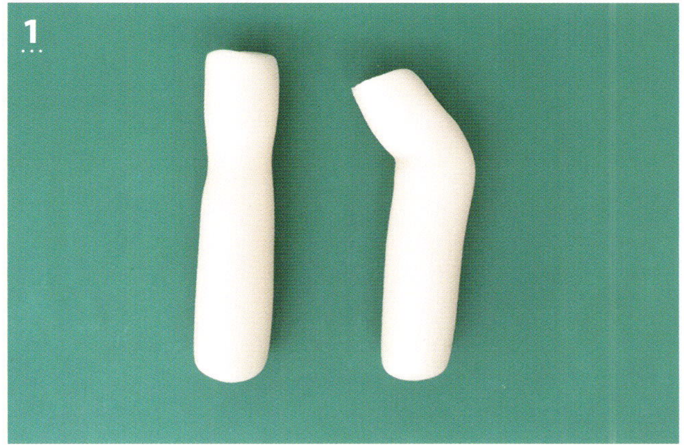

Making the basic leg shape.

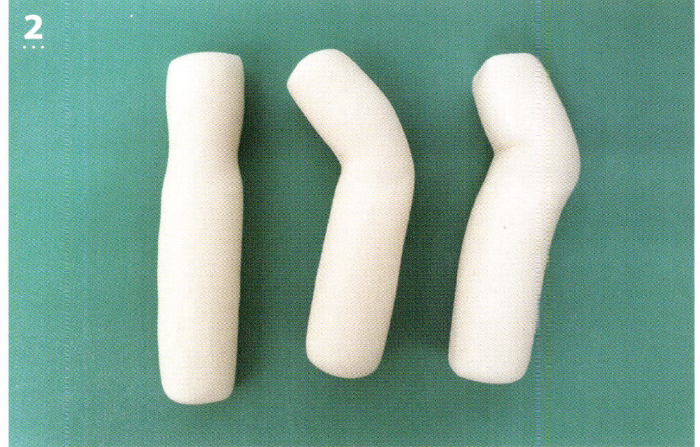

This shows the three stages for creating each leg.

Making and Adding Football Socks

To make the football socks, roll out a rectangle of red paste with the small rolling pin, to a thickness of approximately 2mm. Fold over the top edge carefully with your finger. If you have a knitted effect mould or impression mat, you could use it to texture the rolled-out red modelling paste before adding it to the leg, to give a more detailed effect.

Turn the paste over and place one leg in the middle of the paste, positioned so that the top of the sock sits just below the knee. Trim any excess paste below the end of the leg with a sharp knife. Wrap the paste round the leg so that it joins at the back, trimming away any excess at the join with a sharp knife. Run your finger along the join to smooth and neaten it. Repeat for the second leg.

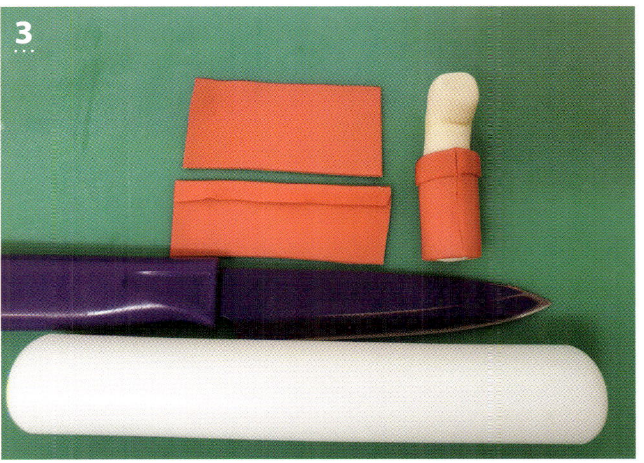

Making and adding football socks to the legs.

Making and Adding the Football Boots

Using 5g of black modelling paste for each boot, first roll into a smooth ball, and then into an oval (fat sausage) shape. Gently stroke the oval downwards with your finger to flatten and elongate it a little at one end.

Press down into the deeper area of the shape with a ball tool, to about half the depth. Wiggle the ball tool around to widen the hole, so that the end of the leg will fit into it. Gently pinch the paste around the edge of the hole to thin and shape it.

Paint a small amount of edible glue or water into the hole and insert the bottom of the leg into the boot. Be careful not to use too much glue or water, as it can cause the coloured paste to 'bleed'.

Then, with a small ball tool, indent the bottom of the boot and add 4mm sugar pearls to make the studs. If you don't have the sugar pearls, you can roll tiny balls of black paste to use instead. Fix in place with a tiny dab of edible glue. Be careful not to add too much as it will get very messy! Set the completed legs aside whilst you work on the shorts.

Making the basic shapes for the football boots.

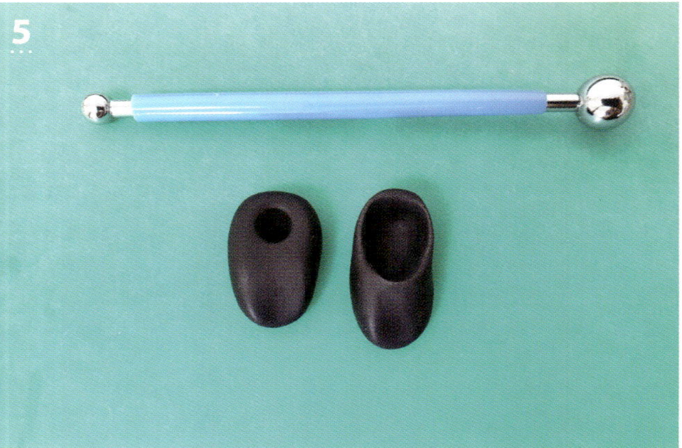

Creating an indent in the football boots to fit the legs.

Attaching the football boots to the legs and adding the simple stud details at the bottom.

Roll 25g of red modelling paste into a ball, smoothing away any cracks with the warmth of your hands. Apply a slight pressure to the top of the ball, whilst rolling between your hands (positioned at a 45-degree angle to each other) to form a gentle, tapered cone shape. Be careful not to make the shape too long or pointy. Lay the paste on your workboard and press the top of it slightly with your palm to flatten it a little.

With a sharp knife, cut a V-shaped piece of paste out of the wider end of the flattened cone shape to make the two leg parts of the shorts. Then, using a medium-sized ball tool, create an indent at each side of the cut. Move the ball tool in a circular motion to shape the inside of the leg areas. Use your finger and thumb to gently pinch and smooth the outside edges, thinning and shaping them. Place the legs just into the shorts to measure the size of the opening, and adjust where necessary. The legs need to fit inside the holes comfortably, without too much gap around the edges.

Brush a small amount of edible glue or water inside the shorts and attach the two legs in place, so that the knees are bending outwards away from each other.

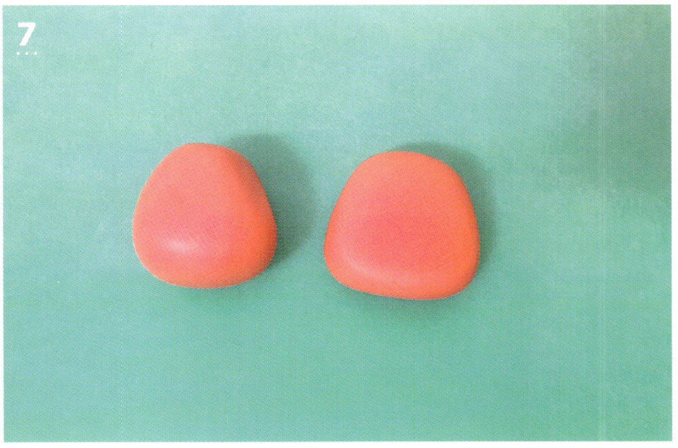

The shorts are created in one piece with coloured paste, rather than being added to the body shapes separately.

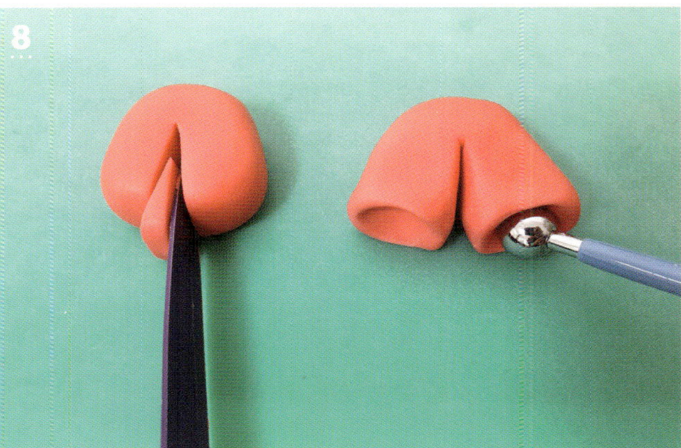

Creating the shape for the shorts, including the space for the legs to fit inside.

Attaching the shorts and legs together.

Making the Mini Football

Roll 5g of white modelling paste into a smooth ball and set aside to firm up slightly. Roll out a small amount of white-and-black modelling paste to a thickness of approximately 2–3mm. Cut out several circles from each colour, using a 10mm circle cutter, then roll the circles into balls. This method enables you to produce balls that are all equal in size.

Start by placing a small black ball on to the larger white ball you made earlier, then surround with six small white balls to replicate the pattern of a football. Continue the pattern using the black-and-white balls until you have covered the entire ball. The paste should stick to itself, but if the small balls are falling off, use a tiny amount of edible glue to keep them in place. Once the ball is completely covered, roll it around gently between your palms until it is smooth, with no remaining bumps. Set the ball aside to firm up, whilst you work on the body.

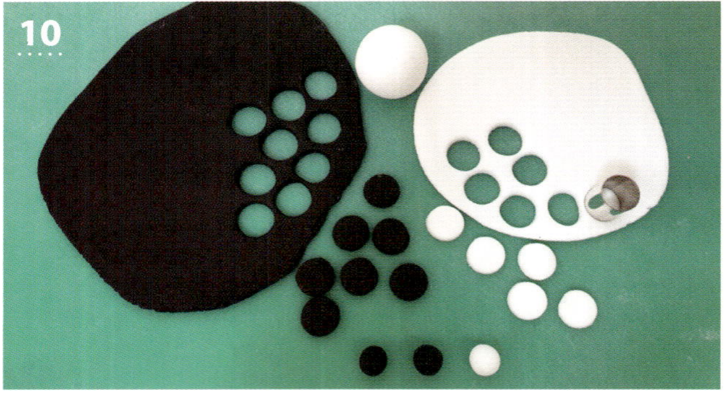
Prepare the pieces you will need to make the football.

Position the tiny balls of black-and-white paste to make the traditional patterned football, then smooth them together with your hands to create the football.

Making the Body of the Figure

Using 70g of white modelling paste, first roll into a ball, smoothing any cracks with your palms. Then position your hands at a 45-degree angle, rolling the paste between them to taper the top part of the ball slightly. Place the paste on to your workboard and press down gently with one palm to flatten it a little. Use a ball tool to hollow out the bottom of the body, to give the impression that it is the bottom of a T-shirt, and to help fit it over the shorts. You will need to make the back slightly longer than the front, so it covers the back of the shorts.

Place the shorts and legs on to a small cake card (or something similar), to make it easier to move around whilst you are working on it. Position the body over the top of the shorts, using a little edible glue to attach if necessary. The back of the shirt should cover the back of the shorts, whilst the front will be a little higher and should just rest on the shorts.

Place the ball between the legs and adjust their positioning if required, so that each leg is resting against the ball, to keep it in place.

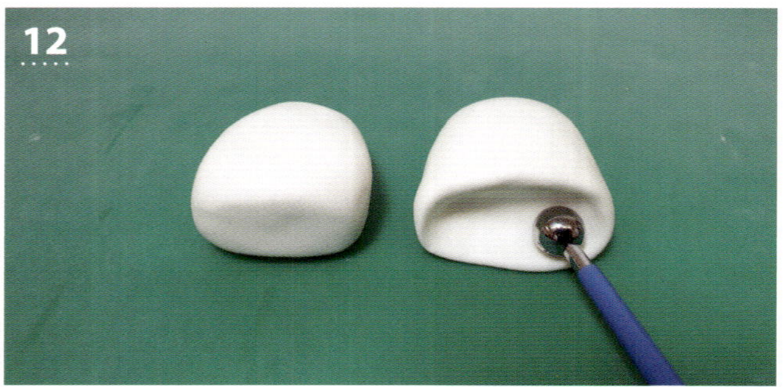
The body is made with white paste to look like the football shirt, rather than making body and shirt separately.

Adding the body to the legs, positioning the football between them.

Making the Arms

Forming the Sleeves

Roll 12g of white modelling paste into a smooth ball, then roll into a sausage shape, measuring approximately 5cm (2in) in length. Cut in half diagonally with a sharp knife, using a sawing motion, as for the legs.

Use a medium-sized ball tool to hollow out the sleeve, on the flat edge underneath the diagonal cut, ready to insert the lower arm. Use your finger and thumb to gently pinch and thin the outer edge.

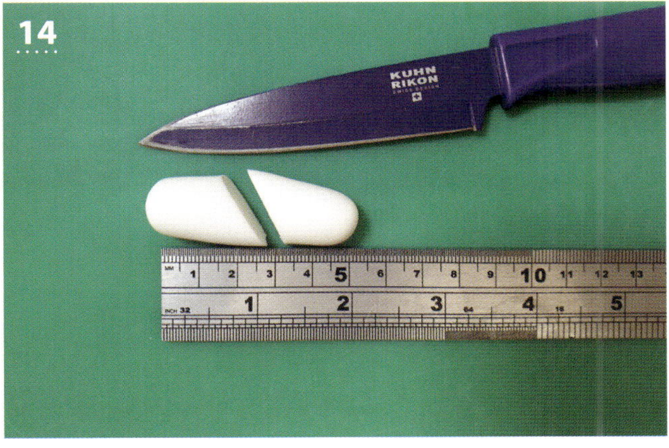

Starting to form the sleeve shapes with white modelling paste.

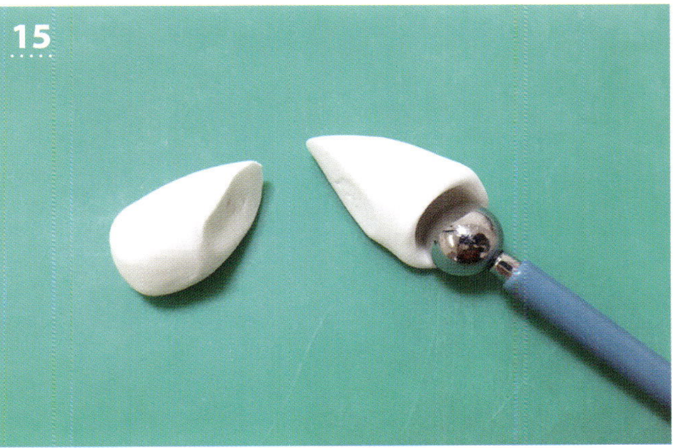

Creating a space to add the lower arms.

Forming the Lower Arms

Roll 15g of skin-tone coloured modelling paste into a ball and then into a sausage, measuring approximately 10cm (4in) in length. Cut in half diagonally to make two arms. Holding each arm just above the diagonal cut, roll the paste gently between your thumb and finger to form a slight indent for the wrist area.

Flatten the paste below the wrist slightly with your finger to form the hands, then use a scalpel to cut a V shape from each to create the thumbs. Be sure to make the cuts at the opposite side on each hand in order to make a pair, rather than two identical hands. By making both at the same time, it makes this easier. This is the simplest type of hands to make, and are ideal for beginners or for when you require a very simplistic style of figure. By not creating individual fingers, they are not so fiddly or time-consuming to make.

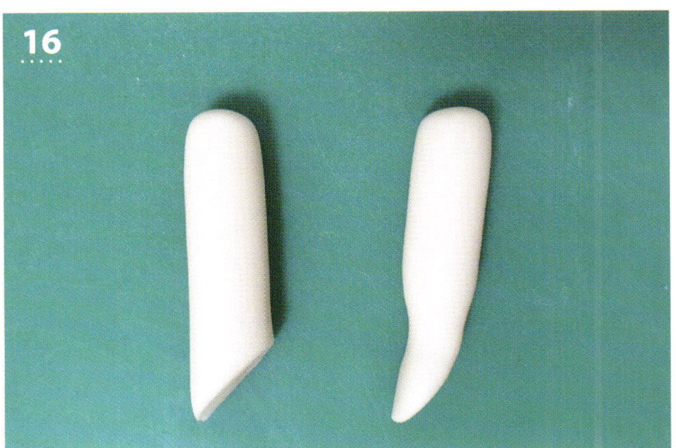

Making the lower arms.

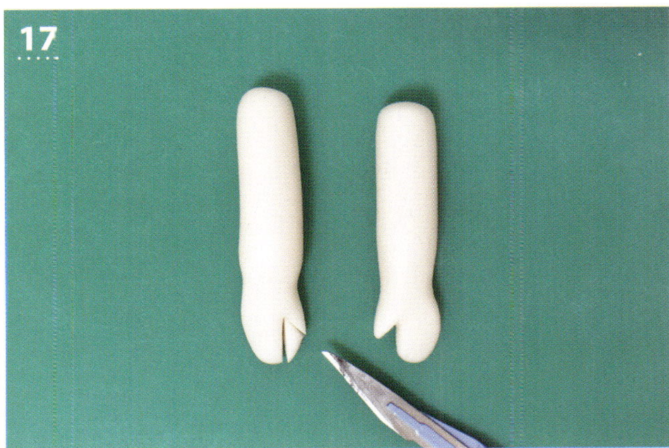

Forming the simple hand shapes.

Bend the top of each arm slightly to form the elbow, then attach inside the sleeve with a little edible glue or water. Again, bear in mind the positions of the hands, to make sure you have a pair of opposite arms. The thumb will be closest to the body on each side.

Roll out a small piece of white modelling paste, and cut two thin strips. Position these over the join between the arm and sleeve, and trim any excess at the back. You shouldn't need to use any glue or water to attach, but if they are not sticking you can use a tiny amount.

Attach the arms to the body with a small amount of edible glue, positioning the hands to rest on the football. You can add a little edible glue where the hands touch the ball, to secure them in place.

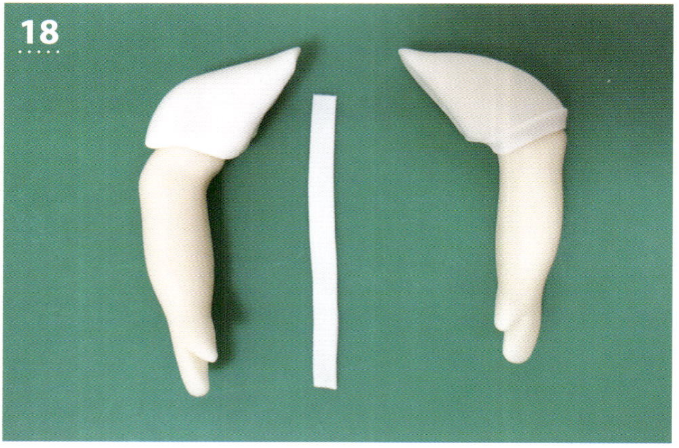

Joining the arms and sleeves together.

Attaching the completed arms to the body.

Creating the Neck and Support for the Head

Use a medium ball tool to create an indent at the top of the body to hold the neck. Roll a short sausage of skin-tone coloured modelling paste for the neck, and secure it into the hole with a little edible glue or water. Smooth the edges down to meet the shirt.

Make a thin strip of white modelling paste (the same as for the bottom of the sleeves) and fit it around the join between the neck and body to neaten. Insert your support by twisting it gently between your thumb and finger as you push downwards, through the neck and body, until it hits the cake board under the figure. Trim the top of the support with scissors or pliers, leaving approximately 3cm (1in) above to support the head in place.

You could use a cake pop stick to form the support for the head, as these are easy to cut with scissors or small pliers, as well as being food safe, but you could also use dried spaghetti or a wooden skewer instead.

Creating the neck area and support for the head.

Creating a Simple Style of Head for your Figure

Roll 35g of skin-tone modelling paste into a smooth ball and then shape into an oval by rolling gently between your hands. Using the handle of your ball tool (or other modelling tool), create an indent across the halfway point of the head, to mark the positioning of the eye area. You can also use your little finger to indent the paste if you prefer.

Use a ball tool to make dents for the eye sockets, pushing the paste gently towards the middle to form a simple nose. Roll a tiny piece of skin tone modelling paste into an oval shape, and position at the bottom of the nose area, using a little edible glue or water to hold in place if necessary.

Use a small ball tool to make a hole in the centre of each eye socket, and add a 4mm black sugar pearl (or roll a 4mm ball of black modelling paste). If you do not have a ball tool small enough, you can use the end of a paintbrush to make the hole. For added detail, you can draw two tiny lines coming from the outside edges of the eyes to look like creases, using the narrow end of your Dresden tool.

Use the smile tool to create the indent for the mouth. Insert it approximately 2–3mm into the paste, moving it up and down slightly to create a wider indentation.

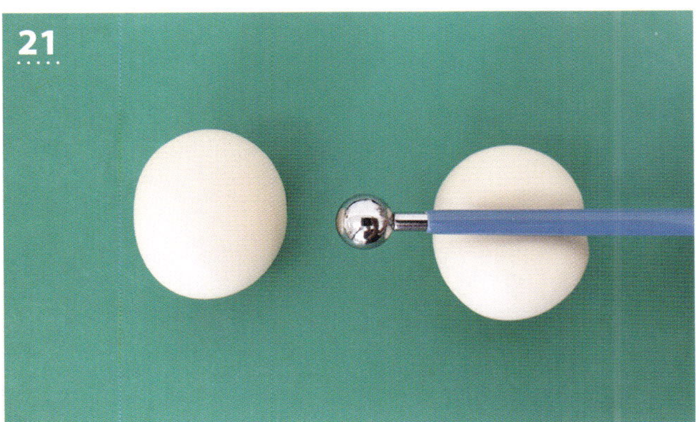

Making the shape for the head.

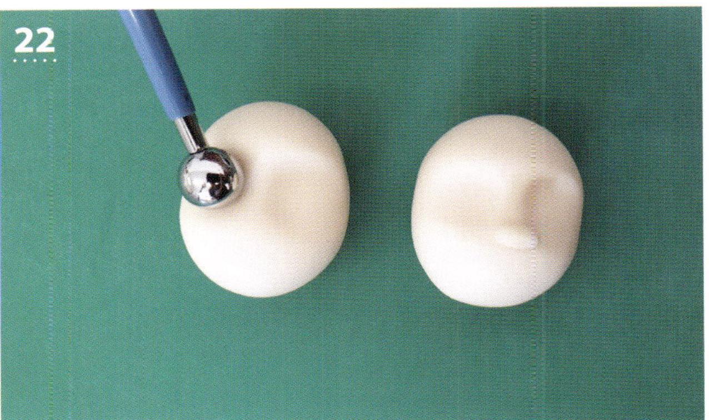

Creating the eye sockets and nose.

Adding simple eye detail.

Creating the shape for the mouth.

To make the ears, roll two small balls of skin-tone modelling paste, then roll into small sausage shapes. Flatten slightly with your finger, and use a small ball tool to make the ear markings.

Attach the ears to each side of the head with a little edible glue, positioning them so that the bottom of the ear is parallel to the bottom of the nose.

Roll a small ball of black modelling paste, and thin one end by rolling between your finger and thumb. Starting with the thin end of paste above the outer edge of the eye, make into an eyebrow shape and trim above the inner edge of the eye using a scalpel.

Brush a small amount of edible glue on top of the neck and over the support stick. Push the head onto the support stick, twisting as you push gently down, so as not to distort the shape.

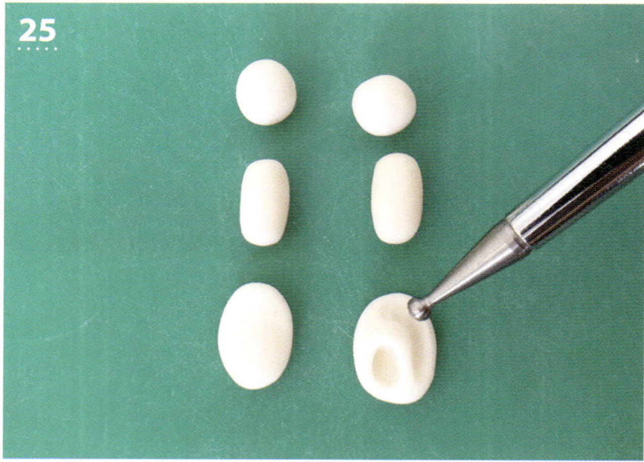

Making the ears and adding detail.

Attaching the ears in the correct place on the head and creating the eyebrows.

Fitting the head securely on to the figure using the support already in place.

Making the Hair

The hair will take approximately 15g of black modelling paste altogether. Roll around half of this amount into a ball and flatten with your hand, thinning the edges between your finger and thumb. Place the disc of paste over the head, bringing any excess to the back and trimming with small, sharp scissors.

Use the thinner end of the Dresden tool to create texture for the hair, by drawing lines into the paste.

To make the fringe area, roll two smaller balls of black modelling paste into cone shapes and flatten with your fingers. You can make them the same size, or have one slightly smaller, depending on your preference for the style. Mark hair texture with the thinner end of the Dresden tool as before.

Attach the two sections of hair to the front of the head with a small amount of edible glue, bending and positioning them into place with your fingers.

Using a soft-bristled brush, add a little touch of pink dust to the cheek areas, to give the figure rosy cheeks. Tap any excess dust off the brush before applying, to prevent the risk of adding too much colour.

Attaching the base part of the hair.

Texturing the hair.

Making the fringe parts of the hair.

Finishing off the hair at the front.

Applying some colour to the cheek area with edible dust.

Adding a Number to the Back of the Shirt

If you wish to personalize the model's football shirt with the player's number or perhaps their age, roll a thin piece of red modelling paste and use a number cutter to cut out the correct number/s. Attach to the back of the shirt with a small amount of edible glue. (This addition is optional.)

Personalize the figure by adding a player number or their age to the back of the shirt.

Adding a scarf just gives that bit of extra detail to the figure, complimenting the football/sport theme.

Roll a strip each of red and white modelling paste to the same width (approximately 3cm/1in). Cut the red strip into even-sized pieces and lay them at intervals along the white strip of paste to form a striped pattern.

Cover the paste with a piece of plastic wrap (cling film) and roll over it in the same direction as the stripes (up and down). This blends the paste together, whilst keeping the stripes as even and straight as possible.

Trim the edge of the scarf straight with a sharp knife. Cut into each end to make a fringe effect.

Wrap the scarf round the model's neck – start by matching the middle of the scarf to the front of the model, then cross over the two sides at the back, bring each side round over the shoulders, and finally cross them over at the front.

What could be a better cake to accompany this footballer figure, than an actual football made of cake? Due to the rounded top of the cake, you would be advised to make the figure once the cake is covered, so that it can be positioned as soon as it is completed. If the legs dry in a straight position, they will stick up from the top of the cake, rather than fit to the curved contour.

Bake a Madeira sponge in two 15cm (6in) half sphere tins, then fill and crumb coat with ganache. Cover a 30cm (12in) square cake board with green sugar paste, then attach the cake to the centre of the board with ganache or royal icing, ready to decorate.

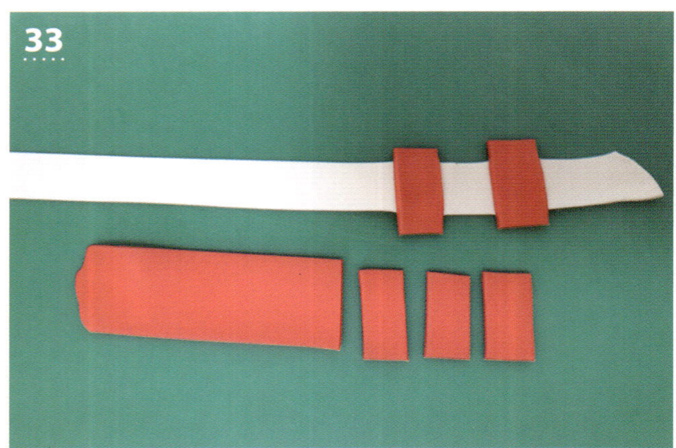

33

Cut and place stripes to make the scarf.

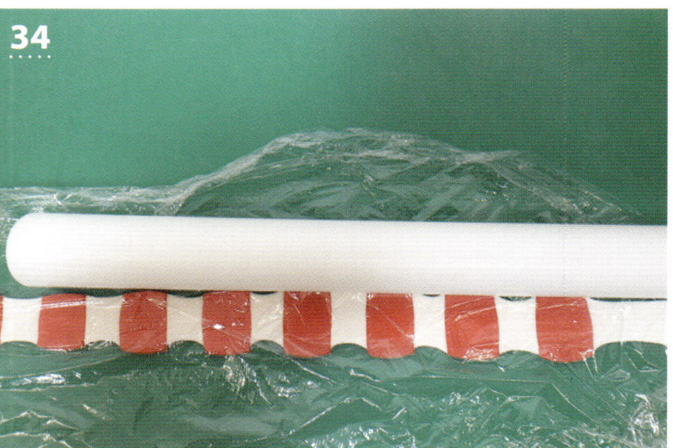

34

Blend the different coloured pastes into one piece.

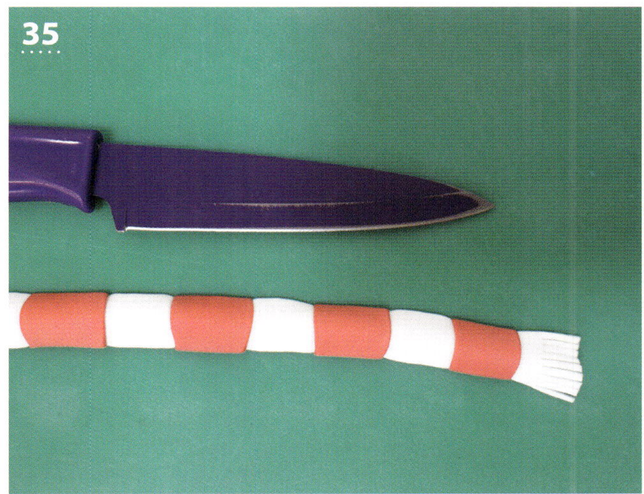

Trim the edges and cut fringes at each end of the scarf.

Positioning the scarf on to the figure.

This football-shaped cake is perfectly suited to the footballer figure, sitting on a football pitch-themed cake drum; it can be personalized with a name, age or birthday message.

Covering the Football Cake

When cutting out the hexagons and pentagons to cover the cake, you need to make sure that the different coloured pastes are rolled out to the same even thickness, to create a smooth finish. Long wooden skewers can be used as a guide when rolling out the paste to the correct thickness. You can also use marzipan spacers, but these are a little too thick for using with sugar paste. Roll out the white and black paste in this way, ready to cut out the shapes.

Using a set of football shape cutters, cut out a number of white hexagons and black pentagons, resting them on the flat side of a foam dimpled pad to firm up a little, before adding to the cake. If they are too soft, they are more likely to go out of shape as you handle them. You can buy sets of football cutters that are scaled to fit the size of sphere cake you are using. Alternatively, for a 15cm (6in) sphere cake,

you can use templates to cut the shapes using a sharp knife.

Apply a thin layer of white vegetable fat (Trex) over the surface of your ganached cake to attach the sugar-paste shapes. Alternatively, you can use cooled boiled water if you prefer. Arrange the shapes on to the sphere cake with a pentagon in the centre, surrounded by hexagons, then continue the pattern over the rest of the cake until it is covered. You may find that the pattern is more difficult to keep correct towards the bottom of the cake, but we will be covering this part with a scarf, so don't worry too much about this area. Add stitching detail around the outside edge of each shape to give more realism to your football cake. It is rather fiddly and time consuming, but the result is well worth the effort.

Preparing the paste for covering the football cake, by rolling to an even thickness.

Using a set of football cutters to cut out white hexagons and black pentagons for the football pattern.

Arrange the black-and-white shapes on the cake in the correct way to achieve a football pattern effect, before giving it a more realistic look with added stitching details.

As mentioned, the bottom of the football cake can be difficult to cover whilst keeping the pattern accurate, so creating a scarf to cover this area will help to hide any imperfections. The scarf is made in the same way as for the model, just on a larger scale.

Roll out white and red sugar paste into two long strips, then cut the red strip into thinner pieces. Lay the red pieces of paste on top of the long white strip to create a striped pattern. Place a piece of cling film (plastic wrap) over the top, and gently roll with a large rolling pin to combine the two colours together. Trim the edges of the scarf straight, then cut into the ends to give a fringe effect.

Here, a knitted effect silicone mould by Karen Davies is used, to texture the scarf for added detail, but this is optional.

Wrap the scarf round the bottom of the cake, securing with a little water or edible glue where it touches the cake.

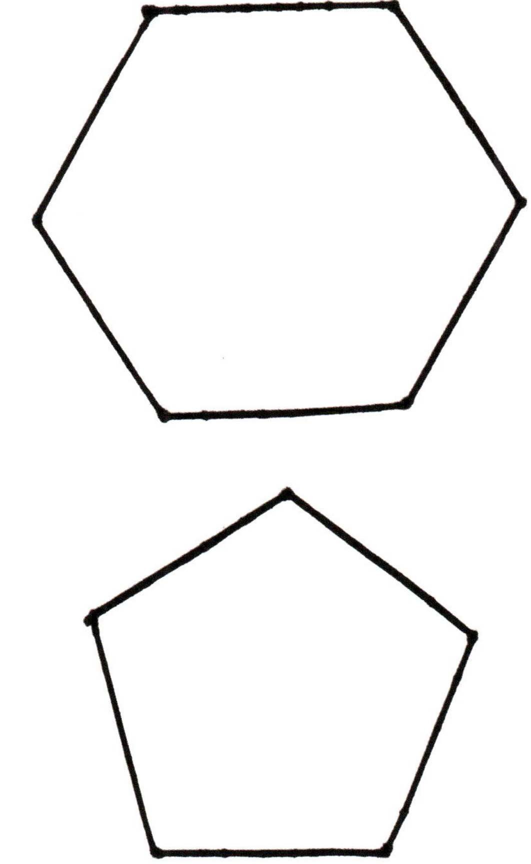

This template can be used to cut out the correct-sized shapes to cover a 15cm (6in) sphere cake if you don't have the cutters. Increase by 200% to obtain the correct size.

FINISHING TOUCHES

To give the board a football-pitch effect, pipe thin white lines of royal icing around the edges, adding rounded corner markings at each corner.

Personalize the board if you wish, by cutting out letters and numbers from white paste. White flower paste (gum paste) works better for cutting out letters, as sugar paste can be a bit too soft, although you can add some Tylose powder to sugar paste. Roll it out thin and leave it to firm up for approximately ten minutes, before cutting out your letters and numbers. Attach the personalized message to the cake board with edible glue or water.

To finish, add 15mm green ribbon to the edge of the board, using a non-toxic glue stick or double-sided tape.

Create a larger version of the football scarf to wrap round the bottom of the cake.

Adding the finishing touches to the cake drum, to personalize and complete the cake design.

CHAPTER 5

Female Figure in Sitting Pose

Using basic modelling tools and simple techniques, this is another ideal starter project for those new to modelling figures. The proportions and sizing of this figure are to resemble a younger child, but these can be adjusted to suit the look of an older person if required. This sitting figure has her legs dangling over the edge of the cake, but can just as easily be made with straight legs to sit on top of the cake (as for the footballer figure). You can also use the techniques shown in the wedding couple figures to make a standing version. The model is pictured sitting on the edge of a 10cm (4in) round cake.

MAKING THE SITTING GIRL FIGURE

Making the Legs

Roll 40g of blue modelling paste into a smooth ball, then extend into a long, even-sized sausage shape measuring approximately 14cm (5.5in) in length. Bend in half at the middle to form the trousers.

Make a mark halfway down the back of each leg with a sharp knife (don't cut in too far, just make an indentation). Turn the legs over, bend each one at the mark, and squeeze slightly with your fingers and thumb just above and below to form the knee shape. Slightly hollow the bottom of each leg with a ball tool, ready to attach the shoes later.

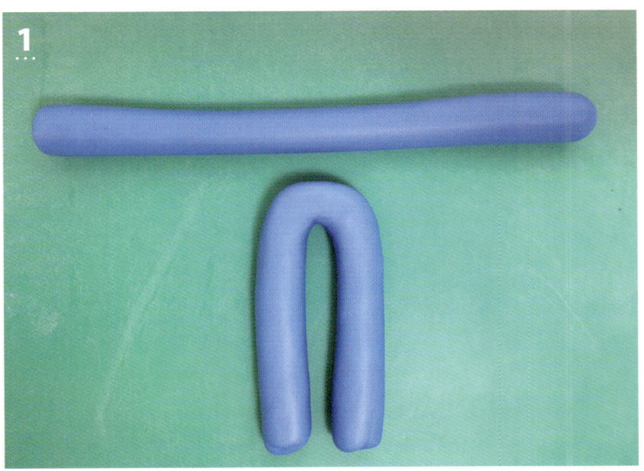

Making the legs and trousers in one piece with coloured paste.

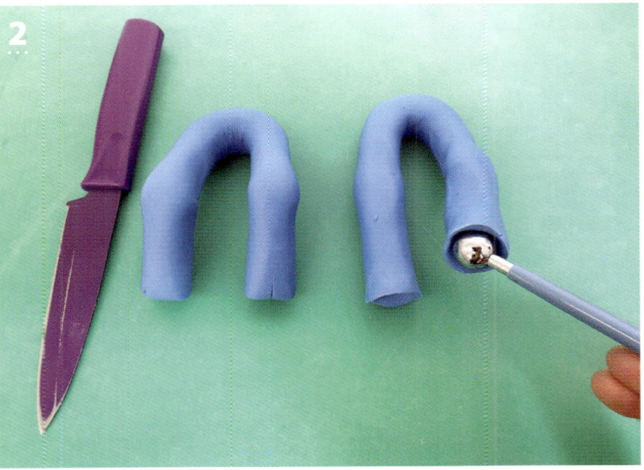

Creating the knee shaping for the legs, and hollowing out the bottoms.

◀ This cute little girl, with her lovely curly hair, sits over the edge of a cake, but she could just as easily be made with straight legs to sit on top if preferred.

Sit the legs on the edge of the dummy or cake, so that they dangle over the edge, whilst resting on the side of the dummy/cake for support. Use the thinner end of the Dresden tool to mark diagonal creases above and below the knee area at both sides, where it meets the edge of the dummy/cake. If you are constructing your model directly on to your covered cake, you will need to secure the legs with a little dab of royal icing, or some edible glue. You don't need to do this if you are working on the model on a dummy cake, as you will be transferring it later, so will need to be able to lift it off.

Positioning the legs on the edge of your polystyrene dummy or cake.

Making the Sitting Girl Figure

Equipment

- small rolling pin
- sharp knife
- scalpel
- ball tools (variety of sizes)
- Dresden tool
- metal ruler
- small, sharp scissors
- kitchen scissors or pliers
- circle cutters (10mm and 25mm)
- 35mm blossom cutter (or similar)
- small plunger blossom or flower cutter
- 60mm round fluted pastry cutter
- paintbrushes for water and for dusting cheeks
- cake pop stick for supporting the head (or use a wooden skewer)
- extra cake pop sticks/wooden skewers for creating hair spirals

Materials

- 70g skin-tone modelling paste
- 45g yellow modelling paste
- 50g white modelling paste
- 40g blue modelling paste
- 60g orange modelling paste
- 10g red modelling paste
- 6g black modelling paste
- pink petal dusts for cheeks (I used Fractal Kitty Nose Pink)
- 2 × 7mm black sugar pearls (optional)

I have used a polystyrene cake dummy to support the figure whilst making it, before transferring to the finished cake. This method is easier, as you don't risk damaging your actual cake whilst making the figure; however, you can build it straight on to a covered cake if you prefer.

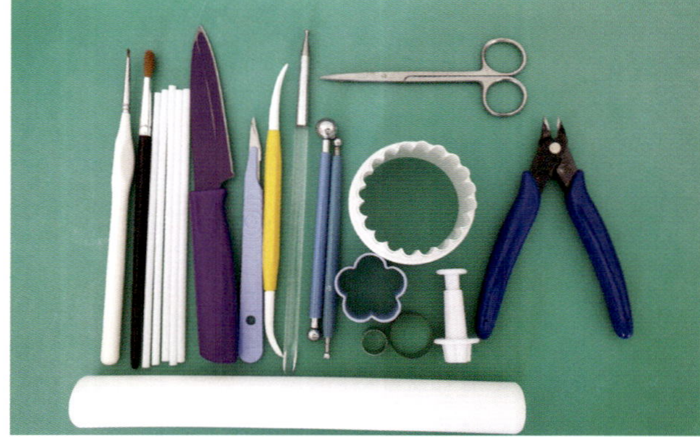

A basic tool set and general cake-decorating equipment is all that is required to make this little girl figure, with a few optional extras to add further detail if you wish.

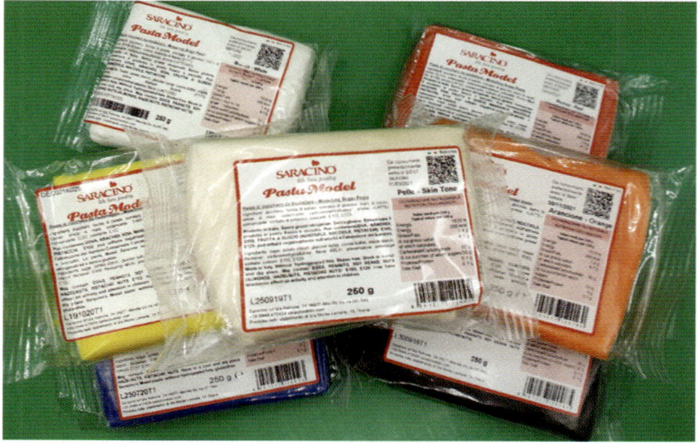

Ready-coloured Saracino modelling paste in skin tone, yellow, white, blue, orange, red and black was used to create this model. You can substitute different colours for the clothing and hair if you wish, when creating your figure.

Making the Shoes

Using 3g of black modelling paste for each shoe, roll each into a small ball and then into a short sausage shape, ensuring that both pieces are the same size and shape. Place on your board and press down on the top to flatten slightly with your finger. Use a sharp knife to make an indentation to mark the heel area on the underneath edge of the shoe.

Use a small amount of edible glue to attach the shoes to the bottom of the legs. You may find it helps to let the glue sit for a minute before attaching, to allow it to go slightly tacky. This will help it to stick more securely to the bottom of the leg. With the narrow end of the Dresden tool, mark creases into the bottom of the trousers.

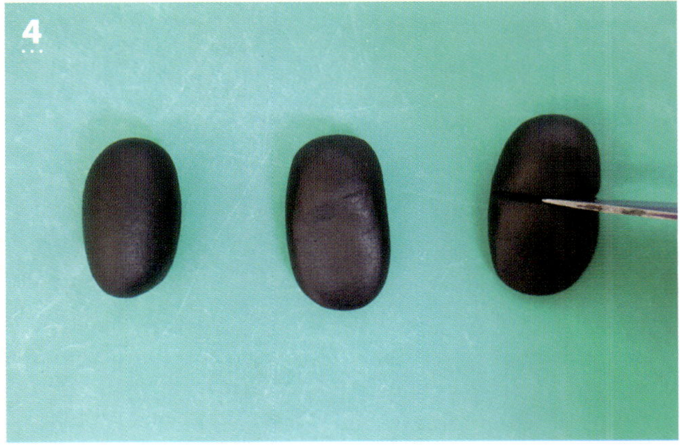

Making a very simple form of shoe – you can add more detailing to the shoes if you wish, such as shoe laces.

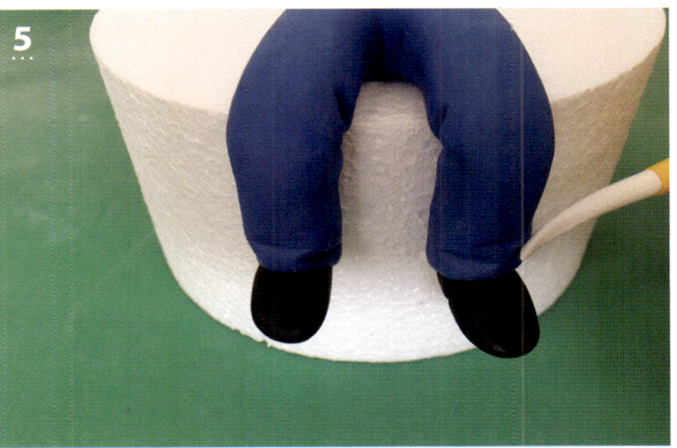

Attaching the shoes securely to the legs (you may need to hold them for a few seconds until they bond, or use a small box to prop them up until the glue dries).

Making the Body

This model is wearing a tunic-style top, which will cover the body and be created in coloured paste. Start by making the lemon-coloured paste by mixing together 45g of yellow and 45g of white modelling paste (you may want to adjust the ratio depending on the shade you require, or you may prefer to use a different colour altogether).

Roll 70g of lemon-coloured modelling paste into a ball, removing any creases, then into a cone shape. Flatten slightly with the palm of your hand, and use a large ball tool to hollow out the bottom of the paste. This will allow the body to fit over the legs.

Thin the edges of the paste between your fingers and thumb, stretching it slightly to lengthen the paste. This will allow it to fall over the legs and around the back of the model like the fabric of the tunic.

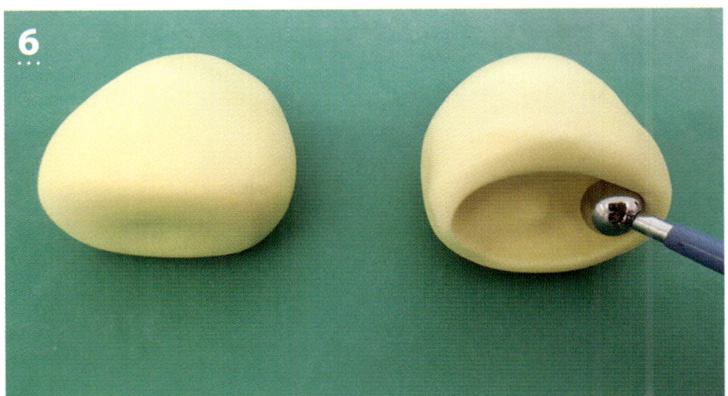

Creating the shape for the body/tunic-style top.

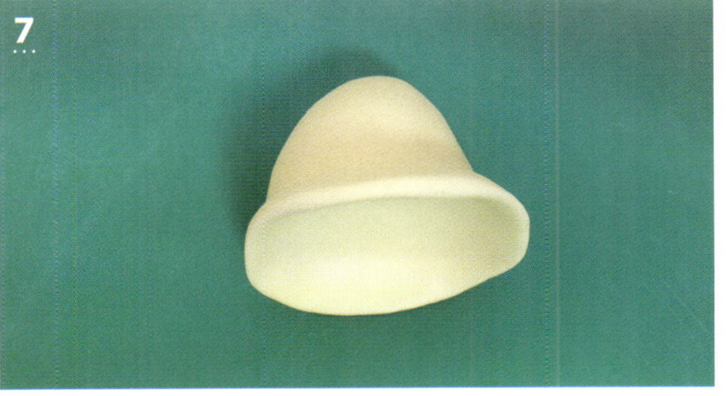

Thinning the bottom edge of the paste will give it a fabric effect to drape over the legs.

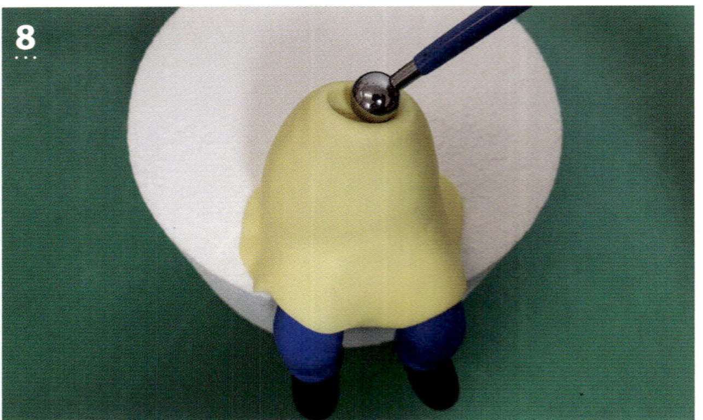

Positioning and securing the body on to the legs.

Position the body over the legs, attaching with a little edible glue if required. Make sure the thinned edge of the paste falls over the legs and round the back of the model to cover the top of the legs completely. Use a medium ball tool to indent a hole in the top of the body for the neck.

Making the Decorative Details for the Tunic

To make the ribbon to go round the waist area of the figure, roll a long rectangle of lemon-coloured modelling paste and cut out a thin strip with a sharp knife. Attach round the waist area with a little edible glue.

Make a small bow by cutting one longer and one shorter strip of the lemon paste. Fold each edge of the longer strip into the middle, and then wrap the shorter piece round to cover the join. Indent each end with the narrow, pointy end of the Dresden tool to give it a little shape and movement.

Attach the bow on top of the strip join at the back of the dress with a little edible glue.

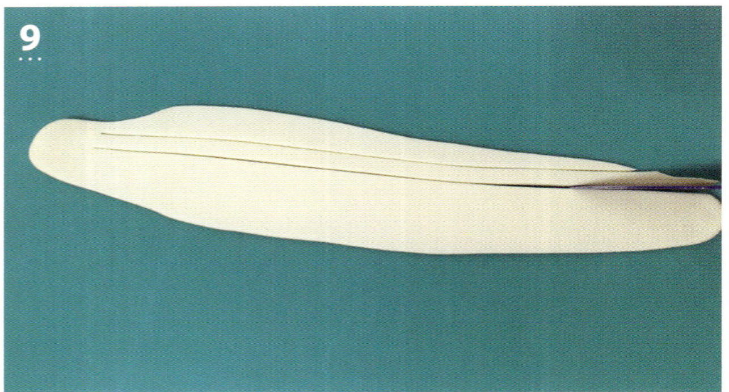

Making a ribbon to go round the waist area.

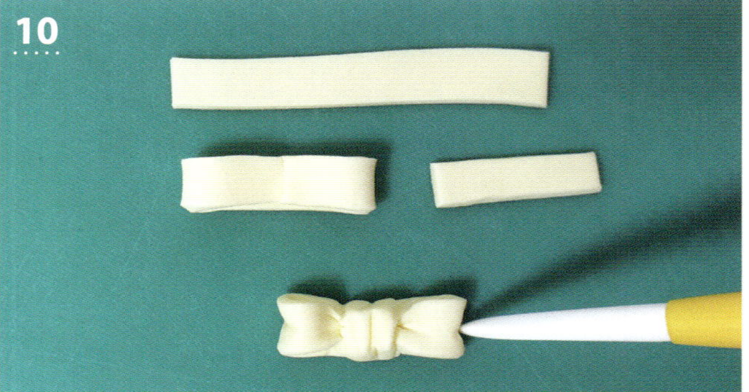

Making a simple bow detail without using a mould.

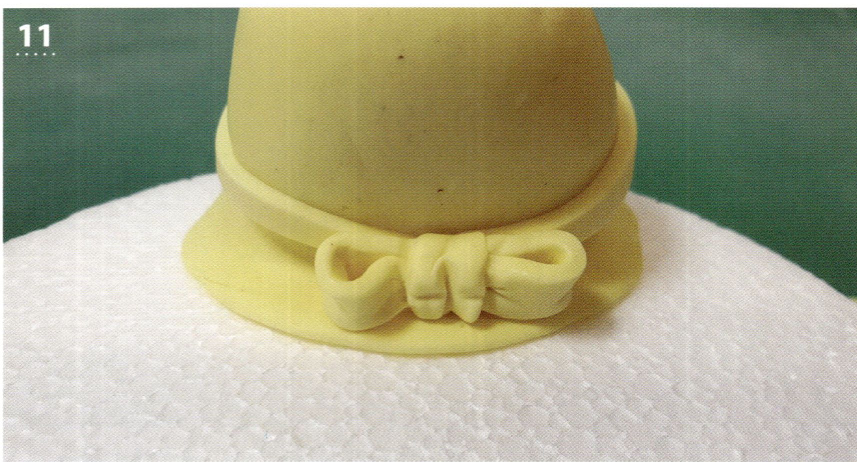

Attaching the bow to the back of the figure.

Finishing the Neck Area

Roll a small ball of skin-tone modelling paste into a sausage, and gently pinch out some of the paste at one end to widen it. Insert it into the hole you made earlier at the top of the body.

Roll out a small piece of lemon modelling paste and use the 35mm blossom cutter to cut out a flower shape. Remove a circle of paste from the centre of the flower with a 12mm circle cutter. Lower it over the neck and position it at the top of the body to make a collar to neaten up the neckline area.

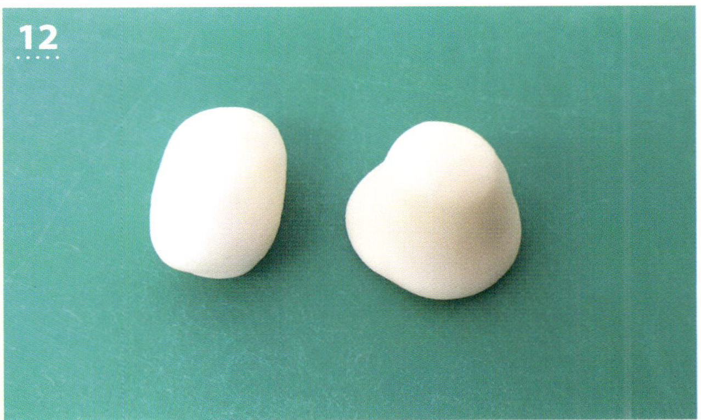

Forming the neck and attaching it to the figure.

Adding a collar detail to finish off the neckline.

Making the Arms and Sleeves

Roll 25g of skin-tone modelling paste into a ball and then into a sausage, measuring approximately 14cm (5.5in) in length. Cut in half diagonally (at approximately a 45-degree angle), ensuring that both arms are the same length. This diagonal cut edge will be attached to the body at the shoulder.

Roll your little finger across the arm approximately 2cm (¾in) from the bottom of the cut edge to begin forming the elbow, and approximately 1cm from the end of the arm to indent the wrist area. Bend the arm to make the elbow, squeezing the paste gently between your thumb and fingers at each side of the bend, to emphasize the elbow shape.

Flatten the end of the arm, below the wrist, ready to create the hands.

Place the two arms next to each other, working on them simultaneously to ensure that you create a pair of hands, rather than two of the same. Cut a V shape in each hand at opposite sides to form the thumbs. Use the thinner end of the Dresden tool to mark three lines for the fingers. Start with making a line in the centre, and then one on each side to make them equal. Having both hands in front of you to work on simultaneously helps to make sure you end up with a pair of hands, rather than two left or two right ones!

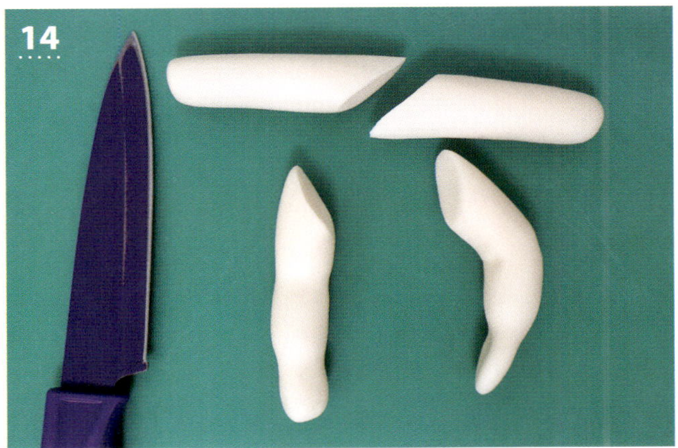

Making the arms, complete with elbow and wrist.

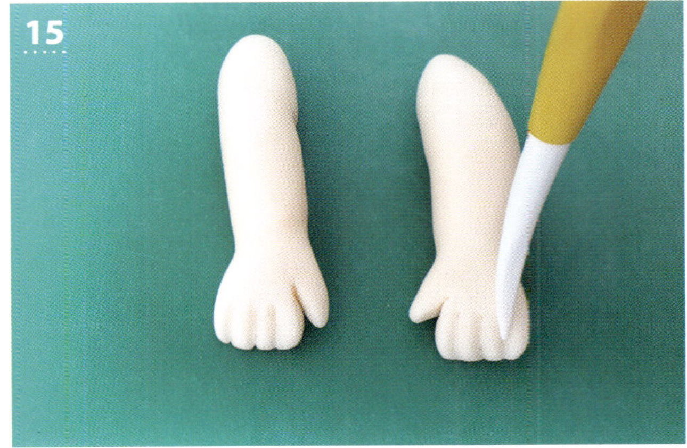

Working on the hands for your model: creating thumb and finger details.

To create the sleeves, roll out a piece of lemon-coloured modelling paste and cut out a circle with a 60mm fluted circle cutter. Cut the shape in half with a sharp knife to make both sleeves, wrapping each of them round the top of an arm. Ensure that the join is on the inside of the arm, and trim any excess paste at the join with small, sharp scissors.

Attach the arms to the body using a little edible glue, positioning the hands on the figure's knees (or however you choose to position them). You can add a little edible glue on the insides of the hands to keep them in place if necessary.

Insert a cake pop stick through the neck and into the body. Trim with small pliers to leave approximately 3cm (1in) above the neck, to support the head. Alternatively you could use a wooden skewer for the support.

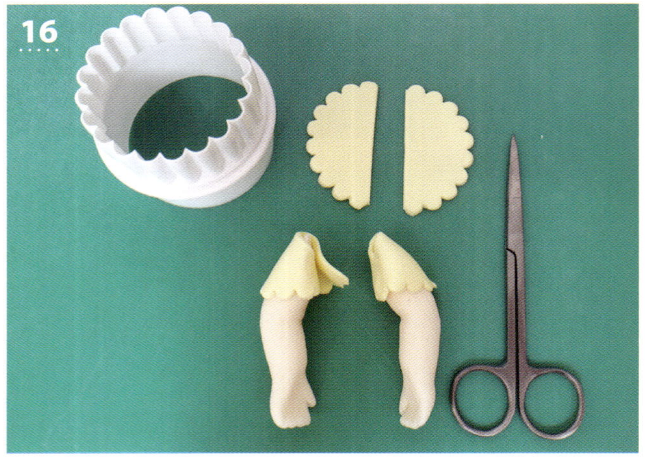

Making and attaching the sleeve detail to the arms.

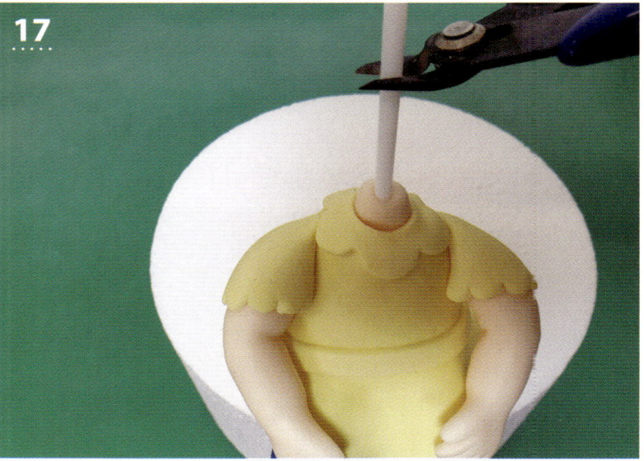

Attaching the arms to the body and inserting a support for the head.

Making the Head

As this figure is based on a younger child, the head proportions are slightly larger than those in adult models. The cartoon style of this model also lends itself to having a larger, rounder style of head.

Roll 45g of skin-tone coloured modelling paste into a ball, smoothing out as many creases as possible, and then roll gently between your hands to form a slight oval (like an egg shape). Use your thumbs (or a large ball tool) to indent the eye sockets at the halfway point of the face.

Roll a tiny ball of skin-tone modelling paste into a small oval and attach to the bottom of the flat area between the eye sockets for the nose. Use a 25mm circle cutter to indent a large smiling mouth shape into the paste, and make an indent at each end with a small ball tool. Alternatively you can use the narrow end of the Dresden tool to draw the mouth on to the face.

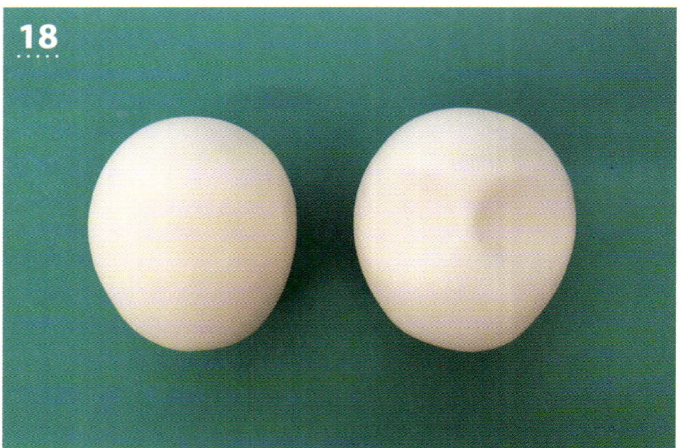

Making the shape for the head and creating eye sockets.

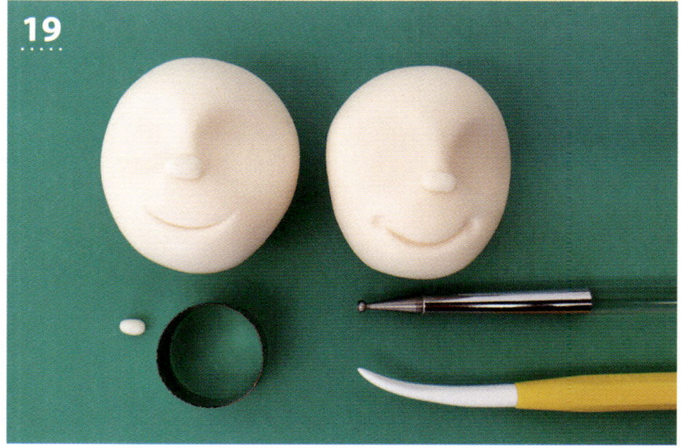

Creating a simple nose and mouth for your model.

Use a small ball tool to indent two holes for the eyes, adding a 7mm black sugar pearl into each hole. If you don't have black sugar pearls, you can roll small balls of black modelling paste and use these instead. You shouldn't need to use any glue to secure the eyes, as they should sit snugly into the holes, but if they are a little loose, you could use a tiny amount of glue to hold in place. Use very sparingly, as it can cause the black colour to bleed from the sugar pearl.

For the ears, roll a small ball of skin-tone modelling paste into a short sausage, flatten slightly with your finger, and cut in half lengthways. Attach the cut edge to the side of the head, so the bottom of the ear is parallel to the bottom of the nose. Use a small ball tool to indent a hole for the ear canal towards the bottom of each ear.

For the eyebrows, roll a small ball of orange modelling paste. Place in your palm and use your finger to roll one end really thin. Paint a thin line of water or edible glue along the top edge of the eye socket, and position the paste, starting at the outer edge of the eye socket. Trim the eyebrow to size with a scalpel or sharp knife. Repeat for the other side. Using the thin end of the Dresden tool, mark two small lines at the outer edge of each eye for extra detail.

Using a clean, soft paintbrush and pink edible petal dust, add a bit of blush colour to the figure's cheeks and inside her mouth.

Helpful Tip

When adding colour to a model's face, make sure you remove excess dust from your brush by wiping it on to a piece of kitchen paper – better to keep adding a little at a time, rather than putting on too much to start with. However, if you do add too much colour, it can easily be removed with a damp cloth – but wait until the surface dries completely before reapplying.

Using black sugar pearls to create simple eyes.

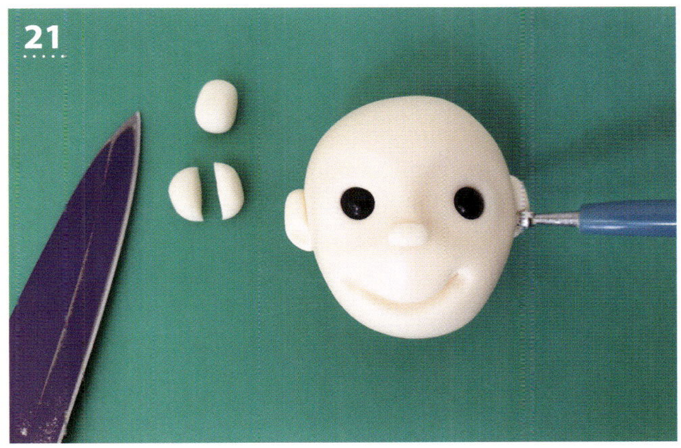

Because of the style of the hair, you don't really see the ears; however, it is best to make simple ears, just in case they are not completely covered by the hair.

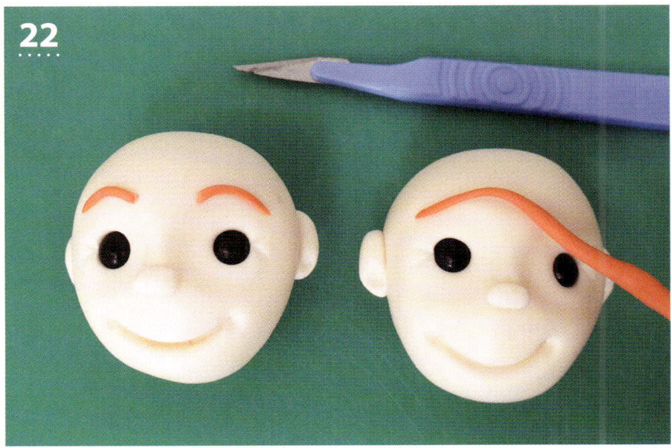

Creating and adding simple eyebrows to your figure's face. The shape of the eyebrows can be adjusted to add extra character and expression to your model.

Using edible petal dust to add colour to the cheek area and inside the mouth.

Attaching the head to the figure, being careful not to distort the shape.

Add a little edible glue to the top of the neck. Carefully position the head over the cake pop-stick support, and twist from side to side as you gently push it down over the stick: this helps to prevent distorting the shape of the head.

Making the Hair

Here we will make these gorgeous ringlets and curls, but of course you could choose to make a different style of hair. To make the orange-coloured paste a little deeper in colour, mix together 60g orange and 10g red modelling paste.

Roll 10g of the orange/red mixed paste into a ball, then flatten it with your hands. Continue to thin the edges with your fingers until you have a circular shape, big enough to cover the back of the head. Starting towards the front of the head, position the paste to cover the top, sides and back, almost like a shower cap, with the excess paste gathering at the back. Cut off the excess paste with scissors and smooth the join with your fingers.

By covering the head with the same colour paste as the hair, it will hide any potential gaps when adding the individual strands of hair.

Roll small pieces of orange modelling paste into balls, then elongate them into long pointed strings of paste. Wrap the paste around a cake pop stick or wooden skewer to create a spiral. Leave in place for a few minutes until it holds its shape, then remove from the stick.

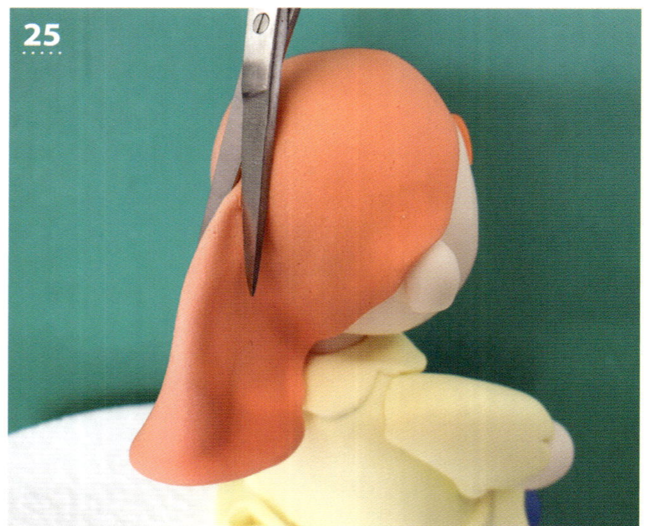

Applying a base layer of hair-coloured paste to the head.

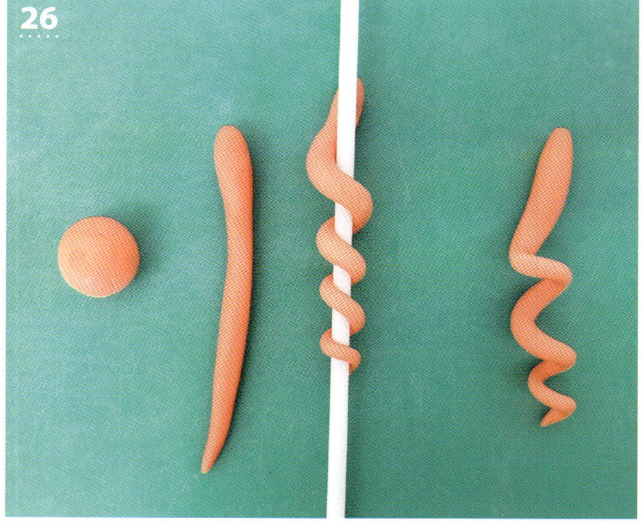

Making spirals of paste for the individual strands of hair.

Continue to make the spirals until you have quite a few ready, then trim off the ends at an angle to remove some of the bulk.

Apply a thin layer of edible glue over the coloured area of paste on the head. Attach the first layer of hair, one piece at a time, towards the bottom of the head, from one side right round to the other. This will give the appearance of a longer hairstyle.

Continue to add layers of hair, so that each overlaps the top of the previous layer. You will need three to four layers of hair, until you reach the crown area of the head.

Attach one or two long strands of hair at each side of the head, so they fall over the ears and in front of the shoulders. You will also need to make some smaller ringlets for the fringe area in between.

Leave a space between the front and back of the hair to fit the hairband.

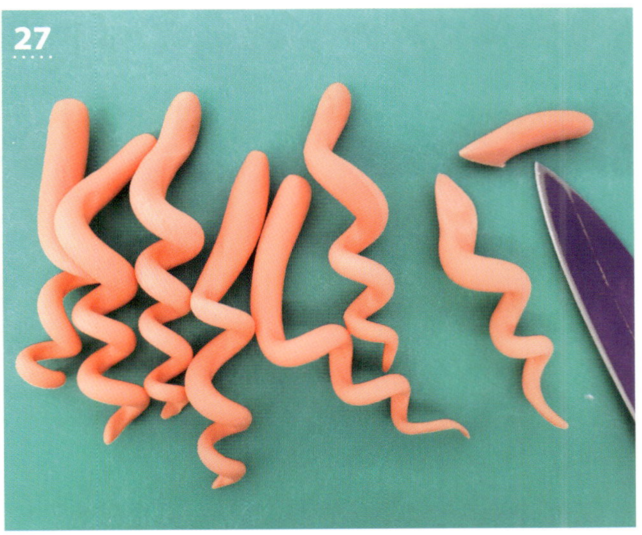

Preparing the hair to attach to the model.

Working on the first layer of hair, which will create the appearance of longer hair.

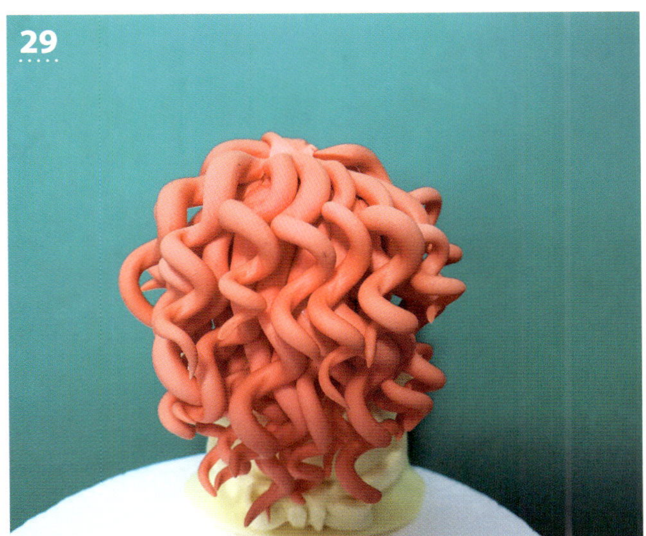

Continuing to add layers of hair to the back and sides of the head.

Adding hair to the front of the head, over the ears and shoulders, moving across the fringe area.

The Finishing Touches

Cut a strip of lemon modelling paste, and trim one end to a point. Measure the size on your figure (it needs to reach over the top of the head, from one ear to the other), and trim to fit. Attach in place with a little edible glue in the gap left between the front and back hair.

Roll out a thin piece of white modelling paste, and using the small plunger blossom cutter, cut out four flowers. Add a tiny ball of lemon paste for the centre of each flower.

Attach three flowers to the hairband and one to the front of the waistband on the tunic.

Roll two tiny balls of white paste to add as highlights for the eyes. Use a small dab of water or edible glue to attach them to the eyes, flattening them slightly with your finger as you stick them in place. Alternatively you could use a white edible marker pen or white edible paint to draw the highlights on to the eyes.

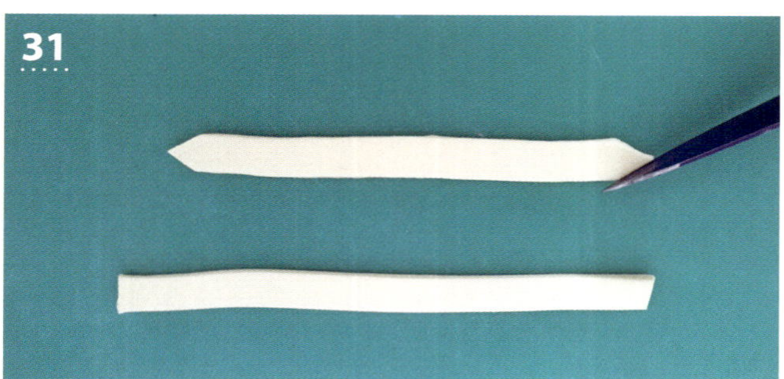

Making the hairband to fit over the head and in between the hair.

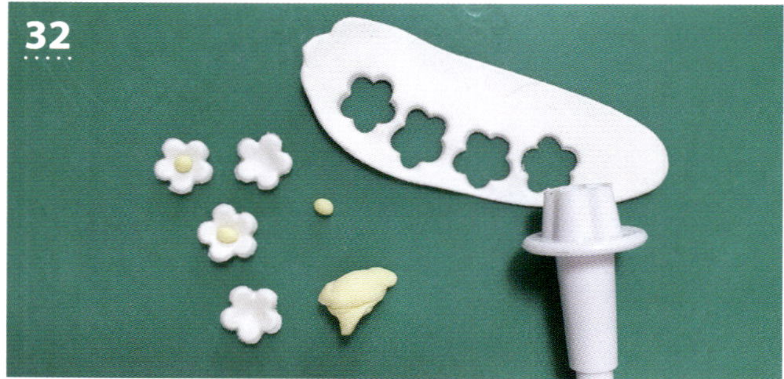

Making the flower details for the headband and waistband.

Adding the final finishing touches to complete your figure.

This two-tiered cake design uses the same colour scheme as for the figure's hair and clothing, and gives a co-ordinated look. You could, of course, go for contrasting colours instead.

Cover a 15cm (6in) round cake and a 10cm (4in) round cake with white sugar paste, then stack them together, using royal icing to secure them, on a 25cm (10in) round cake drum. Make sure to add dowels in the bottom tier to give support.

Use a 15mm orange ribbon to trim the bottom of each cake, securing it with a dot of royal icing at the back. The cake drum is trimmed with the same ribbon, attached using a non-toxic glue stick or double-sided tape.

Using the same colours as the model to decorate this cake gives a co-ordinated look, although you could easily change these to represent the recipient's favourite colours.

Preparing the Circle Decorations

Roll out lemon- and orange-coloured modelling pastes (the same as are used for the figure's dress and hair) to a thickness of approximately 1–2mm. Cut out a selection of different-sized circles from both colours. Remove the centre of some of the larger circles using a smaller circle.

Applying the Decorations to the Cake

Using water or edible glue, attach the circles in a random pattern all over both tiers of the cake. Position some of the circles over the edge of the cake, whilst cutting others in half and positioning them at the top of the ribbons, to vary the look.

Attaching the Figure

Add a small amount of royal icing to the top of the cake, just a little in from the edge of the cake. Be careful not to use too much, or it will push out from underneath the edges of the model. If this does happen, remove any excess royal icing with a clean, damp paintbrush.

Add the figure to the cake, positioning it so that the legs rest against the side of the cake. As the wooden skewer is food safe, it can be inserted straight into the cake. This will offer extra support to keep the model in place whilst the royal icing dries.

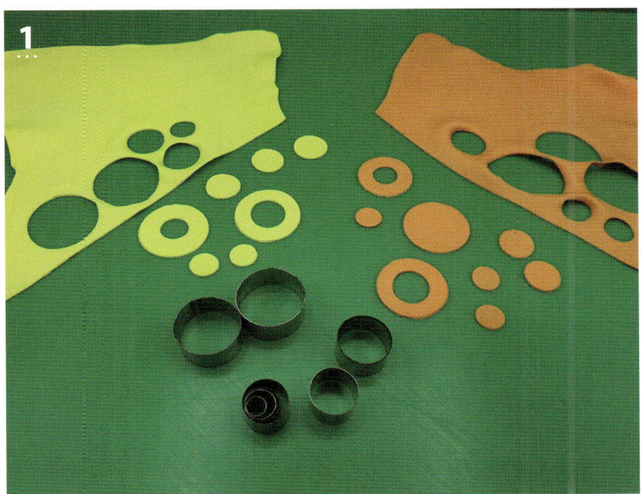

Preparing the coloured circle decorations, in varying sizes, for the cake.

Adding the circle decorations in a random pattern to the cake.

Use royal icing to prepare the cake for adding the figure.

Positioning the figure on top of the cake.

CHAPTER 6

Simple Figure in Reclining Pose

Using basic modelling tools and techniques, this is the final figure in this series of simple figure models, perfect for those first starting out in figure modelling. I have styled this figure to be reading a book, but you could change this for other accessories, such as a toy. The model is pictured lying on its front on a 20cm (8in) round cake.

MAKING THE BOOKS

Open Book Style

Start by rolling 20g of white modelling paste into a smooth ball, then into an even-sized sausage shape. Press to flatten slightly with your fingers. You can roll with a small rolling pin if you prefer.

Use your finger and thumb to pinch each of the four corners, and flatten the edges to create the 'pages' section of the book. With a sharp knife, mark an indent in the middle of the book pages.

With the narrow end of your Dresden tool, mark round each edge to create the illusion of the separate pages in the book. You can also cut gently into the corners of the book pages and lift them slightly, to give the impression of turned up corners/edges.

◀ This little boy figure, busy reading his books, fits perfectly on top of a cake. This style of figure is simple to make and could also be made lying on its back or side, depending on the design of your cake.

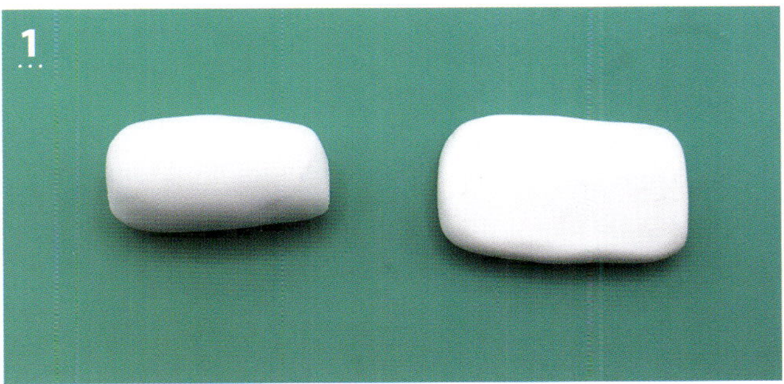

Making the inside pages for the open-paged style of book.

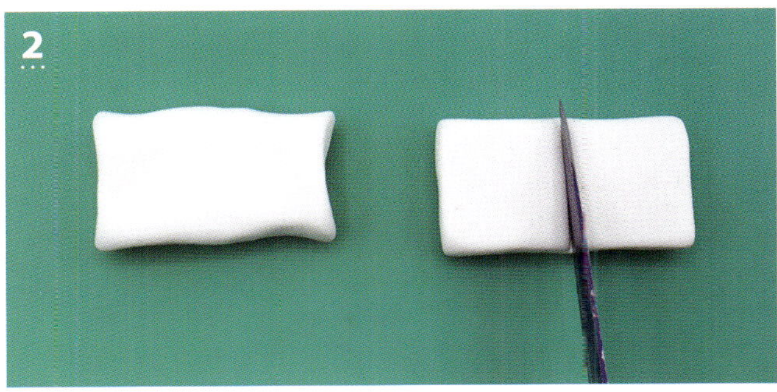

Shaping the open book pages.

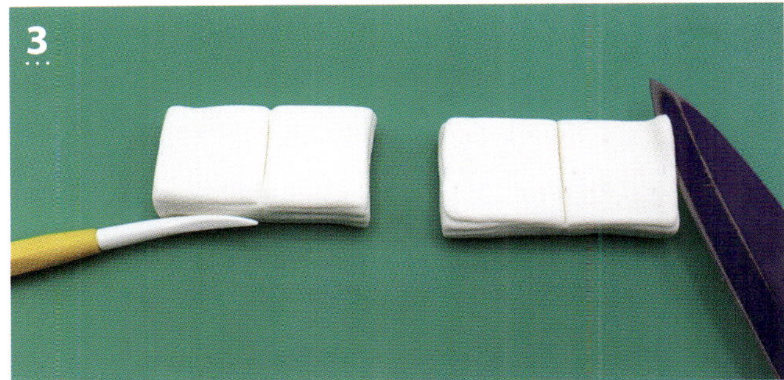

Adding detail to create the illusion of pages in the book.

Making the Reclining Boy Figure

Equipment

- small rolling pin
- sharp knife
- scalpel
- ball tools (variety of sizes)
- Dresden tool
- small, sharp scissors
- metal ruler (optional)
- kitchen scissors or pliers
- paintbrushes for water and for dusting the cheeks
- cake pop stick for supporting the head (or use a wooden skewer)
- dried spaghetti strands (for attaching limbs)
- small foam wedges (you can use make-up wedges)

Materials

- 35g skin-tone modelling paste
- 10g brown modelling paste
- 50g black modelling paste
- 75g red modelling paste
- pink petal dusts for the cheeks (I used Fractal Kitty Nose Pink)
- 2 × 4mm black sugar pearls (optional)

For each book use 20g of white paste for the pages and 15g of different-coloured modelling pastes for the book covers. For this reclining figure we will start by making the books first, to give them time to dry, ready to use when positioning them with the arms later.

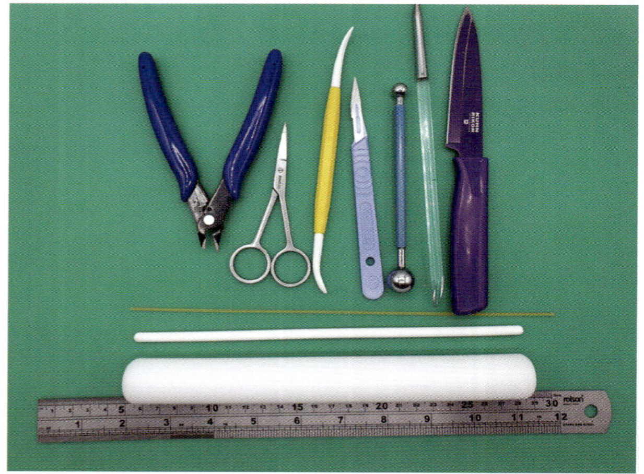

A basic modelling tool set, and some general cake-decorating equipment, is all that is required to make this reclining boy figure.

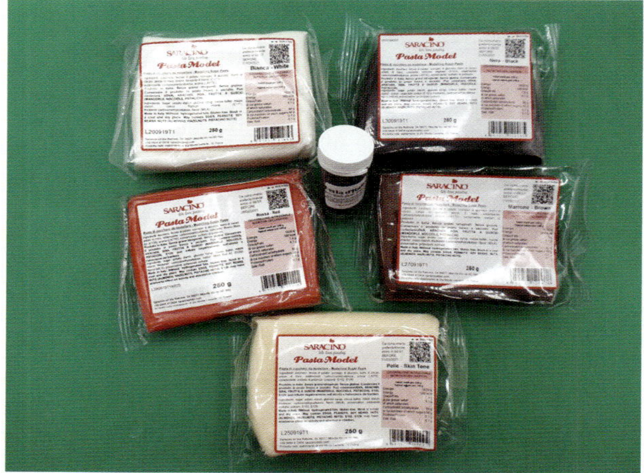

Ready-coloured Saracino modelling paste in skin tone, brown, black and red is used to create this model. You can substitute different colours for the clothing and hair if you wish, when creating your figure.

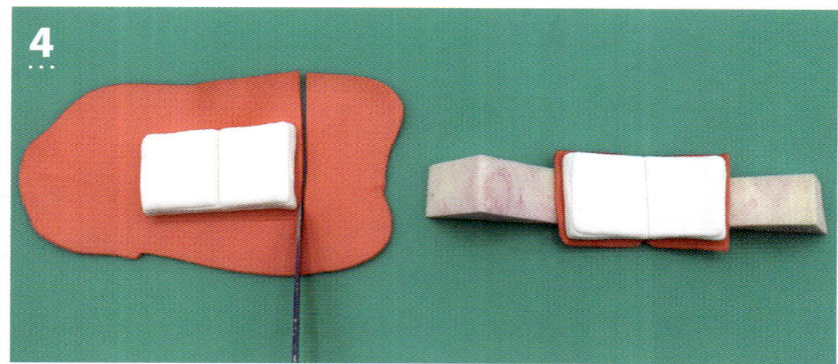

Creating the book cover with your choice of coloured modelling paste.

4

Roll the 15g of coloured modelling paste (red is used here) to a rectangle shape, with a thickness of around 2mm. Place the book pages on top and use a sharp knife to cut round the edges, leaving a small border of coloured paste showing. Bend upwards slightly, and use small foam wedges as support until the paste dries and the book keeps its shape. (Packs of small foam make-up wedges can be purchased cheaply and easily, and are perfect for supporting paste until it is dry and the book holds its shape.)

Closed Book Style

To make the closed book, shape the white modelling paste as before, but this time into a more upright rectangle shape, which is thicker than the open book. For the cover, you need to trim the paste with a small border at the top and bottom, but it needs to be long enough to fold over the top of the white pages. Place the white paste at the right-hand side of the cover and wrap the paste up and over the top.

Use the narrow end of your Dresden tool to mark a line for the spine of the book.

Make an assortment of open and closed books, in different colours, shapes and sizes, using the techniques above. Leave them aside to dry whilst you make the figure.

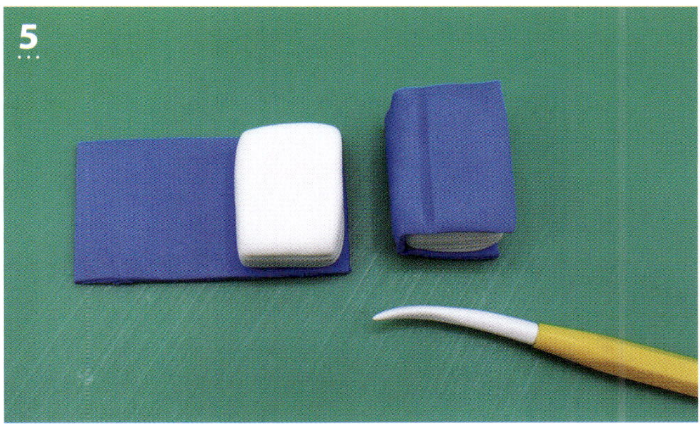

Making the pages and cover for the closed book.

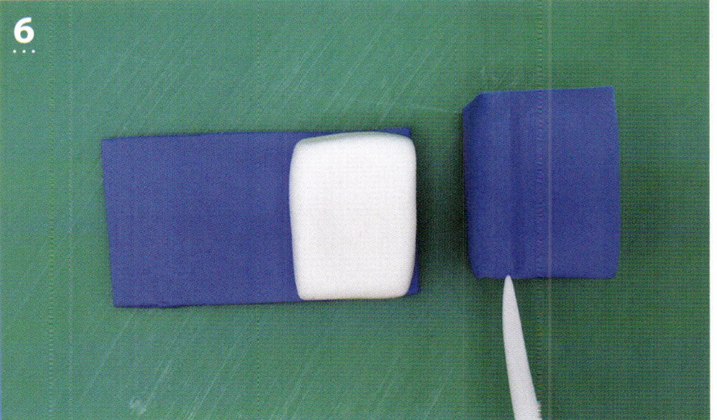

Adding the finishing touches to the closed book for greater realism.

A selection of finished books, ready for adding to your cake later.

MAKING THE LEGS

Roll 50g of black modelling paste into a smooth ball, then into a sausage shape, measuring approximately 16cm (6in) in length. Narrow each end slightly (place one hand at each end and roll gently), leaving the middle section thicker.

Bend the paste in the middle of the thicker section to make two trouser legs. Pinch the paste at each edge on the top section to straighten.

Use a sharp knife to indent the halfway point on each leg, where the knee would be. Bend each leg upwards from this point, pinching at the bottom slightly where the knee would be positioned, to give a little definition.

Use a medium-sized ball tool to press into the bottom of each leg, wiggling it around carefully. This will open up a space to fit the feet into. Gently pinch round the edges with your thumb and finger to thin the paste round the opening.

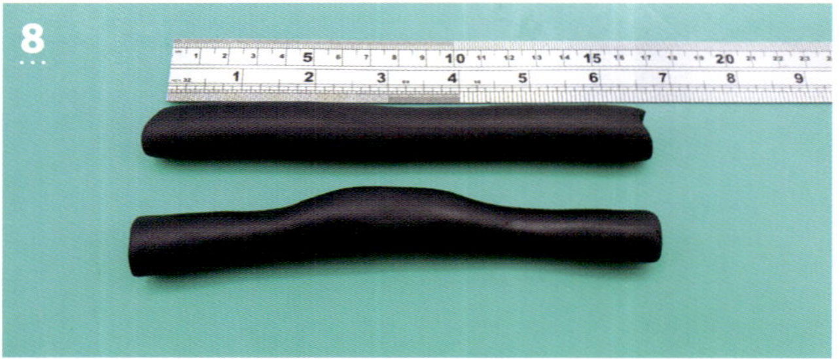

Creating the legs and trousers together with coloured paste.

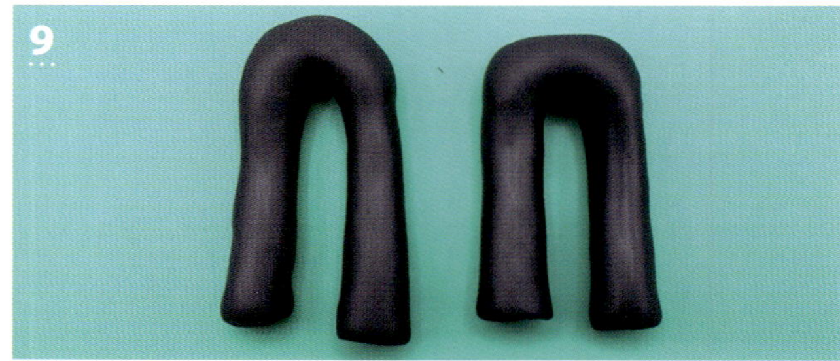

Shaping to form the two legs.

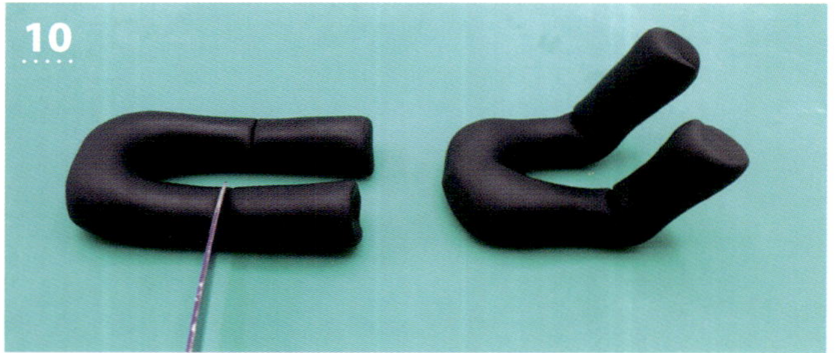

Creating the bent legs and knee area.

Making an opening at the bottom of the trousers to make space in which to fit the feet.

Creating a Different Shade of Skin Tone

Mix 35g skin tone and 10g brown modelling paste together, to create a darker shade of paste. Make sure the two colours are completely mixed together. By varying the ratio of these two colours you can create many different shades. You can find out more about this in the materials chapter of this book, or experiment with your own colour mixes. You can also use gel colours to colour white paste to the skin tone you require.

Using pre-coloured modelling pastes to create a different skin-tone colour.

Helpful Tip

When mixing two or more pre-coloured pastes together to create a different colour/shade (or if adding colouring gels/pastes to white modelling paste), you may find that the modelling paste becomes very soft and a little sticky from overworking it. Leave the paste to rest for a few minutes and you should find it firms back up again, ready to use.

MAKING THE FEET

Roll 8g of skin-tone modelling paste into a ball and cut into two even-sized pieces with a sharp knife. Roll each of these pieces into a ball and then into an oval/egg shape for the feet, making sure that they are both the same size and shape. Work on both feet simultaneously, to keep them uniform throughout the shaping process.

Using your finger, gently stroke the paste downwards at an angle at one side to narrow the toe end of the foot.

Turn the foot over, and use the handle of the ball tool to indent a hollow for the arch of the foot. Smooth with your finger to remove any harsh lines left from the tool.

Use the narrow end of your Dresden tool to mark the toes. You can also use a sharp knife to add further definition if needed.

Break off two small pieces of dried spaghetti and insert one into the bottom of each leg to help hold the feet in place. Brush a thin layer of water or edible glue into the hollow, and add the feet.

Use small sponge wedges to support the legs in place until the paste dries. You will need to keep the supports in place overnight until the paste dries fully, however you can keep working on the rest of the figure whilst the support is in place.

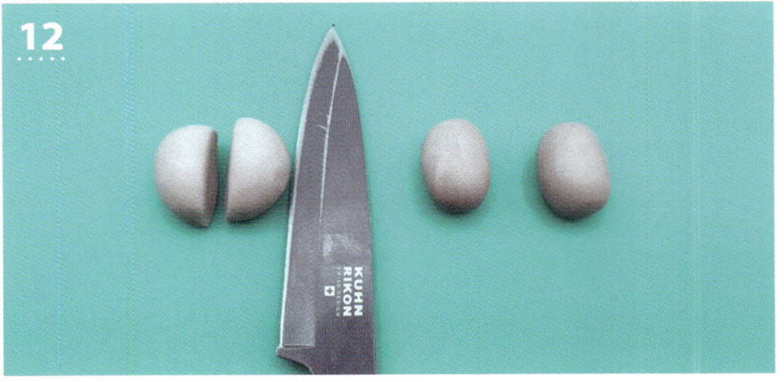

Cutting a piece of paste in half will enable you to make both feet the same size.

Shaping the foot to create a toe area.

Creating the foot arch and smoothing the paste.

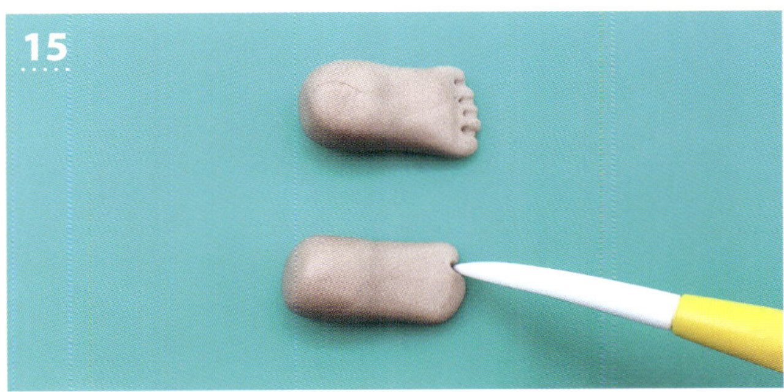

Adding simple details for the individual toes.

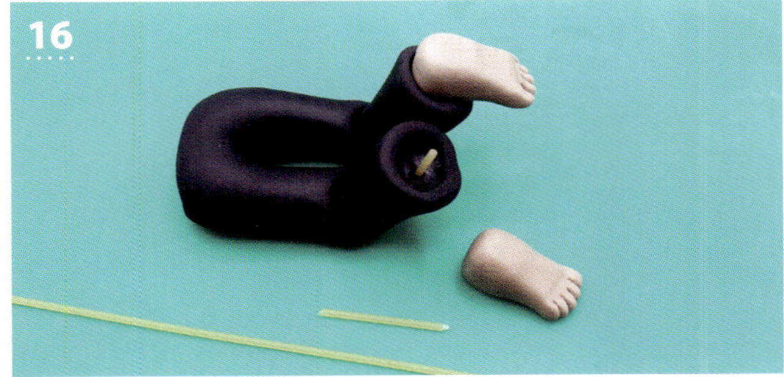

Attaching the feet, using dried spaghetti for additional support.

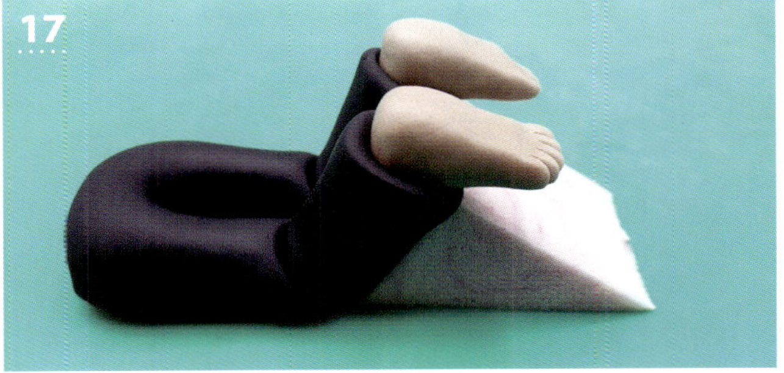

Use foam pieces to support the legs in the desired position until the paste dries.

Making the Body

Roll 50g of red modelling paste into a smooth ball, then into a short, fat sausage. Use a ball tool to hollow out the bottom edge, thinning the edges of the paste between your finger and thumb.

Indent the middle of the body with the side of your hand (or the handle of a ball tool) and bend the front upwards slightly, to make it look as if the back is arching upwards.

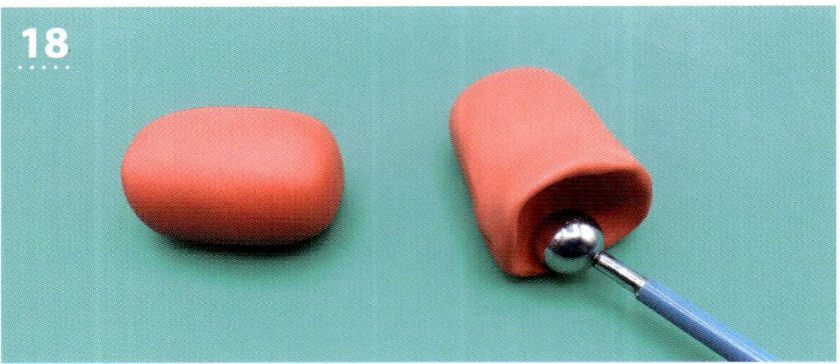

Creating a simple body shape.

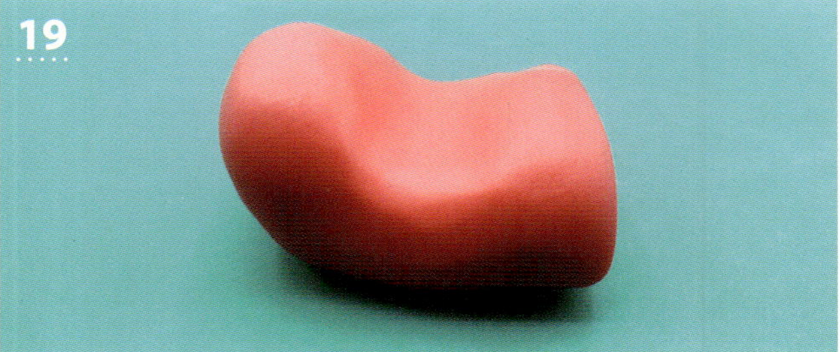

Shaping the body so the back is arching upwards.

Making the Neck

Roll 3g of skin-tone paste into a smooth ball. Thin and elongate it by rolling your finger across one half of the ball, then flatten the bottom and shape the neck by rocking it between your finger and thumb.

Attach the body to the legs with a little water or edible glue, making sure the legs fit neatly inside the hollow you made earlier. Use a ball tool to make an indent at the top of the body for the neck.

Position the neck in place, securing with a little water or edible glue.

Creating and shaping the neck.

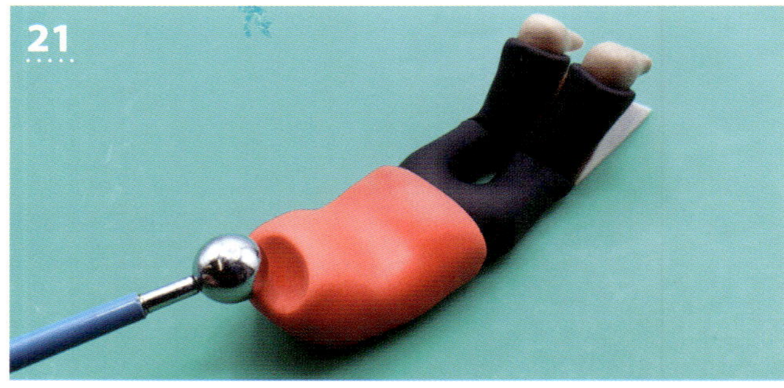

Adding the body to the legs.

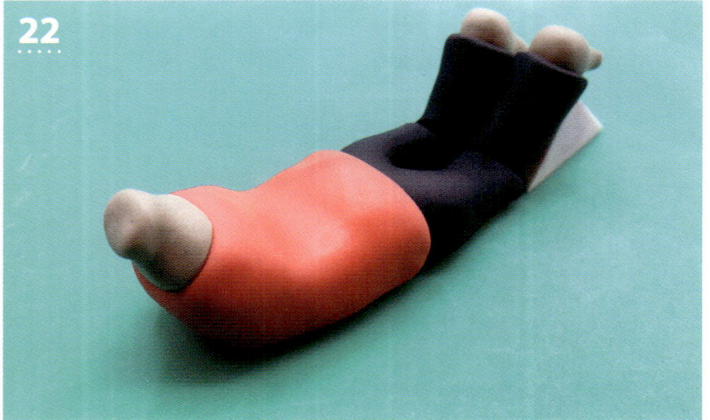

Inserting the neck.

To neaten the join between the neck and body, make a collar by rolling out a thin strip of red modelling paste and trimming the edges straight with a sharp knife. Place the middle of the strip to the back of the neck, trimming any excess so that it joins underneath the neck, out of sight.

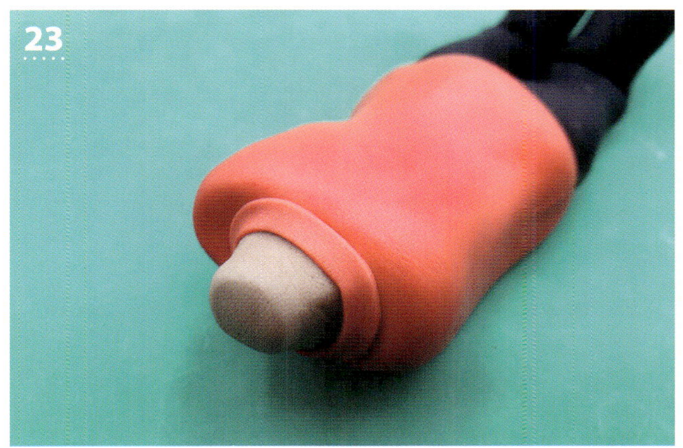

Add a collar to neaten up the join between the neck and body.

Making the Head

Roll 30g of skin-tone modelling paste into a smooth ball, then into an oval/egg shape. Indent two eye sockets halfway down the front of the face, leaving a flat space between them for the nose.

Use a small ball tool to indent two holes for the eyes, inserting a 4mm black sugar pearl in each. Alternatively you can roll tiny balls of black modelling paste for the eyes. Roll a tiny oval-shaped piece of skin-tone modelling paste for the nose, attaching it with a tiny amount of water.

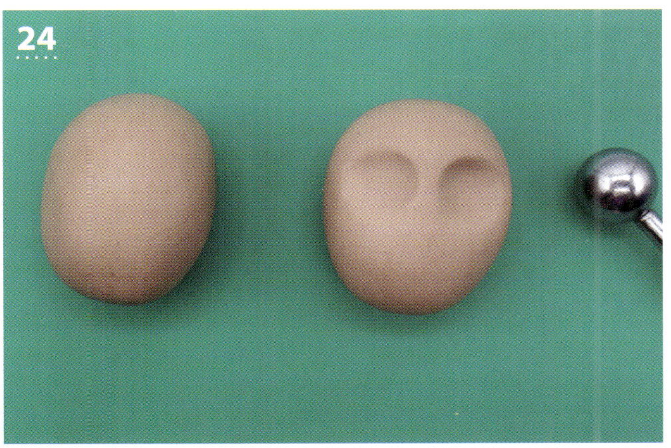

Creating a head shape and indenting eye sockets.

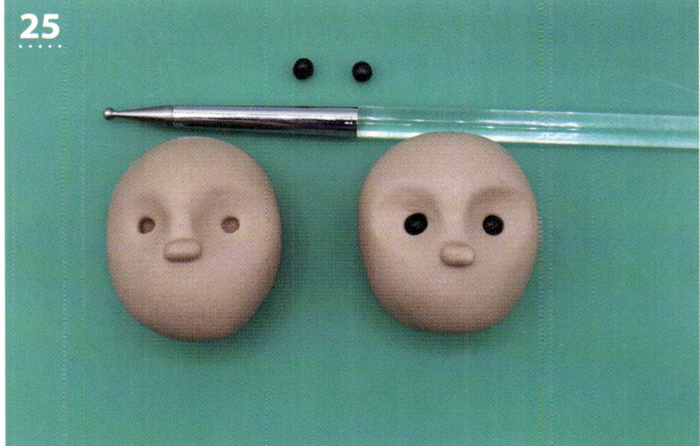

Adding eye and nose details.

Making an Open Mouth

Insert the wider end of your Dresden tool (with the flatter side facing upwards) into the head, halfway between the bottom of the nose and the chin/bottom of the face. Gently pull the tool downwards to open up the mouth cavity. Roll a small sausage of black modelling paste and smooth it to line the open mouth, using your Dresden tool.

To create the teeth, roll a tiny, thin sausage of white modelling paste, attaching it just inside the top of the mouth. If you wish you can leave the strip plain, or mark teeth lines with a small sharp knife or scalpel. Roll a tiny piece of pink modelling paste (mix red and white paste together) to make the tongue. Position it at the bottom of the mouth and gently indent a line down the middle of the tongue with the narrow end of your Dresden tool.

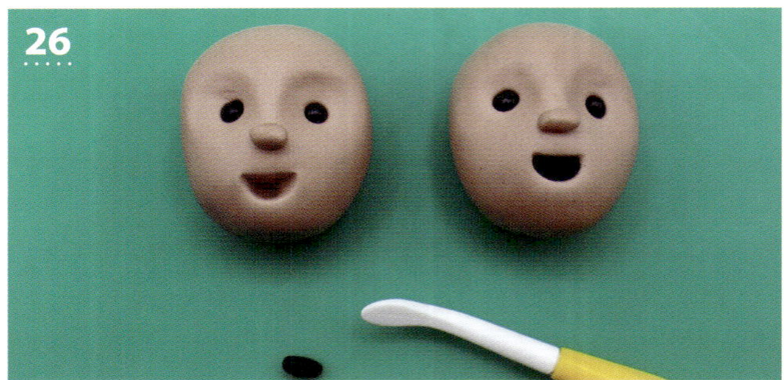

Creating a simple open mouth.

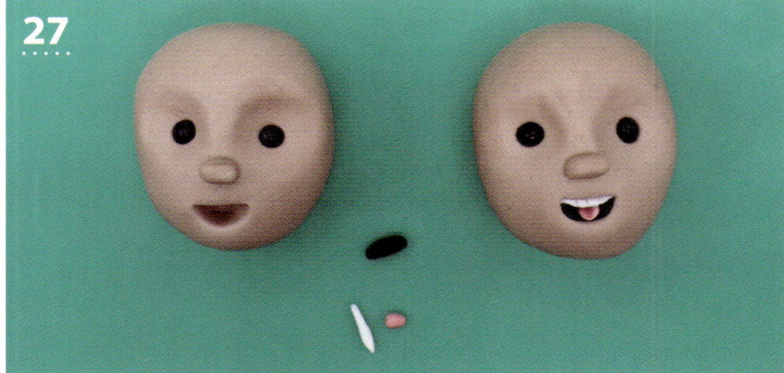

Adding teeth and tongue to finish the mouth.

Making the Eyebrows and Ears

Roll two tiny, thin sausages of black modelling paste for the eyebrows, bend into shape and attach above the eyes with a tiny amount of water. You can experiment with different positioning and shaping of the eyebrows to show different emotions and expressions, giving the impression of the character reacting to the book he is reading.

Roll a small ball of skin-tone modelling paste and cut it in half to make two ears. Shape each ear into a small oval, and indent one end with a small ball tool for the ear opening.

Attach the ears to each side of the head, so that the bottom of the ear is in line with the bottom of the nose.

Making and positioning the eyebrows – you can really change the character and expression of a face by the placement of the eyebrows.

Making two identical ears.

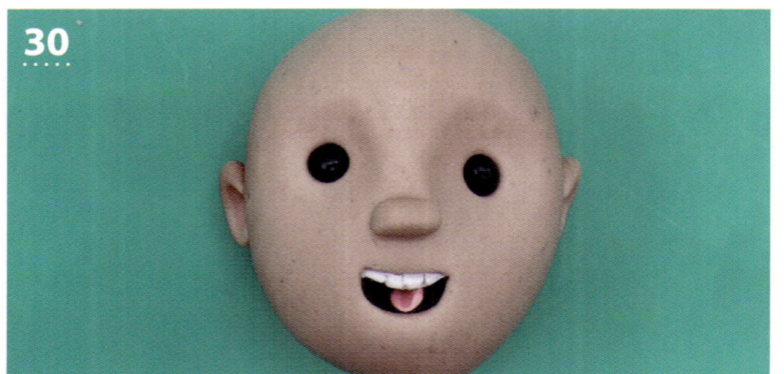

Attaching the ears to the head in the correct position.

Attaching the Head

Due to the positioning of the head, you will need support to keep it in place. Insert a cake pop stick through the neck and into the body, twisting it gently between your finger and thumb as you insert it, so as not to distort the paste. Cut off the excess length with a pair of pliers (or sharp kitchen scissors). Brush a small amount of water on to the top of the neck and over the cake pop stick. Push the head down on to the support, gently twisting from side to side so as not to distort the shape of the head.

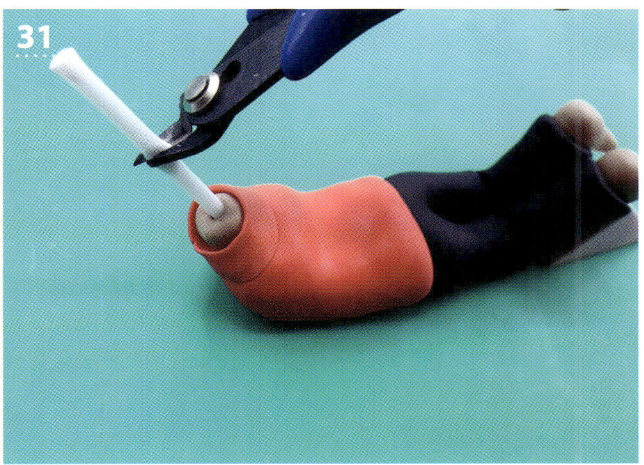

Using support to keep the head in place.

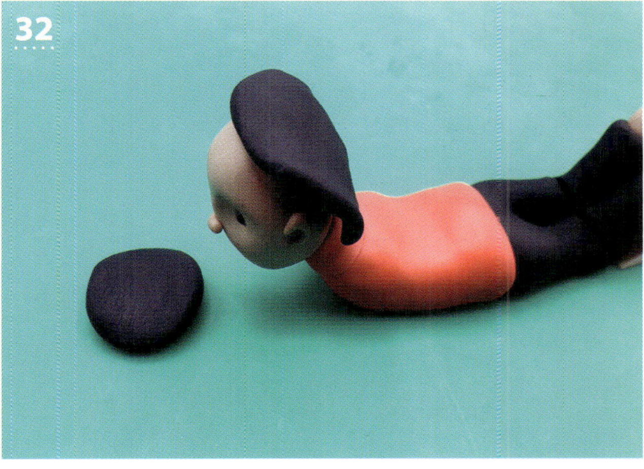

Add the head to the body, and then start forming the base layer of hair.

Making the Hair

Roll approximately 10g of black modelling paste into a ball and flatten into a circle with your fingers until it is big enough to fit over the back of the model's head, like a shower cap. Place the flattened black paste to the back of the head (use a little water to stick it down if needed).

Wrap the paste round to the front of the head, pinching any excess together at the top and trimming with small, sharp scissors. Texture the hair using the narrow end of your Dresden tool to draw lots of lines. Pay particular attention to the direction in which the hair will be facing whilst texturing.

Roll 10g of black modelling paste into a ball and cut it into two pieces, splitting it into approximately one third and two thirds. Roll each piece into a cone and flatten with your fingers. Use the narrow end of your Dresden tool to texture the pieces of paste in the direction of the hair growth.

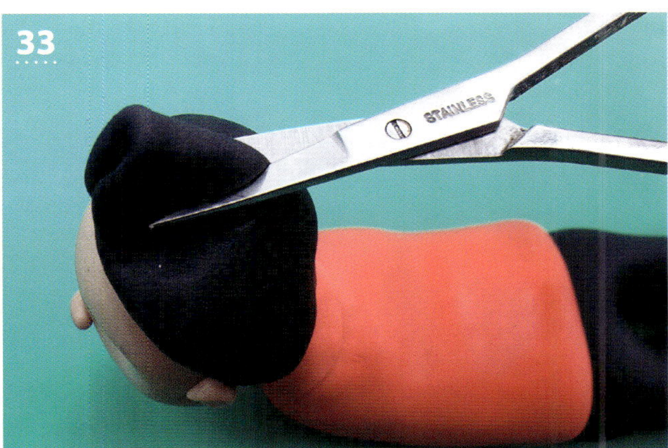

Shaping the hair to the head and texturing.

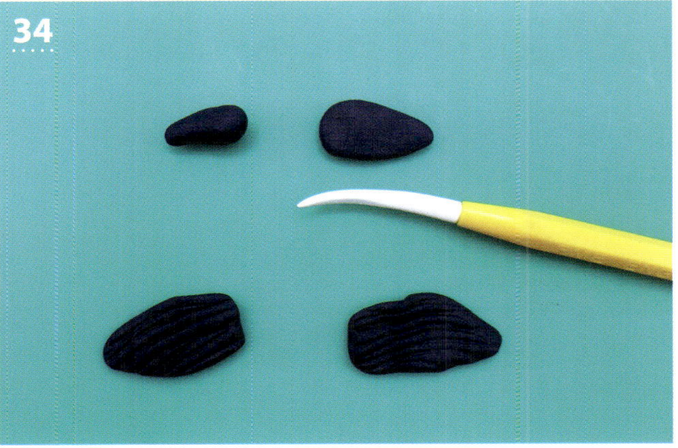

Making extra pieces of hair to style the front of the model's head.

Finishing off the hairstyle to complete the head.

Attach the two pieces of paste to the front of the head, bending and shaping them round the sides of the ears to complete the hairstyle.

Making the Arms

Roll 20g of red modelling paste into a smooth ball to remove creases, then roll it into a sausage, and cut it in half diagonally with a sharp knife to form the two arms/sleeves. Roll your finger across the half-way point on each arm, bending at this point to shape the elbow. Pinch the paste gently with your finger and thumb to define the elbow shape. Use a ball tool to open up the flat end of each sleeve slightly, ready to insert the hands.

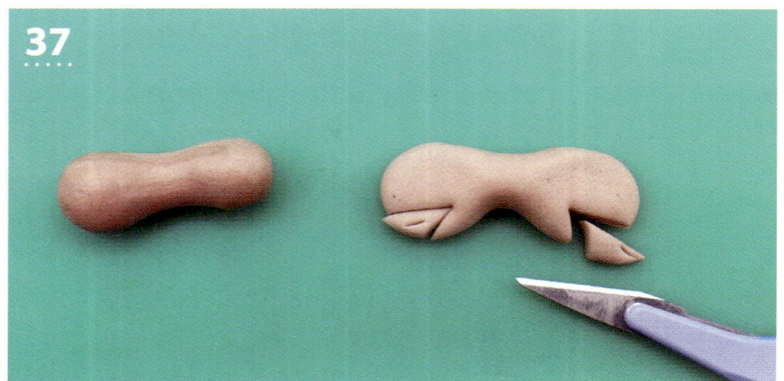

Making and shaping the arms/sleeves.

Making the Hands

Make both hands together from one piece of paste to ensure you make a pair of hands that are the same size and shape.

Roll 3g of skin-tone modelling paste into a ball, then a sausage. Roll your finger across the middle to narrow the paste a little, then flatten each end slightly. Cut a V shape from each end using a scalpel, to form the thumbs.

Using the scalpel, cut the remaining paste to form fingers. First divide in half, then cut each of those in half to create four fingers. Separate the individual fingers, then shape and elongate them by gently rolling and twisting each finger between your finger and thumb. Be very gentle when doing this, as you do not want to pull the fingers off!

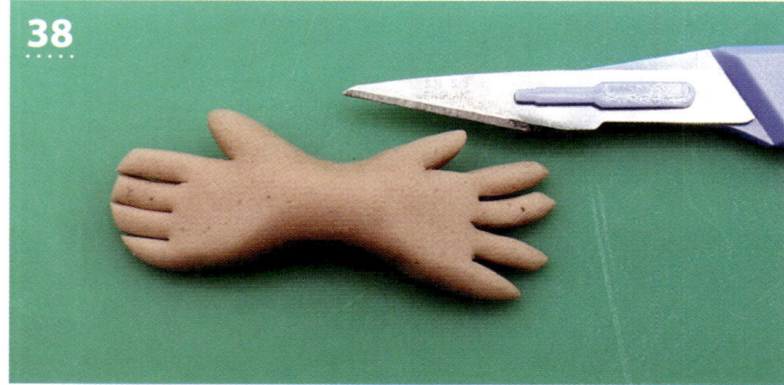

Make both hands together in one piece, to ensure you end up with a pair of hands.

Shaping the fingers on each hand, being careful not to damage them in the process.

Cut the paste in half to separate the hands. Hold the wrist part between your finger and thumb, then roll backwards and forwards to shape.

When attaching the arms, you will need one of the open books to ensure the placement is correct. Place the book just in front of the figure, then add the arms and hands (securing each with a little water or edible glue), positioning them to look as if they are resting on, or holding the book, as preferred. Allow all the pieces to dry completely before removing any foam supports and adding the pieces to your cake.

This design would be fabulous for any book lover! Decorated to resemble a collection of books, you could add titles to the book spines to really personalize this cake design to the recipient.

Cover a 20cm (8in) round cake with white sugar paste, securing it to a covered 30cm (12in) round cake drum with royal icing.

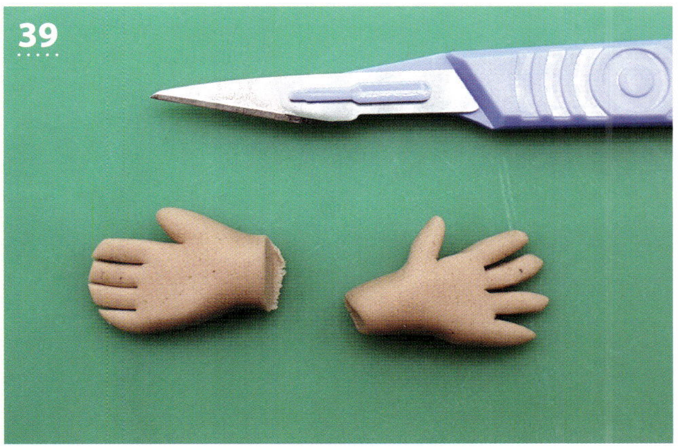

Separating the hands and shaping the wrists.

Positioning and securing the arms to complete the figure.

This cake, decorated as a collection of books, is perfectly in theme with the boy figure, who is lying down to enjoy his favourite book.

Preparing the Book Spines

To work out the size for each book spine (if you want them to be equal in size round the cake), first you need to measure the circumference of the cake. For this 20cm (8in) round covered cake, I needed thirteen spines, each measuring 5cm (2in) wide. The height for each needs to be just a little taller than the height of the cake, so they stick up slightly over the top. A variety of different coloured books is made here, two each of five different colours and three of another.

Roll out your different coloured sugar pastes to an even thickness (*see* the football cake for details on how to do this), then trim to size using a metal ruler and a pizza roller cutter or sharp knife. Cut out all the pieces, then leave them to firm up slightly on a foam pad before adding to the cake, so they are easier to handle.

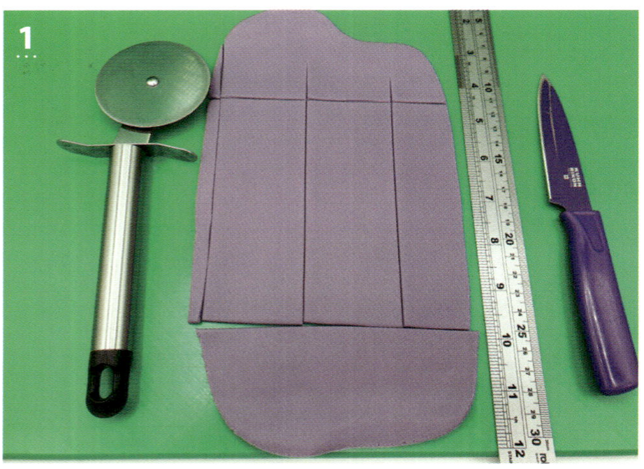

Measuring the cake to calculate the size for each of the book spines, before cutting them from various coloured pastes.

Decorating the Cake

Use edible glue or water to attach each of the book spines to the covered cake. Ensure they are placed in an upright position, and that the tops sit a little above the cake, without any gaps.

Add detailing to the book spines, using a variety of equipment – for example, different sized oval cutters or a metal ruler/Dresden tool to press into the paste to leave an indent.

Positioning the coloured book spines round the side of the cake and adding detail to them.

To continue the book detailing on to the top of the cake, cut narrow strips of coloured paste, two for each book. Measure the strips so that they reach from the outside edge to the middle of the cake. The ends of the strips that will be in the centre of the cake will need to be trimmed on the diagonal to fit. Secure the strips with a little edible glue or water, then fill the hole left in the centre with a small ball of black sugar paste.

Adding Extra Details to the Book Spines

Add extra detail to the book spines using edible paint in metallic colours. Either use ready-made edible metallic paint, or make your own by mixing lustre dust and rejuvenator fluid. Paint the indented areas with the edible paint carefully, using a fine brush. Support your wrist with your other hand to keep it steady as you paint.

Attach the reclining figure to the top of the cake, using a little royal icing. You can also add some additional small modelled books to the cake drum, then trim the edge with 15mm ribbon in the colour of your choice to finish.

Continuing the book details on to the top of the cake.

Adding extra details to the books with metallic edible paint.

Making Figures with Additional Furniture

Sometimes it is useful to create a model sitting on a piece of furniture, rather than directly on the cake itself. This is particularly useful if the cake topper is to be kept as a memento or keepsake, as it can be designed to fit on a separate cake drum, placed on top of the decorated cake, making it easy to remove.

In this chapter, I will show you how to use Rice Krispie Cereal Treats (also known as RKT), to create an edible armchair, before modelling the figure to fit. The figure sitting in an armchair is pictured on a 6" (15cm) round cake.

MAN SITTING IN AN ARMCHAIR

This man sitting in an armchair is quick and simple to make, using basic modelling tools and techniques. It can be made with any age or gender of figure; however, it is very well suited for retirement cakes or milestone birthdays.

Additional figures could be added around the chair to represent children or grandchildren for a larger cake. A pet cat or dog could also be included, perhaps sitting on the figure's knee.

Children and pets can also be added around the seated figure if appropriate.

◄ This elderly gentleman, sitting reading in his armchair, makes a fabulous cake topper for a retirement or milestone birthday cake. It can easily be adapted for other ages too though.

Man Sitting in an Armchair

Equipment

- Small rolling pin
- 24-gauge black florist wire
- Plastic dowel (or round handled tool)
- Wooden skewer
- Sharp knife
- Scalpel
- Ball tools (variety of sizes)
- Dresden tool
- Pliers
- Spare cake card/drum
- Paintbrushes for water and for dusting cheeks

Materials

- 4 x Rice Krispie cereal bars
- 250g brown sugar paste
- 30g white sugar paste
- 70g blue modelling paste
- 45g black modelling paste
- 15g brown modelling paste
- 125g white modelling paste
- 60g skin tone modelling paste
- Petal dusts of your choice for cheeks (I used Sugarflair rose)

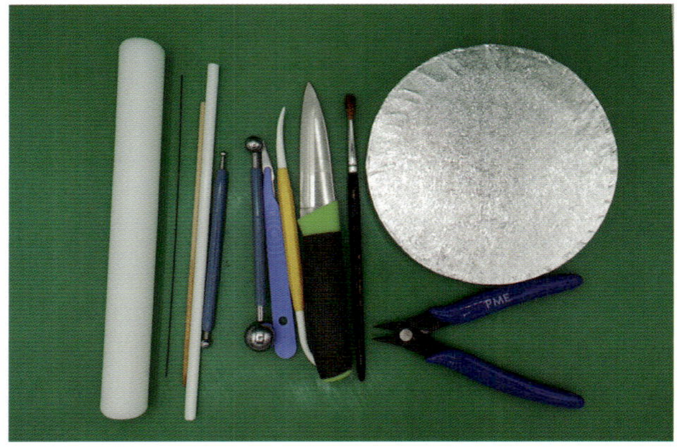

A basic tool set, and general cake decorating equipment is all that is required to make this figure sitting in an armchair, with a couple of optional extras to add further detail if you want to.

I used ready coloured Saracino modelling paste in skin tone, white, blue, brown and black to create the modelled figure. Ready made Rice Krispie cereal bars were used to create the chair, and pre-coloured brown sugar paste for covering.

Modelling the armchair

Rice Krispie Treats (RKT) are easy to sculpt and shape, and very widely used in cake decorating. As a modelling medium, it is light, which makes it particularly useful for larger cake toppers, since it is not adding too much weight to the top of the cake.

RKT also last very well, making them perfect to use for toppers that are designed to keep as a memento, although they are equally good to eat, making them a very popular choice, especially with children!

DIY RKT

If you prefer not to use commercially available Rice Krispie cereal bars, you can make your own.

Melt 60g of marshmallows in the microwave for approximately one minute, then stir in 60g of Rice Krispies until completely coated.

Leave to cool for approximately five minutes before shaping by hand.

If you wish, you can press the mixture firmly into a square greased tin, allow to set and then carve into shape.

Using a sharp knife, divide the Rice Krispie cereal bars as follows:

- Cut approximately 1cm from one end of two of the bars
- Cut one bar in half lengthways to create two thin slices
- Leave one bar full (uncut)

Stack the cereal bars together, placing one of the thin slices on top of the full bar to create the seat of the chair. Add the two longer pieces to the back, followed by the two shorter pieces at each side of the seat to create the arms.

You will have one thin slice of cereal bar left over.

Slice the remaining thin layer into three pieces, adding two along the top of the top of the chair back to add a little extra height. You will be left with one small piece of cereal bar, which you will not need.

Compress the cereal bars together with your hands to ensure they are stuck together, and also to round off the edges slightly. You should not need to use anything to stick the bars together, as they are naturally quite sticky. However, if the shape is not holding together, you can use a small amount of melted chocolate as a 'glue' between the separate pieces.

Cutting the Rice Krispie cereal bars to size for the armchair.

Arrange the pieces of cereal bars to form the basic shape.

Adding extra height to the chair back with the leftover piece of cereal bar.

Place the armchair onto a spare cake drum (or card) while working on it. This will make it easier to handle without damaging.

Roll out the brown sugar paste to a thickness of approximately 3–4mm, then drape it carefully over the armchair. Gently smooth the paste over the back and arms of the chair, and into the corners of the seat.

Trim the excess paste around the bottom to approximately 1cm away from the chair, then tuck this paste underneath.

Neaten the bottom edge of the chair with the narrow end of your Dresden tool. Wrap a small piece of brown paste in a double layer of cling film, to use as a smoother. This will help to smooth around the curved shape of the chair, as well as getting into the tricky corners of the seat.

Use the narrow end of the Dresden tool to add markings on the armchair. These are typically around the front of the chair arms, along the front of the chair, towards the bottom, as well as around the sides of the lower seat area. (You may find it helpful to look at pictures of armchairs to get an idea of different styles for inspiration.)

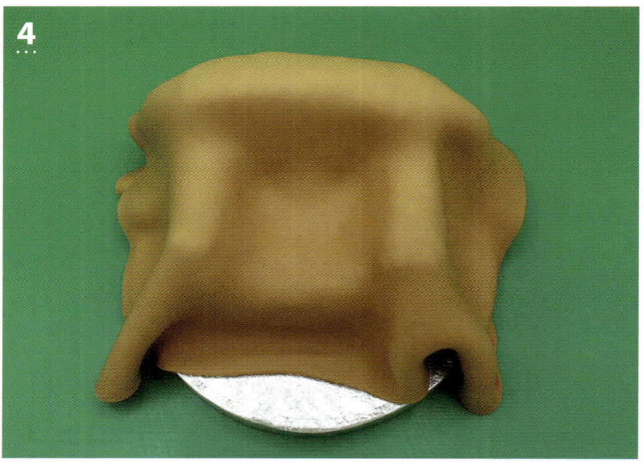

Covering the armchair with sugar paste.

Smoothing and neatening the sugar paste layer.

Adding extra detail to the armchair with a Dresden tool.

Modelling the cushions

Use some of the leftover brown sugar paste to shape two cushions, one for the seat of the chair and one for the back. You will need to measure these to your armchair, and keep adjusting the shape to ensure a good fit.

Secure the cushions in place with a little water (or edible glue). Use the end of a small rolling pin to create hollows in the centre of the back and seat cushions where the figure will be sitting.

Create crease lines along various points of the cushions, using the narrow end of your Dresden tool. Again, you can refer to pictures of armchairs to help with this part if necessary.

Mix 30g of white sugar paste with a little of the leftover brown sugar paste, to create a very pale brown shade (you can use a different colour if you prefer).

Split the paste in half, and roll into two balls. Shape these into cubes with your fingers, then flatten to create smaller cushions. Mark around the edges of the cushions with the narrow end of your Dresden tool to create a line, giving the impression of a seam or join.

Position the two smaller cushions on the chair, but do not secure in place, as you may need to adjust the positioning around the figure as it is modelled.

Modelling the chair cushions.

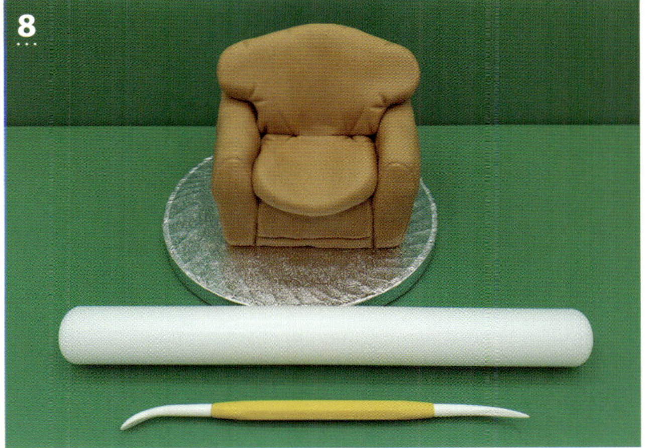

Attaching and adding detail to the chair cushions.

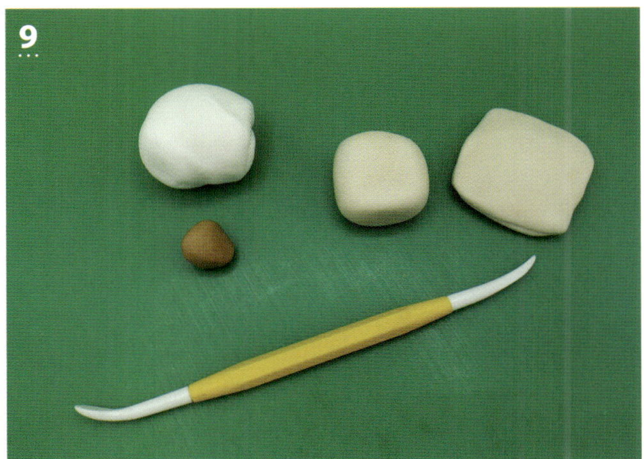

Creating smaller cushions to add to the chair.

Adding the cushions to finish the chair.

Making the legs

Mix together 70g of blue and 10g of black modelling paste to create a deeper, more denim-like colour for the trousers. If you don't mix the colour through completely, it will give you a streaky look, like some jeans have, but this is purely optional. If you prefer to use a solid colour, just keep mixing until totally combined.

Roll the 80g of dark blue modelling paste into a ball and then into a long sausage, measuring approximately 20cm in length.

Fold in half and shape the top of the trousers, by pinching the outer edges gently between your finger and thumb, to make them a little squarer. Flatten the two bottom edges by pressing with your finger.

Turn the trousers over and use the back of a knife to indent a line halfway down each trouser leg. Bend the legs at this point, gently pinching the front to create a bent knee area. Use a ball tool to open up the bottoms of the trouser legs slightly.

Using the narrow end of the Dresden tool, mark crease lines at the top of the trousers, around the knee area and also along the bottom edge, where the trousers will gather above the shoes.

Creating a denim style colour for the trousers.

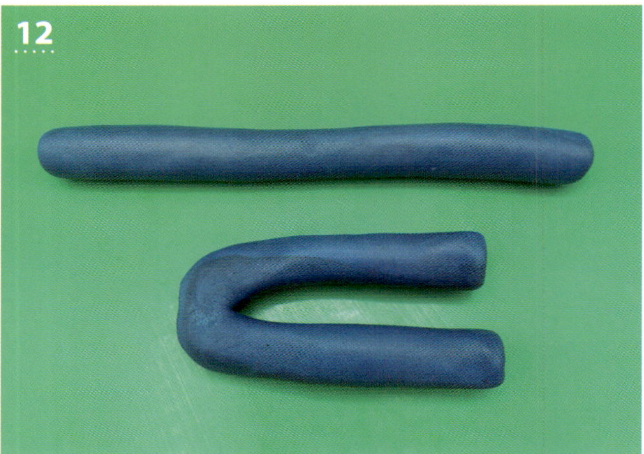

Shaping the trousers.

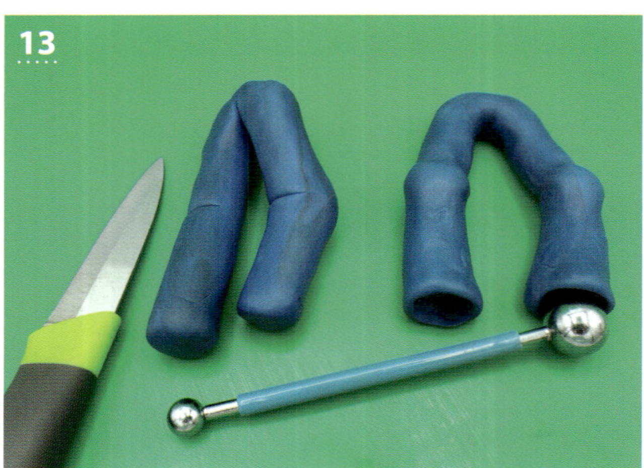

Creating the knee area and shaping the bottom of the trousers.

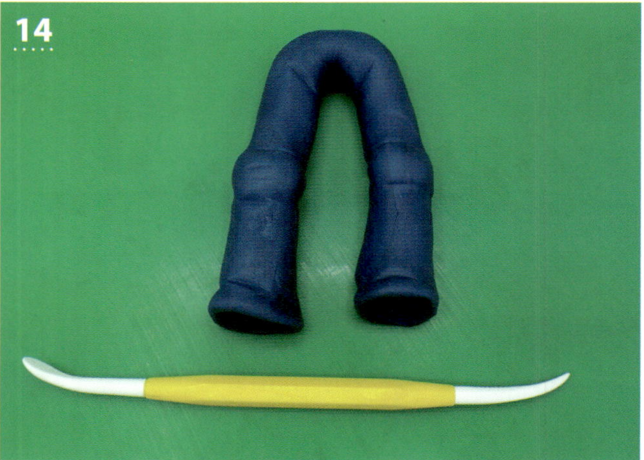

Adding further definition to the trousers.

To make the shoes, roll 15g of brown modelling paste into a ball, then cut in half to create two equal pieces. Roll these two pieces of paste into balls, then narrow slightly into ovals. Stroke the paste downwards with your finger along the front half of the shoe, leaving the other half untouched.

Mark a line down the front of the shoe, with the narrow end of the Dresden tool, then turn over and mark the heel of the shoe at the bottom.

Position the legs onto the chair, adjusting the two smaller cushions if necessary, and secure with a little water (or edible glue). Brush a little more inside the bottom of the trousers, and secure the shoes in place, so that they rest onto the cake card.

Creating the shape for the shoes.

Adding detail to the shoes.

Positioning the legs and shoes onto the chair.

Creating the grey modelling paste colour for the body.

Modelling the body

Mix together 100g white and 25g black modelling paste to create a medium grey shade (the ratio can be adjusted depending on the shade required).

Forming a simple shape for the body.

Roll 75g of the grey modelling paste into a ball, and then in to a cone shape. Flatten the top half, towards the narrower end, to create a flatter chest and more rounded tummy area.

Flatten the bottom of the body onto the board, so that it will fit better over the legs. Use a ball tool to create an indent at the top for the neck to be added later.

Add the body to the top of the legs, using a little water (or edible glue) to secure in place. Add crease marks to the body using the narrow end of the Dresden tool.

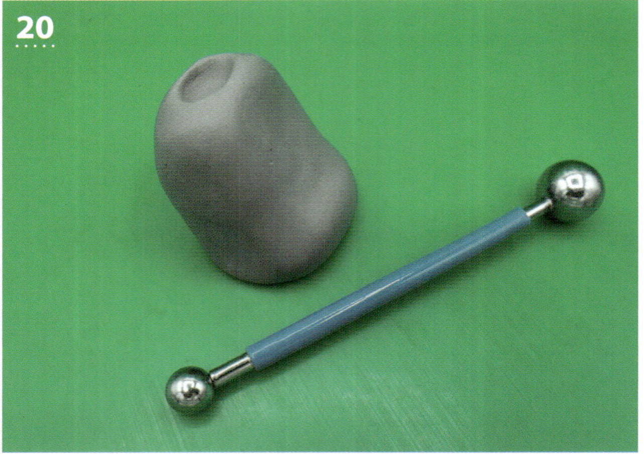

Adding more shape and detail to the body.

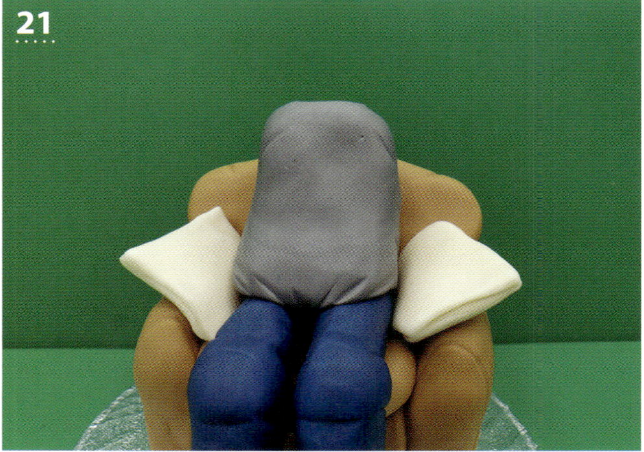

Positioning the body onto the legs and adding extra definition.

Making the arms

Roll 30g of grey modelling paste into a long sausage, measuring approximately 15cm in length.

Cut in half, at a 45-degree angle, with a sharp knife. Use a sawing motion with the knife whilst cutting, to prevent distorting the shape of the paste.

Starting to create the arms.

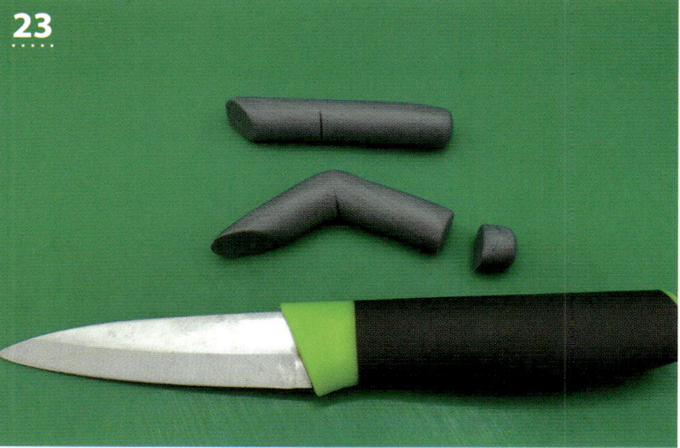

Creating the elbow shape for the arms.

Use the back of the knife to indent a line for the elbow crease, bending the paste and pinching gently to form the elbow. Trim the bottom of the paste flat, to create the end of the sleeve.

With a ball tool, indent the flat ends of the sleeves slightly, in order to make space for the hands to be added.

It is better to model both hands together, in order to ensure that you create a pair of hands, rather than two identical ones by mistake.

Roll 4g of skin tone modelling paste into a ball and then into a short sausage shape. Gently roll your little finger over the middle section to narrow slightly, leaving the two ends untouched.

Flatten each end of the shape gently with your finger, to create the hands.

With a scalpel, cut out a triangle of paste from each hand (at the same side), gently rolling the narrow piece of paste between your thumb and finger to create thumbs.

For the remaining paste, carefully square off the rounded edge with your fingers, so it is more evenly shaped.

Divide the remaining paste into four fingers, by cutting in half, then in half again at each side. Gently roll each finger between your finger and thumb to shape and slightly elongate.

Use the wider end of the Dresden tool to press at the end of each finger/thumb to make slight indents for the finger nails.

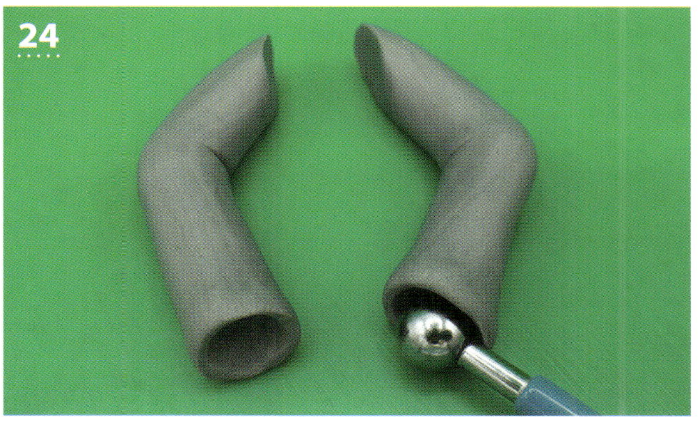

Making space to fit the hands in the arms.

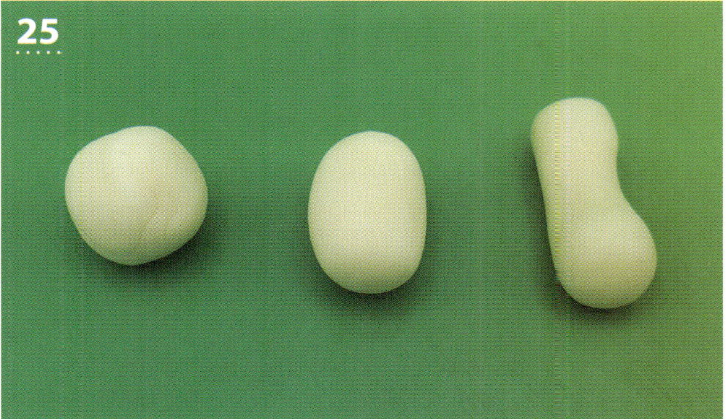

Forming the shape for the hands.

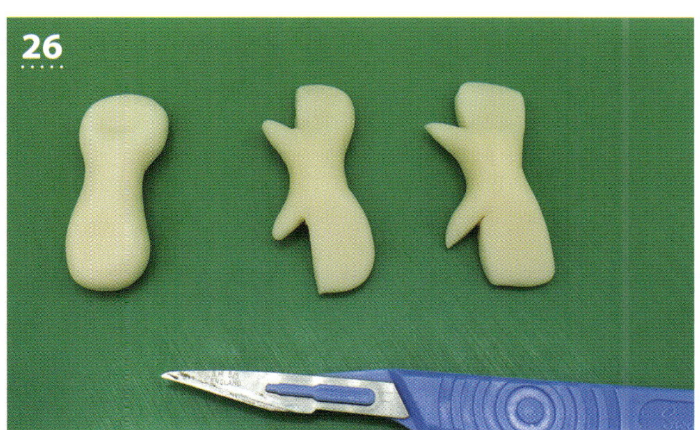

Working on both hands together to create a pair the same.

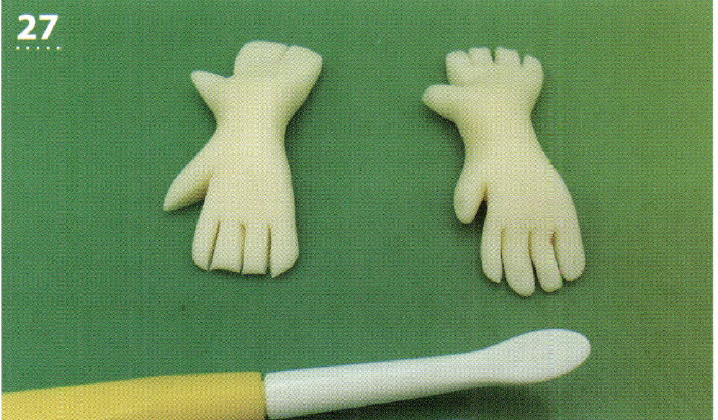

Adding fingers and fingernail details to the hands.

Separate the two hands with a scalpel. Hold each hand, one at a time, between your finger and thumb, rolling backwards and forwards to create a wrist area.

Paint a small amount of water (or edible glue) into the ends of the sleeves, and position hands with the thumbs pointing upwards, whilst resting on the knees.

Using 10g each of white and black modelling paste, model an open book (following instructions on page 59).

Place the book, so it is resting on the model's lap, and secure the hands in place with a little water (or edible glue). The thumbs need to be separated from the fingers, holding onto the front of the book.

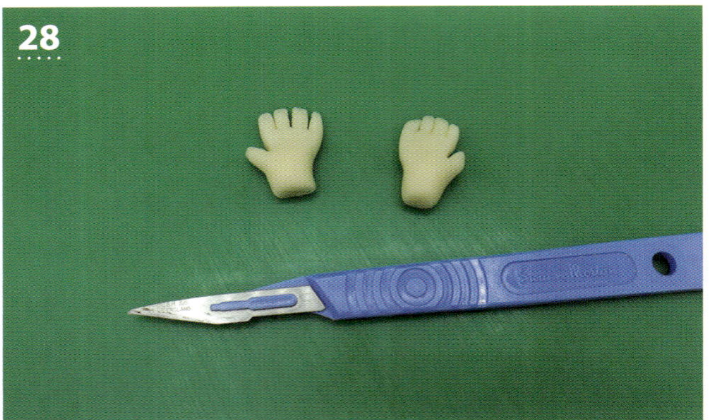

Separating the hands and creating a wrist area.

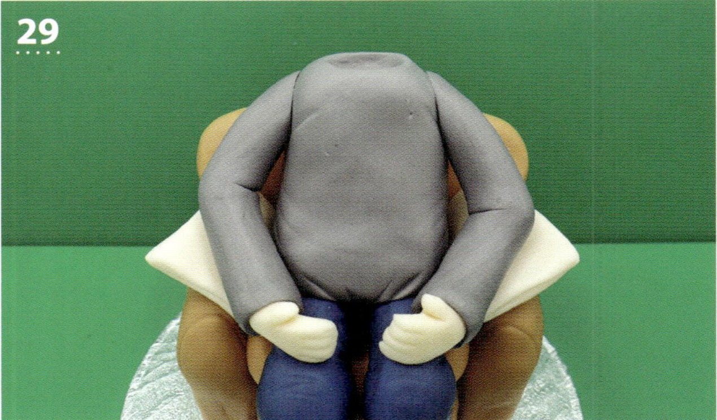

Positioning the arms and hands onto the seated figure.

Adding a book to the figure, ensuring the hands are correctly positioned.

Roll a 3g piece of skin tone modelling paste into a ball, and then into a rounded cone shape to fit into the hollow created earlier for the neck. You shouldn't need to use any water or edible glue to fix into place.

To make a collar, which will hide the join, roll a small piece of grey modelling paste into a long, thin sausage. Flatten slightly with your hand (or you could press down onto it gently with a rolling pin).

Starting at the back of the model, wrap the collar around the bottom of the neck area, trimming it to size at the back to join. Smooth the join gently with your finger to blend together.

To create a support for the head, insert a wooden skewer through the neck, body and down into the chair. Trim with pliers, to leave a length of approximately 2-3cm of skewer above the model.

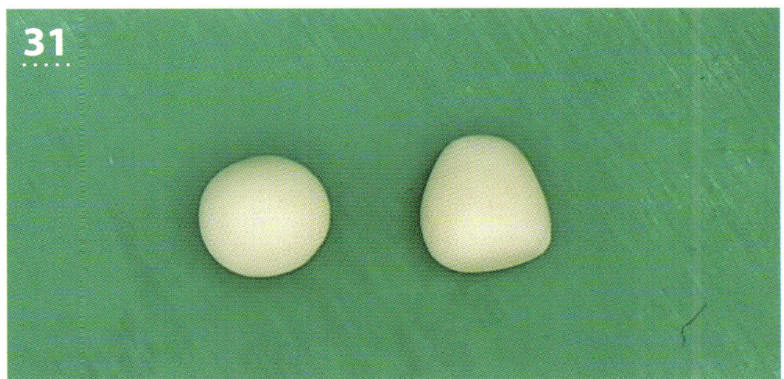

Modelling a neck to add to the figure.

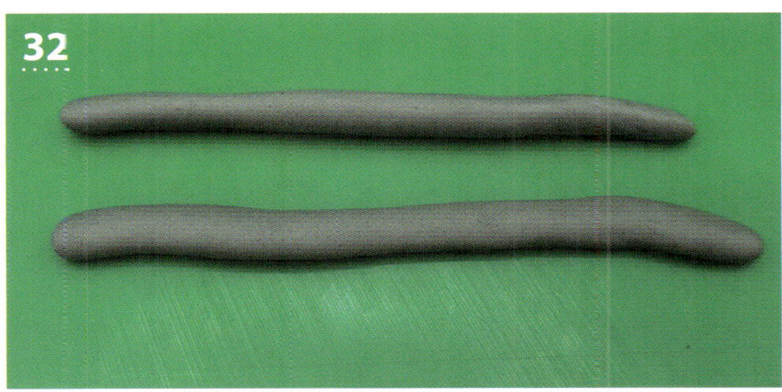

Creating a collar for the model.

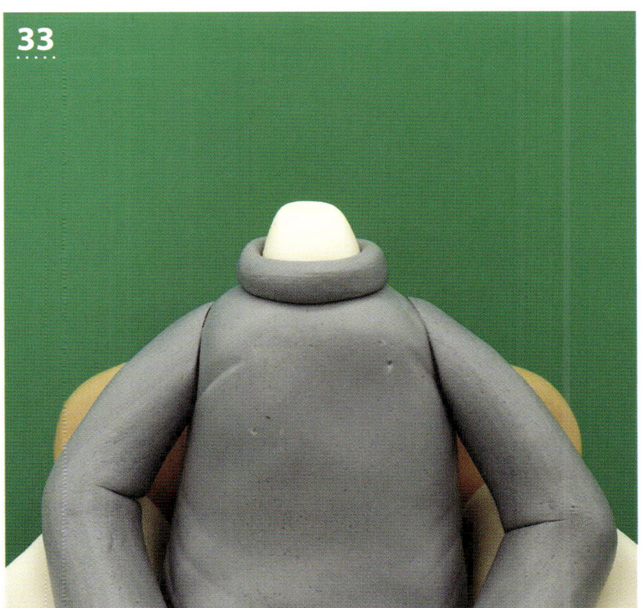

Adding the neck and using the collar to hide the join.

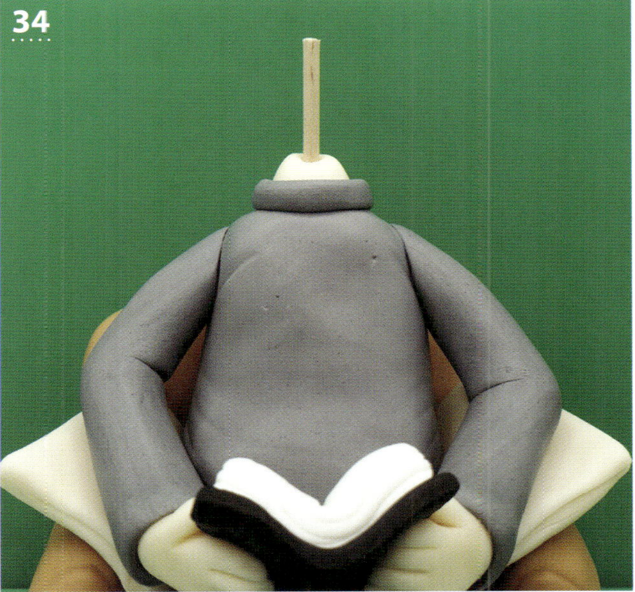

Inserting a support to secure the head.

This model of an older gentleman has a few added wrinkles and creases, as well as being slightly balding on the top of his head. He is also wearing a pair of reading glasses. However, you could substitute one of the other styles of head in the book if you prefer.

Roll 50g of skin tone modelling paste into a smooth ball, then into an oval shape. Use your thumb to stroke the paste at the back downwards a little, so that is sits up away from the workboard. When viewed from the side, the shape looks a little like a traditional loaf of bread.

Make an indentation halfway down the face with your finger or a rounded handle from a modelling tool. This will form the eye sockets and browbone. Soften the edges of the indentation at the top and bottom, so they start to blend into the head slightly.

Use a ball tool to create more definition for the eye sockets, leaving a space between them for the nose to be created.

Roll a tiny ball of skin tone modelling paste into a slight oval, and position between the bottom of the eye sockets, to form a simple nose shape. With a smaller ball tool, create a deeper hole for each eye.

Fill each hole with a small ball of white modelling paste, and press gently to smooth flat with your finger. Create a smaller hole towards the bottom of each white area, filling with a ball of brown paste for the iris.

Repeat the process to create pupils, using a tiny amount of black modelling paste, then add white modelling paste as a highlight for the eyes.

Roll black modelling paste to a very fine point, then attach around the top half of the eye with a little water. Be careful not to add too much water, as it can cause the black paste to bleed.

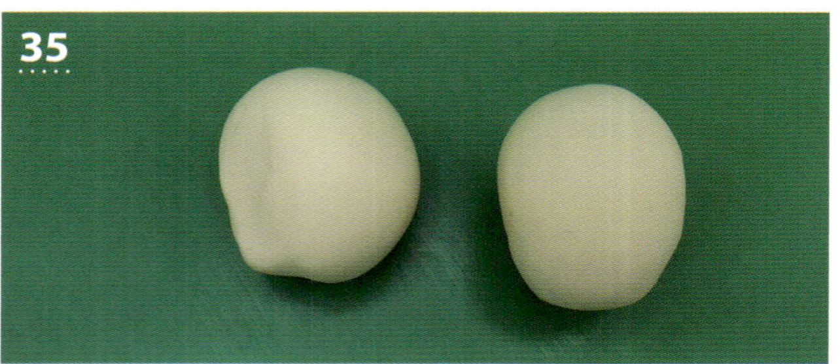

Shaping the skin tone paste into a head.

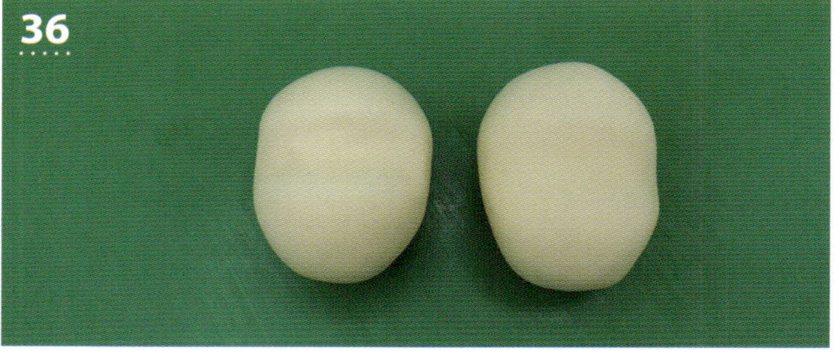

Creating the space for the eye sockets.

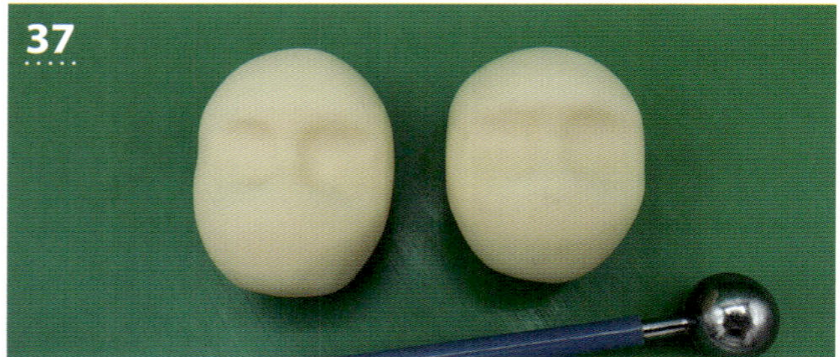

Defining the area for the eye sockets and nose.

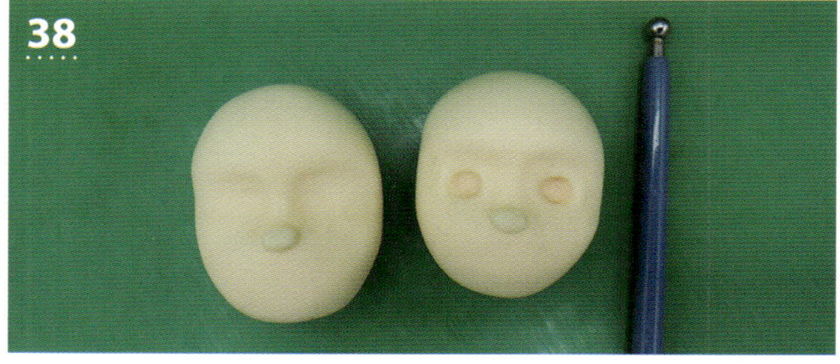

Adding simple nose details and creating a space for the eyes.

Adding the whites and irises to the eyes.

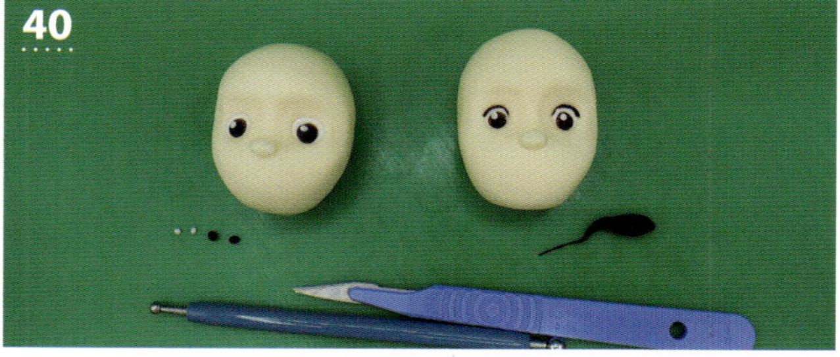

Finishing the eyes with pupils, highlights and eye lash line.

Use a scalpel to cut a straight line for the mouth, cutting to a depth of at least 5mm. Whilst the blade is still in the cut, wiggle from side to side to clean the cut. Then, lift the scalpel blade upwards gently under the paste to form the upper lip.

With the narrow end of your Dresden tool, make a small indent for the philtrum, from under the nose to the edge of the upper lip. Gently press upwards at either side with your finger or the wider end of your Dresden tool to create the 'Cupid's bow' effect of the top lip.

Insert the wider end of the Dresden tool into the mouth, and pull downwards to open the mouth up a little.

Create the bottom lip area by running the wider end of the Dresden tool from one side to the other, approximately 3mm below the cut edge.

Push upwards slightly at each side to create a smile and rub over any harsh lines left by the Dresden tool to soften.

To resize and reshape the face to be in proportion to your figure model, use the rounded end of a modelling tool to mark around the chin area. Continue to push the paste downwards, away from the face, until you are happy with the shape.

Mix a pinch of grey modelling paste into 15g of white modelling paste to create the desired colour for the hair and eyebrows. Roll a small ball into thin strands to create the eyebrows, the outer edge of the eyebrow is slightly thinner, and a little more tapered.

Eyebrows can be used very effectively when creating different expressions for faces, as their shape helps us to illustrate how faces change with a range of emotions. For example, very arched eyebrows can convey surprise, whereas one raised eyebrow suggests confusion or curiosity.

Apply pink petal dust to the cheeks to give a rosy glow, using a rounded paintbrush. Be careful to remove any excess dust from the brush by tapping it onto a piece of kitchen paper. Apply the dust in thin layers to build up the colour gradually. It is very easy to end up with too much colour on the face. If this does happen, remove by blotting with a clean, damp tissue. Wait for the paste to dry completely before reapplying the colour.

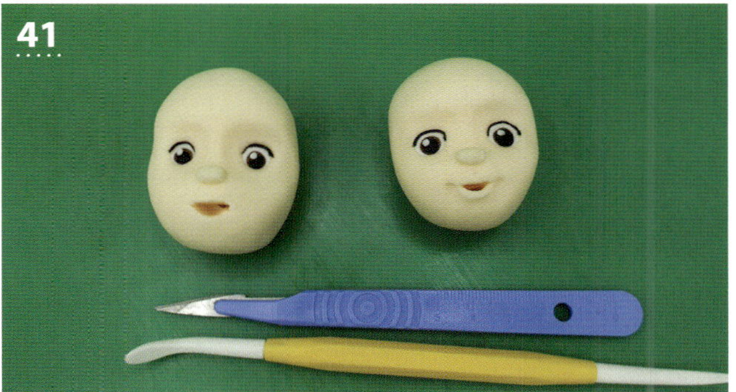

Creating a slightly open mouth with a smile.

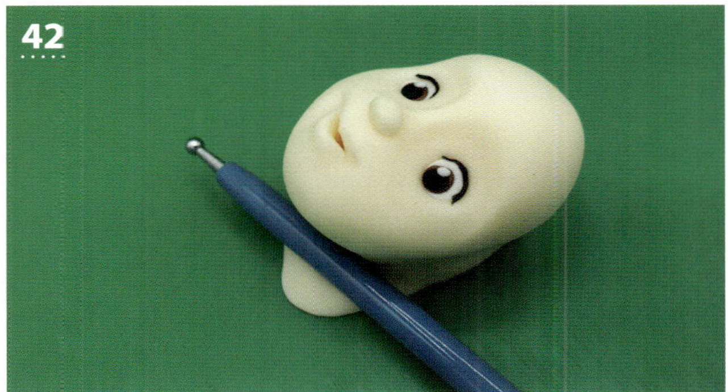

Refining the shape and size of the head to suit the model.

Adding eyebrows to match the hair colour.

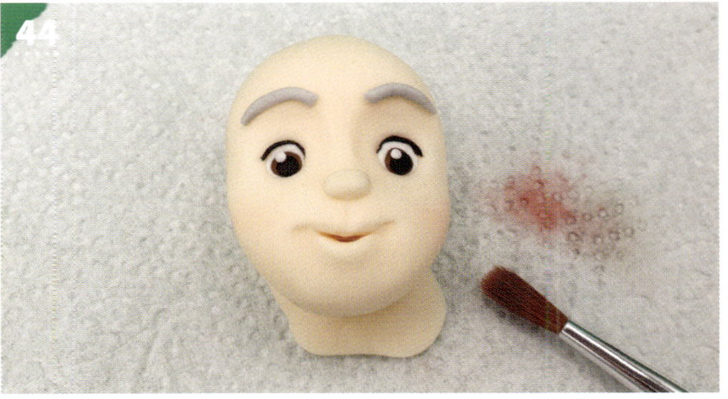

Colouring the cheeks with pink petal dust.

Adding wrinkles and crease lines to age the model's face.

Remove the excess paste at the back of the head with scissors (or a sharp knife) and smooth around the edges with your finger.

Brush a little water on top of the neck and the skewer, then, holding the head gently, push it down onto the support, twisting from side to side as you push carefully downwards.

Use the narrow end of the Dresden tool to mark a few creases and lines on the forehead, edges of the eyes and around the nose.

Tip for Wrinkles

You can add as many wrinkles and creases as you like, but be careful not to press too firmly with the Dresden tool. If the lines are too severe, rub over them gently with your finger to soften.

Making and fitting the glasses

The glasses are created using 24-gauge black florist wire, although you could substitute for other colours if you prefer. You could also use a smaller gauge of wire to create thicker frames, although these can be more difficult to bend into shape.

Cut the florist wire in half with pliers, to make it easier to handle. Bend the wire around a plastic dowel, or the rounded end of a modelling tool to create circles to fit over the eyes. Measure against the model to ensure the positioning is correct.

Bend the wire backwards at each side and cut off any excess (you need to leave enough wire to reach around to the sides of the head and past the ears). Keep trying the glasses against the head to ensure the shaping is correct.

Roll two small balls of skin tone paste for the ears, narrowing slightly towards the bottom, and flatten slightly with your finger.

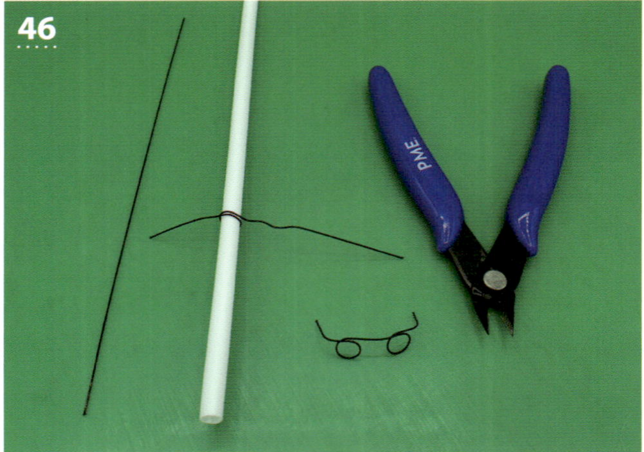
Creating a pair of glasses using coloured florist wire.

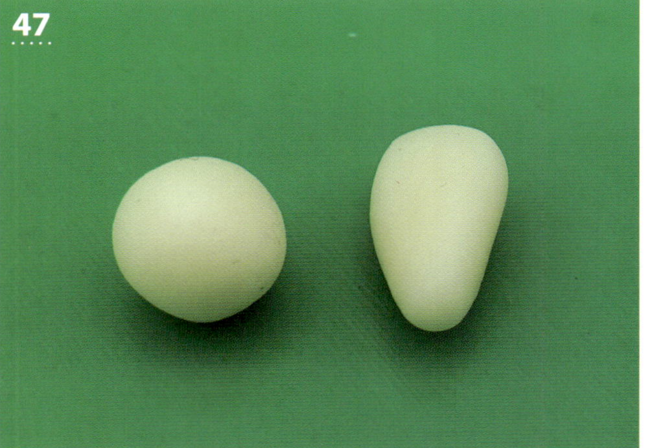
Shaping a pair of ears.

Brush a small amount of water (or edible glue) at each side of the head to attach the ears.

First position the glasses, then attach the ears, so that they cover the wires to hold in place at each side. The bottom of the ears should be in line with the bottom of the nose.

Use the end of a paintbrush (or a small ball tool) to indent a hole towards the bottom of the ears, which will also help to secure them firmly in place.

Attaching the glasses, using the ears to hold securely in place.

Adding the hair

Roll the remaining pale grey modelling paste into a ball, then a fat sausage shape, flattening out into a thin semi-circular shape with your fingers. This helps to give it a more natural look, rather than rolling the paste out with a rolling pin and cutting.

The shaped paste needs to reach from behind the ear at one side, to behind the ear at the other. You can hold it up to the back of the head to measure, adjusting until it is the correct size.

Use the narrow end of your Dresden tool to texture the hair from the top to the bottom, in a downwards motion.

Brush a little water onto the back of the hair piece, then attach to the back and sides of the head. Smooth the paste at the top, adding more texture with the Dresden tool if required.

Roll tiny pieces of paste to attach in front of each ear to form the sideburns, texturing with the Dresden tool.

Your model is now complete and ready to be transferred to your cake.

If you wish, you can place a tiny cake card underneath the armchair when attaching to the cake.

It shouldn't need dowels underneath, but if you have made the topper larger, or if you would rather be a little more cautious, you can add three small dowels underneath for added support.

Use a little Royal icing to attach to the top of your cake, being careful not to use too much so that it seeps out around the edges.

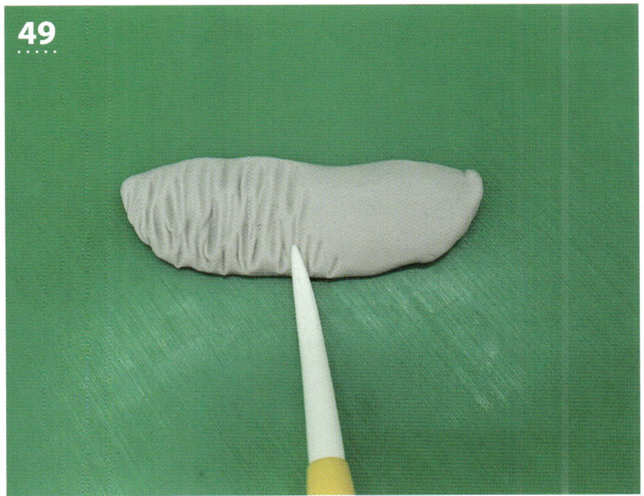

Creating and texturing the hair in one piece.

Adding the hair to the model and creating small sideburns to finish.

CAKE DESIGN IDEA

As mentioned earlier in the chapter, this style of cake topper lends itself very well to being used as a keepsake for a special occasion. If this is the case, you may wish to create it on a decorated cake drum, which can be easily removed from the cake and used to display the cake topper.

From a commercial point of view, you could also create and sell this type of cake topper by itself, for your customer to add to their own cake.

Covering a cake drum with a wooden floor effect

Cover a 15cm (6") round cake drum with white sugar paste, rolled to a thickness of approximately 4–5mm. Trim around the edge with a sharp knife.

Use a piece of crumpled aluminium kitchen foil to texture all over the paste, to create an aged wood effect.

Use a metal ruler to indent lines for the floorboards, pressing all the way down through the paste. Add smaller lines, running in the same horizontal direction, for added texture.

Using a cream or brown gel colour (depending on the effect you are trying to achieve), dilute with a little clear alcohol (such as vodka) and paint between the lines with a small, flat paintbrush. Add a few other lines of darker colour where the Dresden tool has been used.

Dilute the colour with more clear alcohol, and using a wider flat paintbrush, paint the whole board, with long, even strokes, following the same direction as the lines.

Remember to paint around the outside edge of the white paste as well as the top.

Add a brown (15mm) ribbon to the edge of your cake drum, using a non-toxic glue stick or double-sided tape, to finish.

Covering and texturing the cake drum, ready to add more detail.

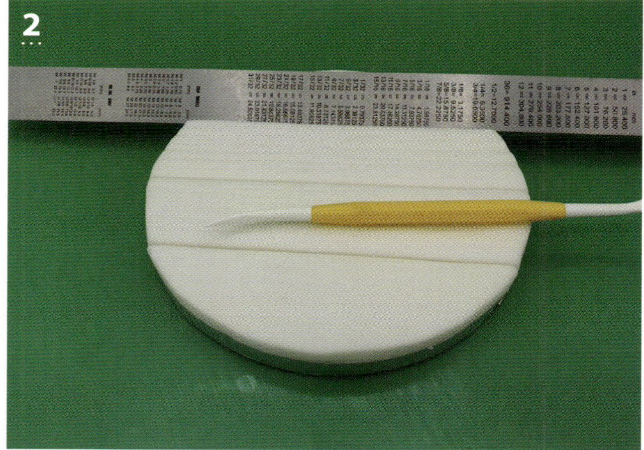

Creating grooves for floorboards and texturing the wood further.

Hand painting the paste to give a realistic wooden effect.

Adding the topper

When adding a cake topper like this to your cake, use dowels underneath to support the added weight of the cake drum and paste.

CHAPTER 8

Male Standing Figure

When making figures that need to stand on top of a cake, a little extra support is required to make sure they stay in place without falling over, or falling apart. It is often easier to build the figures on to a polystyrene cake dummy first, before transferring to your finished cake. This means you can make them in advance, giving them time to dry firmly before moving them.

In Chapters 8 and 9 we will look at standing figures with simple internal support, before moving on to figures requiring more complex internal structures, in the final chapter.

A wedding couple cake topper is a good example of this style of standing figure, and is a popular choice for wedding cakes, as they can be personalized to resemble the happy couple. The wedding couple figures are pictured on a 15cm (6in) round cake.

STANDING GROOM FIGURE

Using simple internal support and introducing some more advanced modelling techniques, this figure is a great way to further develop and improve your modelling skills.

For this standing figure, we will start by making the legs first, and then work our way up the body to the head. The legs and arms will be made with the colour of the suit trousers/sleeves, and the body will be dressed with the suit jacket separately.

This standing male figure, dressed in a suit, uses a simple internal support to enable him to stand on top of your cake. He can be personalized by changing the colour of the suit and tie, his hair/eye colour and hairstyle.

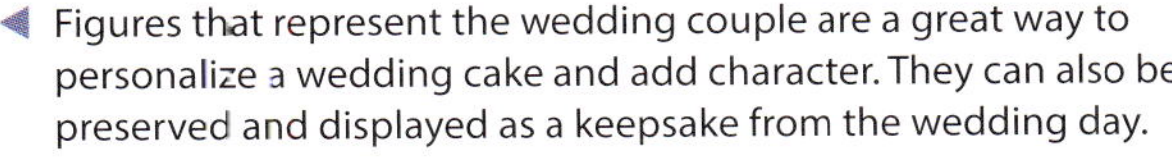

◀ Figures that represent the wedding couple are a great way to personalize a wedding cake and add character. They can also be preserved and displayed as a keepsake from the wedding day.

These wedding figures can easily be personalized to compliment the wedding colour scheme and outfits, as well as the hairstyles and features of the happy couple.

Standing Groom Figure

Equipment

- small rolling pin
- sharp knife
- scalpel
- ball tools (variety of sizes)
- Dresden tool
- stitching tool (optional)
- small, sharp scissors
- small pliers
- 2 x wooden skewers
- dried spaghetti strands
- soft silicone rounded tipped modelling tool
- hard silicone pointed tipped modelling tool
- 12mm circle cutter
- paintbrushes for water and for dusting cheeks

Materials

- 130g blue modelling paste
- 30g brown modelling paste
- 2g yellow modelling paste
- 50g white modelling paste
- 20g black modelling paste
- 40g skin-tone modelling paste
- pink petal dust for cheeks (I used Fractal Kitty Nose Pink)

40g skin tone and 20g brown pre-coloured modelling paste was mixed together to achieve the desired skin tone for this figure.

Additional equipment you may find useful for adding decorative elements to the figure

- Katy Sue Designs 'Blossoms and Birds' silicone mould
- Frankly Sweet 'Multi-mould' silicone mould

Or you may have something similar that you can use instead to achieve a similar result.

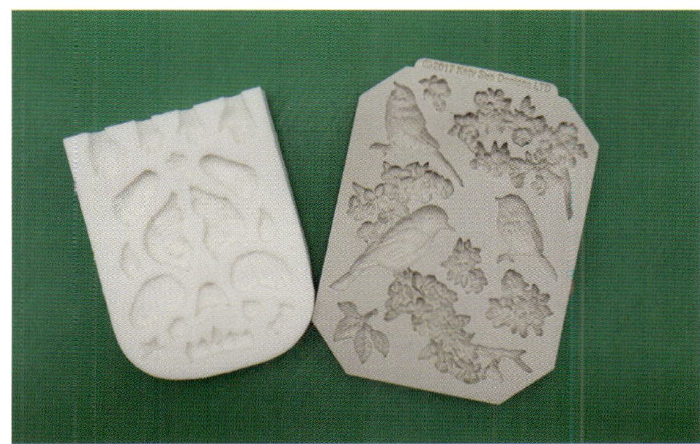

Silicone moulds such as these can be useful for adding other decorative elements to your figures without having to make them by hand.

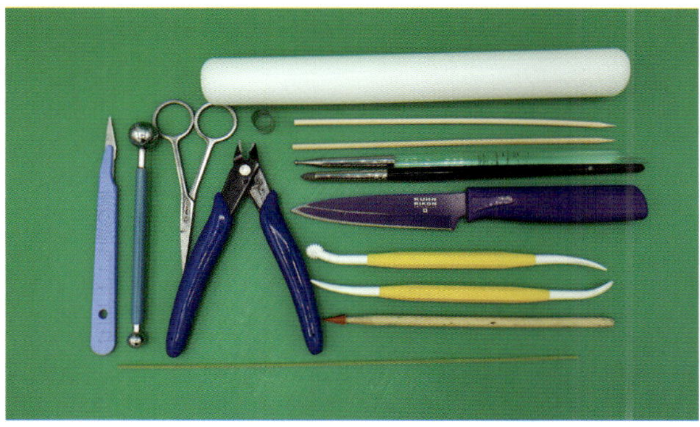

There are a few extra tools that will be useful for achieving the more detailed facial features on this model, in addition to the basic modelling tool set and general cake-decorating equipment that have been used previously.

Ready-coloured Saracino modelling paste in blue, brown, yellow, white, black and skin tone are used to create this model. You can substitute different colours for the clothing, hair and other details if you wish, when creating your figure.

Making the Legs

Roll 60g of blue modelling paste into a smooth ball, then roll with your hands to make a long sausage shape. Bend the shape in the middle and then trim each end straight with a sharp knife.

Halfway down each leg, pinch and push the paste gently with your fingers and thumbs to form the knees. You can also lightly indent the back of the leg with a sharp knife to help define it if you wish. Open up the bottom of each trouser leg with a ball tool, thinning the edges of the paste by pinching gently between your thumb and finger.

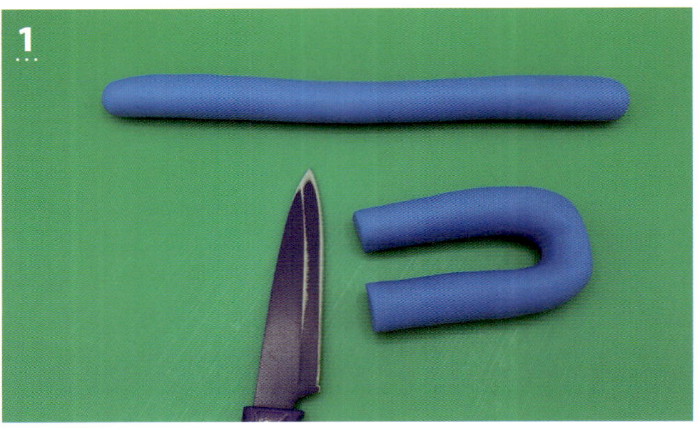

Creating the all-in-one legs and trousers.

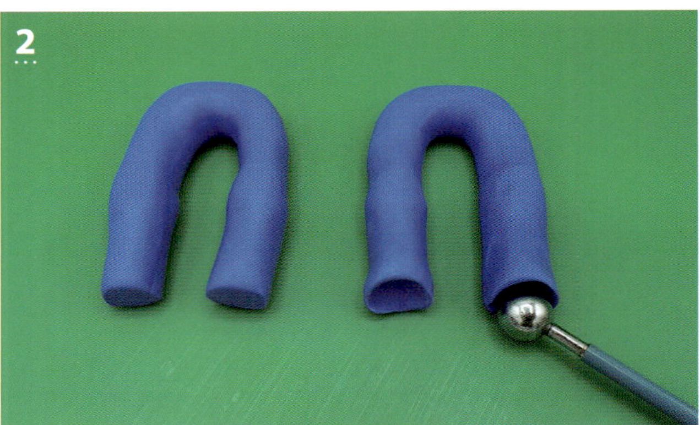

Adding shape to the knees, and opening up the bottom of the trouser legs.

Making the Shoes

Mix together 8g brown and 2g yellow modelling paste, to make a tan colour (or you can just use brown on its own, or even black if you prefer). Roll into a ball and cut in half to make two equal pieces for each shoe. Roll each piece into a smooth ball, then into an oval shape. Use your finger to gently stroke downwards on one half of the shoe so that it slopes down to the front (where the toes would be).

Make an indent at the top of the higher end of the shoe with your thumb (or use a ball tool), then mark a line down to the toe area with the narrow end of your Dresden tool. Turn over and make a line across for the heel with a sharp knife.

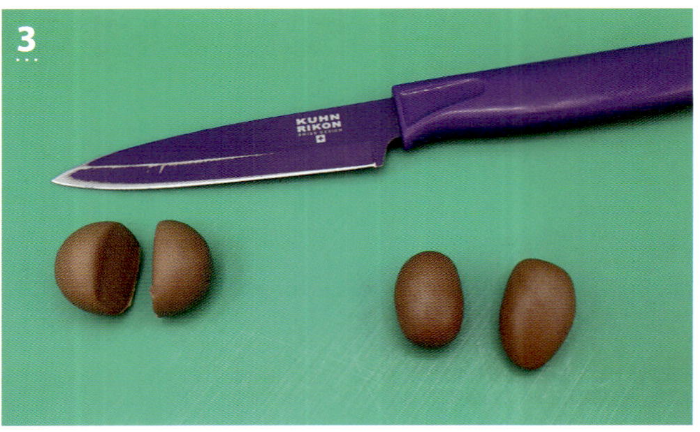

Making a simple shape for the shoes.

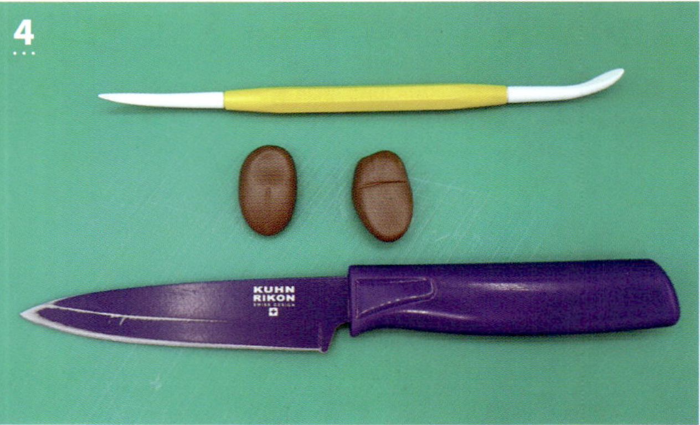

Adding some extra detailing to the shoes.

Attach the shoes to the bottom of the trousers with a little edible glue or water. Using the narrow end of your Dresden tool, mark creases at the bottom of the trousers where they rest over the top of the shoes (optional).

Inserting the Supports into the Legs

Insert a wooden skewer from the top, through to the bottom of each leg. Twist the skewer gently between your finger and thumb as you insert it, so as not to distort the paste.

The skewers need to pass straight through the bottom of the shoes, so that approximately 5cm (2in) of the skewer is visible underneath the model. Push the ends of the two wooden skewers into a polystyrene dummy, to hold the figure upright and in place whilst you are working. These will also help to keep the figure in place when you add it to the cake when it is finished. Trim the top of one of the skewers shorter using the pliers.

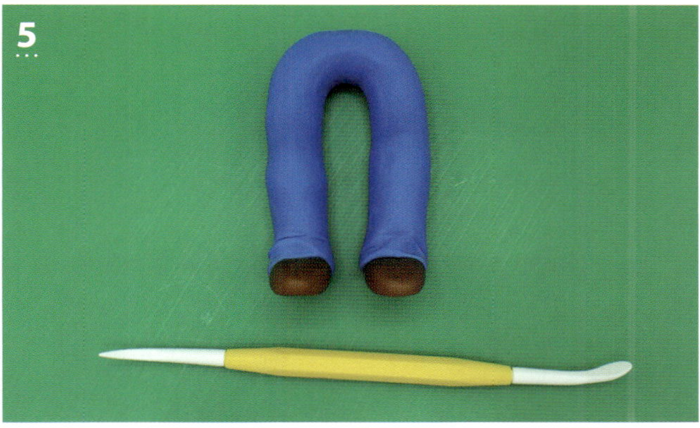

Joining the shoes and trousers together.

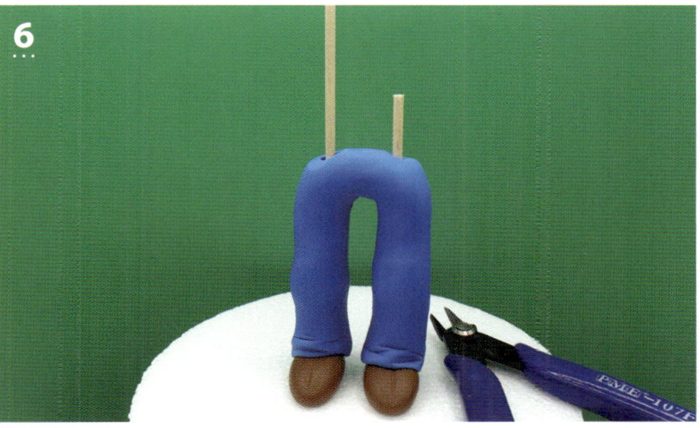

Inserting the supports into the legs, to enable the figure to stand. Use a polystyrene dummy to hold the model stable whilst you work on it.

Making the Body

The main trunk part of the body is made from white modelling paste, to look like a shirt underneath the jacket, which is then added separately.

Roll 40g of white modelling paste into a smooth ball and then into a fat sausage shape. Narrow the middle to create a waist, by rolling between your fingers. Flatten the paste slightly with your hand, then use a ball tool to open up the bottom edge, so that it fits over the trousers.

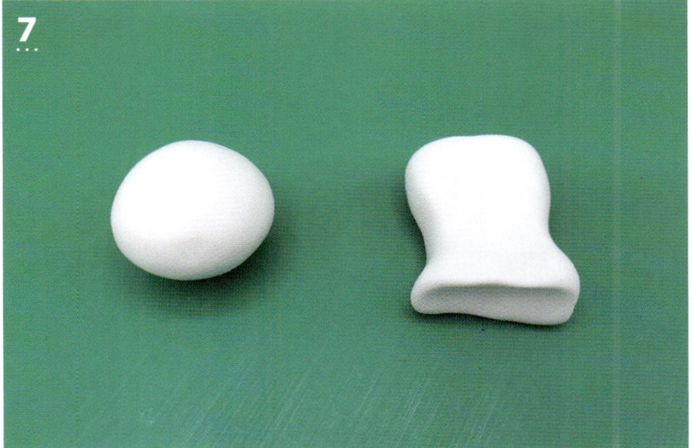

Shaping the main trunk of the body.

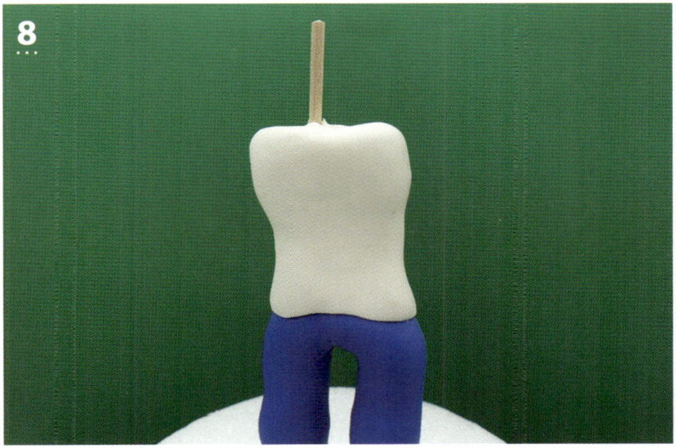

Adding the body to the legs.

Add the body piece to sit over the top of the legs, by pushing it down gently over the wooden skewers. The paste should completely cover the skewer that was trimmed shorter, whilst the remaining longer skewer should come out of the top of the body in the centre, where the neck will be positioned. Use your finger (or a ball tool) to make an indent around the skewer in order to fit the paste for the neck.

Roll 3g of skin-tone modelling paste into a ball, then make a short, wide cone shape for the neck. Push down over the top of the wooden skewer, and use the wider end of your Dresden tool to mark an indent in the neck at the front.

Use the narrow end of your Dresden tool to draw a line down the centre of the body for the shirt detail. If you are leaving the jacket open, you can also add tiny balls of white paste for buttons, but for a fastened jacket, they would not be seen, so there is no need to add them.

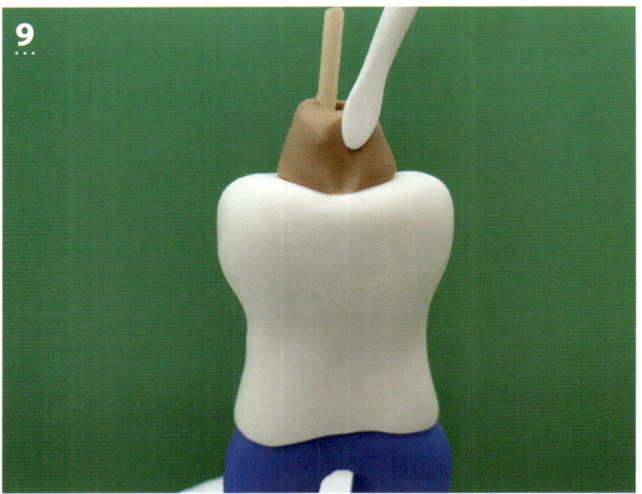

Creating and detailing the neck.

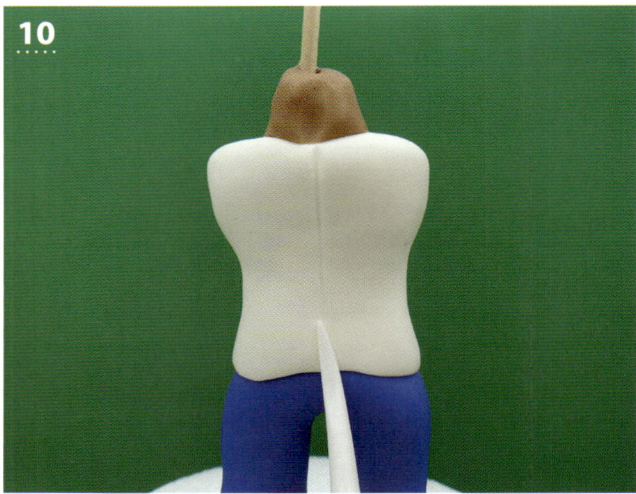

Adding shirt details to the body – if you wish you can also add buttons, but these will most likely be covered by the jacket and tie.

Making the Collar and Tie

Roll a small piece of brown modelling paste to approximately 2mm in thickness with a small rolling pin. Using a sharp knife, cut out a tie-shaped piece, holding it against the body to gauge the correct size. If you wish, you can cut out a template for the tie first, using kitchen paper, which you can then use when cutting the paste.

Cut out a smaller rectangle of brown paste, and wrap it round the top of the tie to look like a knot where it has been tied.

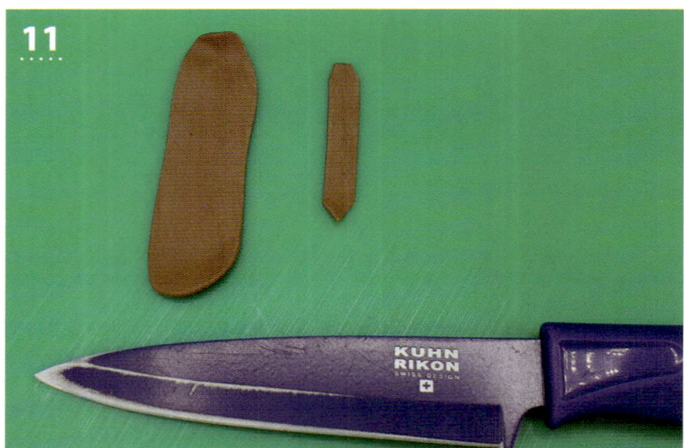

Cutting out the tie shape.

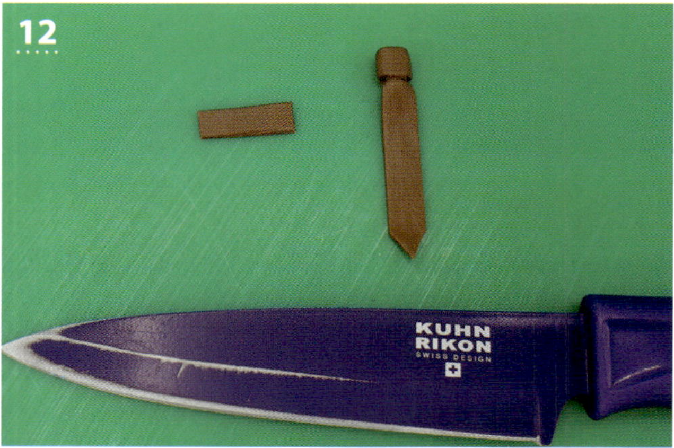

Adding the knot detail to the tie.

Roll out a long piece of white modelling paste, and cut out a thin strip. It needs to be long enough to fit round the neck of the figure. Cut one end at a diagonal.

Fix the tie in place, using a little edible glue or water, then add the collar, trimming at the front with another diagonal cut (I find it easier to use small, sharp scissors to make this cut once the collar is added to the figure).

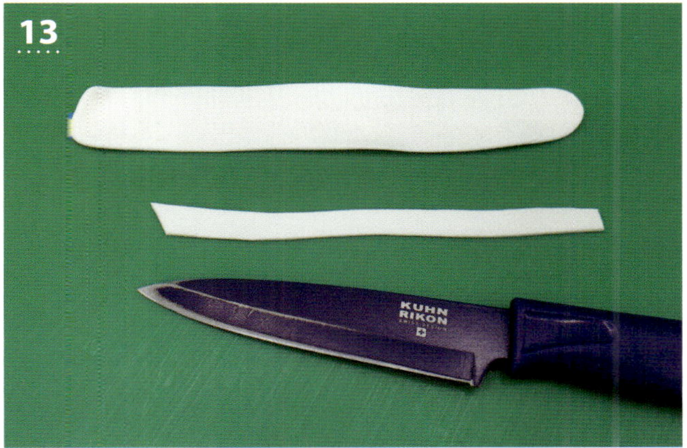

Making a collar for the shirt.

Adding the tie and collar to the figure, trimming to size at the front.

Making the Jacket

Make a simple template for the jacket front and back from kitchen paper (or greaseproof paper); it needs to be a flexible material, so that you can bend it round the figure to measure. Just keep the shape basic, as you can trim the jacket to fit when adding it to the body. It is better to start with a template piece that is too large, and then trim it down to size, rather than too small and have to redo it.

Roll blue modelling paste to a thickness of approximately 2mm, then cut out two pieces of paste with a sharp scalpel, using your template as a guide.

Cut one of the jacket pieces in half, then trim a diagonal piece off each with a sharp knife, to make the two jacket fronts.

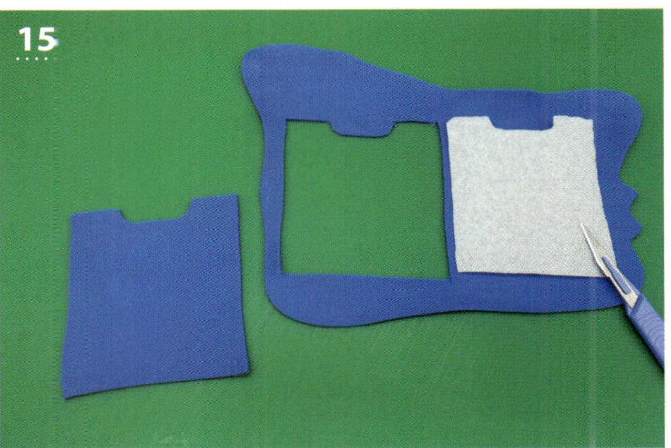

Making a template and cutting out the jacket pieces.

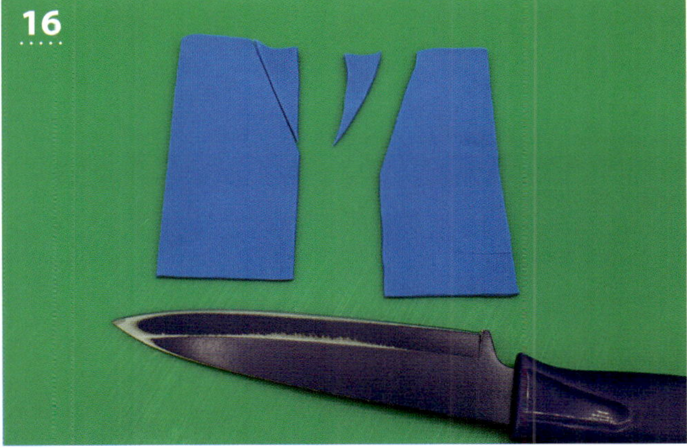

Shaping the jacket fronts from one of the cut-out pieces.

Add the jacket back to the figure, folding the sides round and trimming off any excess paste. The jacket back should reach halfway round the side of the body. Using sharp scissors, cut off the triangular excess piece of paste where the sides and top of the shoulders meet. Rub the cut edge with your finger to gently soften and blend the paste together.

Add the two jacket fronts, overlapping slightly at the front. Trim off any excess paste where the sides and shoulders meet. Gently rub over the joined edges with your finger to blend the seams.

Cut out three small rectangles for pockets, adding a small strip to the top of each. You can use a stitching tool to add a stitched-effect detail to the top of the pockets if you wish. Shape a small piece of brown modelling paste to make a folded handkerchief for the top pocket.

Attach the pockets to the front of the jacket with a small amount of edible glue or water. Be careful not to use too much, or the pocket pieces may slip. If you have added too much, blot away any excess with a tissue before adding the pockets. Roll tiny balls of blue paste for buttons and add to the jacket front. You can indent small holes for the buttons to sit in if you wish.

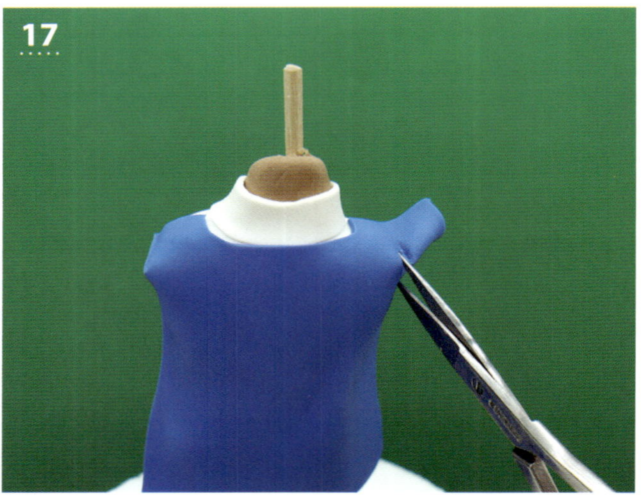

Fitting the back of the jacket to your figure, adjusting the size and trimming excess paste where necessary.

Adding the jacket fronts, trimming and blending in the paste with the back piece.

Making pockets for the jacket, as well as a handkerchief to coordinate with the tie.

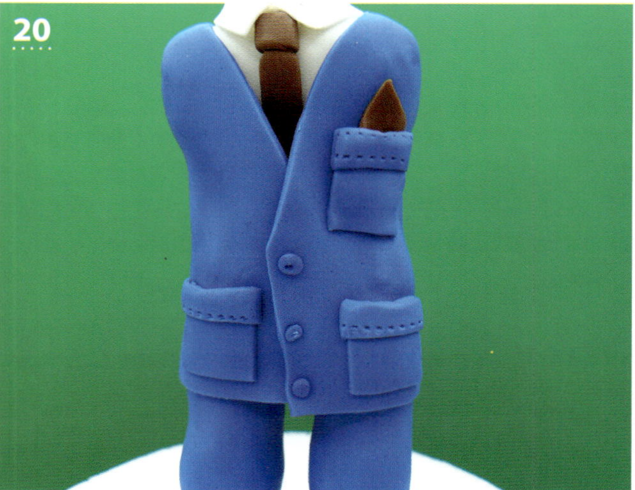

Adding the pockets and buttons.

Make a template for the jacket lapels with a piece of kitchen paper (or similar). Look at a picture of a suit jacket to find a style that you prefer. With a sharp scalpel, cut out two lapels from the blue modelling paste, rolled the same thickness as for the jacket pieces; make sure you turn the template over for one of the pieces to ensure you have a pair, rather than two of the same.

Add the lapels to the front edges of the jacket using a little edible glue or water, overlapping at the bottom and trimming to fit at the back of the neck.

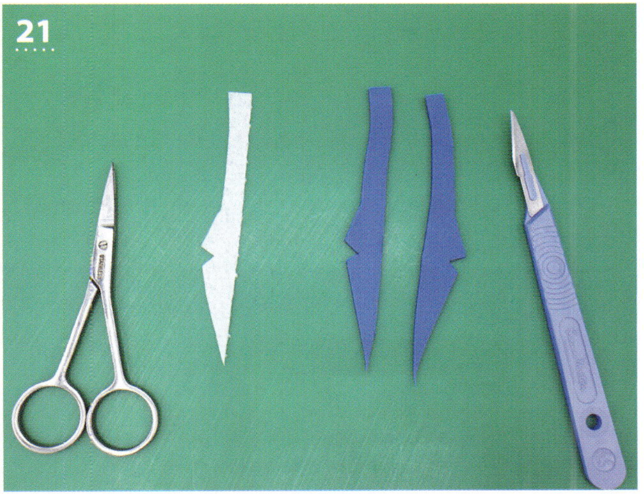

Making a template for the jacket lapels, and cutting them out as a pair from blue modelling paste.

Adding the jacket lapels and trimming them to fit.

Making the Arms and Hands

Roll 30g of blue modelling paste into a smooth ball and then into a long sausage shape. Cut in half diagonally with a sharp knife to make two arms. Mark an indent halfway along on the inside of the arm and bend inwards. Pinch the paste gently with your finger and thumb to sharpen the bend and define the elbow on the outside of the arm. Use a ball tool to open up the end of the arm to make space to fit the hands.

Roll 5g of skin-tone paste into a ball, then a sausage shape. Flatten each end with your finger to make two hands. Cut the paste in half to separate the hands, ensuring that they are equal in size and shape.

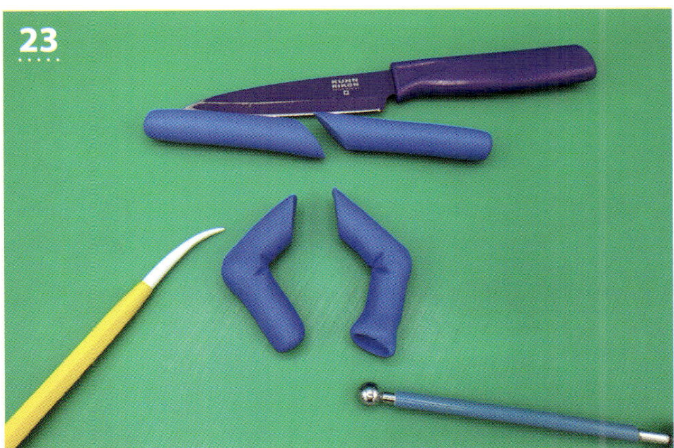

Creating and shaping the arms, including forming the elbows.

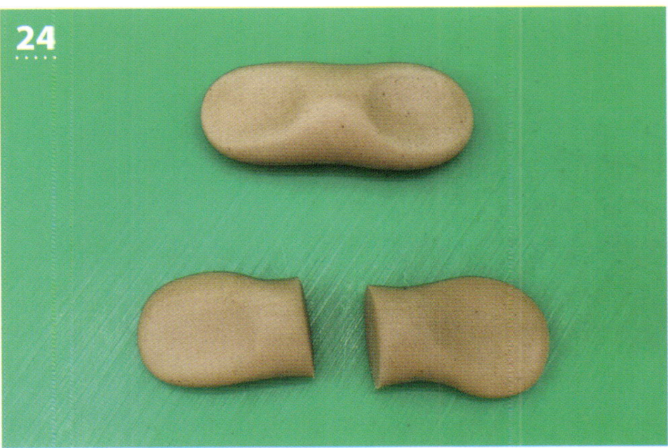

Start by making the basic hand shapes as one piece, before cutting into two separate hands.

Cut out a V-shaped piece of paste from each hand to form the thumb. Place the hands next to each other as you work, cutting from opposite sides to make a pair of hands, rather than two identical ones. Divide the rest of the hand into four fingers – cut into the middle first, then cut each side in half to ensure the fingers are evenly sized and spaced.

Separate the fingers from each other and then twist them gently between your finger and thumb to thin and elongate them individually. Be very gentle, as you don't want to risk pulling a finger off at this point! Use the narrow end of your Dresden tool to mark lines on the hands. Holding the wrist between your finger and thumb, twist backwards and forwards to further define the shape.

Insert the wrist part of the hands into the arms, securing with a little edible glue or water. Pay attention to the positioning of the hands: the thumb needs to be on the same side as the inner arm. Cut out a thin strip of blue modelling paste and use to make a cuff, covering the join between the arm and hand. Trim excess paste from the join at the back with a sharp scalpel.

Break off two short pieces of dried spaghetti to help hold the arms in place. Insert the dried spaghetti downwards into the body at a 45-degree angle, leaving only a tiny amount showing. If you leave too much dried spaghetti sticking out, it may show on the outside of the arm. Use a little edible glue to stick the arm into place. If needed, you can add a little glue to the front of the jacket where the arm touches it for added security.

Add the second arm in the same way; position them however you wish.

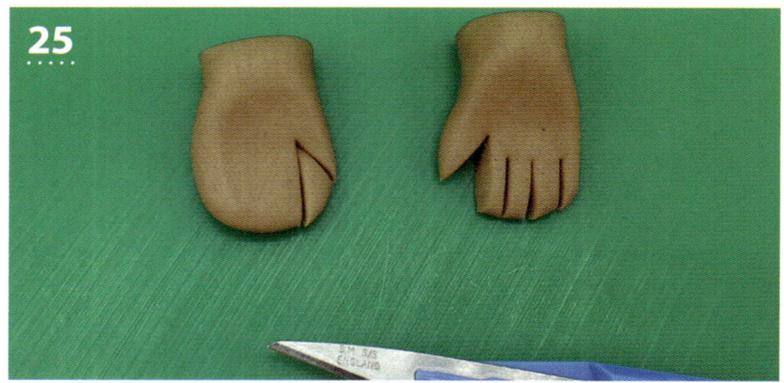

Cutting out the thumb and fingers: be careful to cut them on opposite sides for each hand.

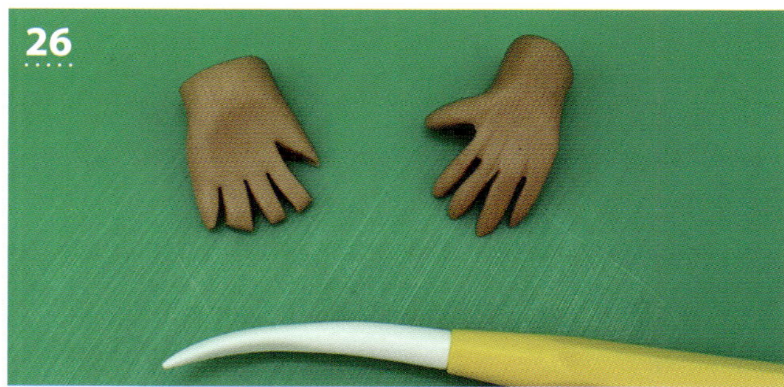

Refining and adding detail to the hands.

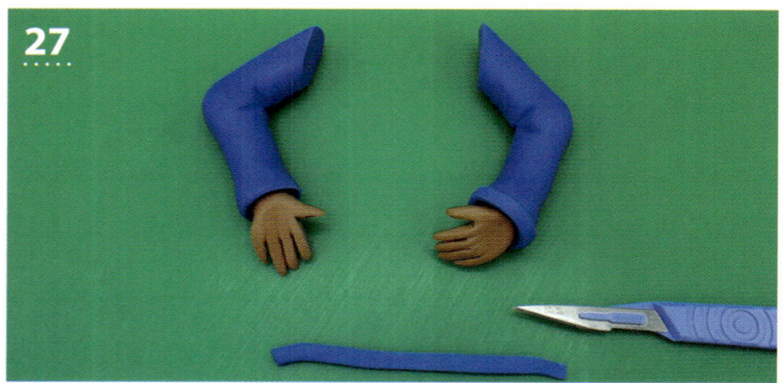

Fixing the hands to the arms, and creating a cuff for the sleeves to neaten the join.

Placing the first arm, using dried spaghetti for extra support.

Positioning the second arm.

Making the Head

Roll 45g of skin-tone modelling paste into a smooth ball, then into an oval/egg shape. Squeeze the paste at the back of the head downwards gently to make a 'foot' to stick to the board as you work. (It will resemble the shape of an old-fashioned loaf of bread from the side.)

Use the side of your hand to create an indent across the middle of the face area (rock your hand backwards and forwards across the paste). You could also use your finger, or the handle of a ball tool, whichever you find easier and most effective. Use a ball tool to create two eye sockets, moving in an L-shaped motion, upwards then outwards at each side within the indented area.

Use the wider end of your Dresden tool to define the nose, stroking down the sides and underneath the nose area, then softening and gently smoothing away any tool marks with your fingers. Build up the shape slowly, moving small amounts of paste at a time. Look at the profile of the nose, and smooth the top with your finger.

Use the sharp-pointed silicone-tipped tool to create the two nostrils. Smooth the paste downwards from under the nose with your finger to flatten it slightly. Continue to define the edges of the nose gently with your Dresden tool, using small movements.

Shaping the head and securing it to your workboard to work on it hands free without flattening the back of the head.

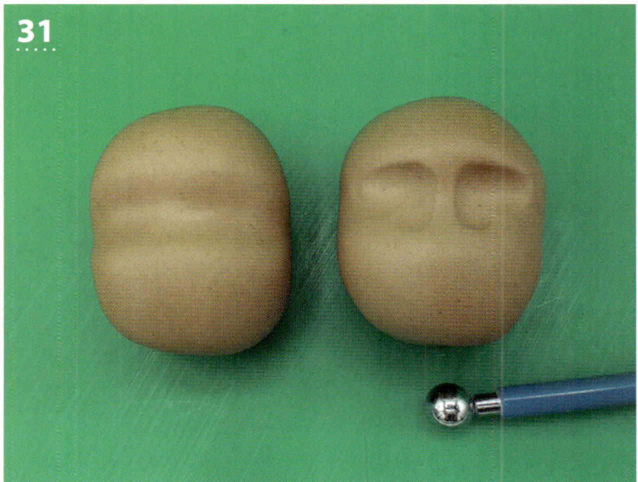

Creating eye sockets within the indented area of the head.

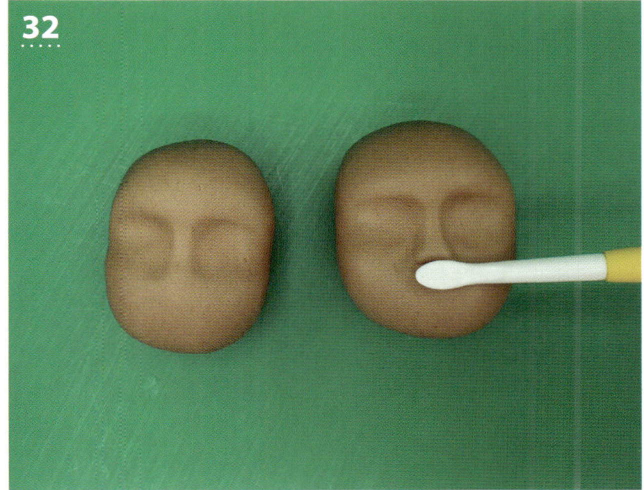

Building up the nose shape gradually.

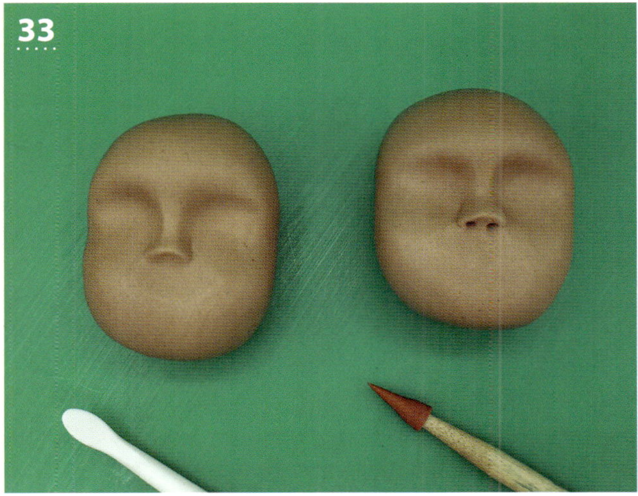

Giving extra definition to the nose and creating the nostrils.

Draw a line for the mouth with the sharp-pointed silicone-tipped tool, halfway between the bottom of the nose and the chin, then cut into the paste with a sharp scalpel. Open slightly with the scalpel blade by moving it backwards and forwards gently whilst it is still in the cut.

Use the wide end of your Dresden tool to gently press the paste to form and shape the top lip area. Mark a line up to the nose with the narrow end, then use the wider end again to draw lines down from the outer corners of the nose and at each side of the bottom lip. Push the paste up gently to form the bottom lip.

Remove any tool marks and gently refine the shape of the mouth and surrounding area, by rubbing gently with your finger to soften and blend. Use the handle of the small ball tool (or any other tool with a smooth, rounded handle) to shape and resize the lower half of the face, pushing the excess paste downwards and under the chin area. Note that the chin area in a male face shape tends to be squarer and more angular than in a female face shape: taking this into account when shaping the face will help to make it more recognizably masculine.

Continue to soften and refine the facial details and shape of the head, using your Dresden tool and your fingers. You can also use a soft-tipped silicone tool to help soften lines and edges, until you are happy with the look of the facial features and shape.

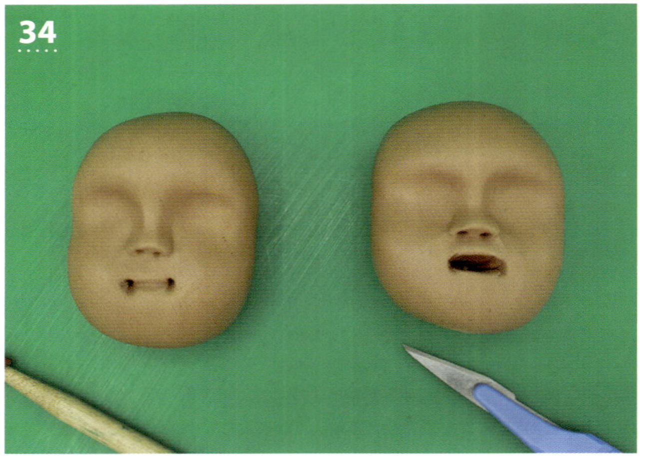

34

Cutting the mouth shape with a sharp scalpel.

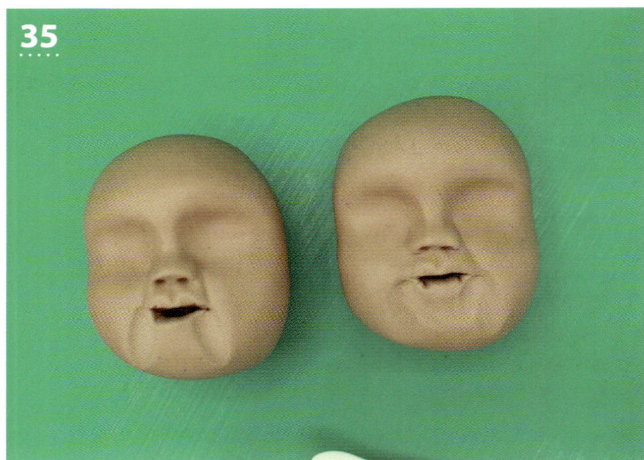

35

Forming the lips.

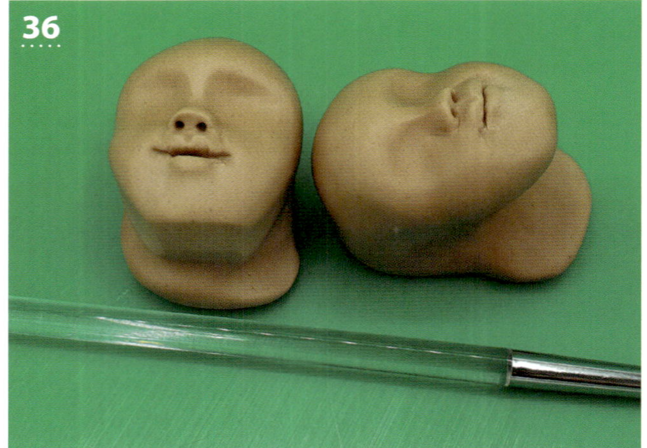

36

Defining the lower half of the head shape, including the chin and jawline.

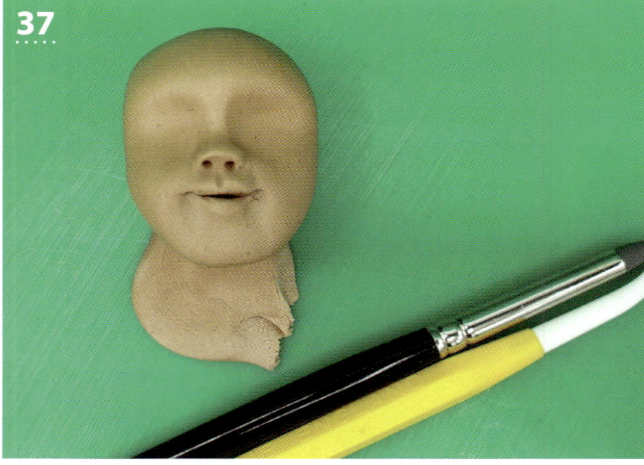

37

Refining the details and shape of the rest of the head.

Use the hard-pointed silicone tool to draw the outline for the eyes, then push the paste inwards with a small ball tool to open up the cavity.

Roll two tiny balls of white modelling paste and fill the eye cavities with these. Make sure that the white paste is not too big: it needs to fit comfortably inside the space, without overlapping the edges.

Make an indent in the centre of the white paste with your small ball tool, and fill with a small ball of brown modelling paste. Smooth with your finger so that it is flush with the white paste. You can obviously change the colour of the eyes to resemble the actual eye colour of the groom.

Repeat to add the pupil, using a smaller amount of black modelling paste.

To create the upper eyelids, roll a small piece of skin-tone paste to approximately 3mm thickness. Cut out two 12mm circles, then use the same circle cutter to cut away the lower area of the circle shape. Use a tiny amount of water to attach the upper eyelid in place, trimming away any excess paste with a sharp scalpel. Use the wider end of your Dresden tool to smooth and blend the paste into the face, softening any lines or marks left by the tool using your finger.

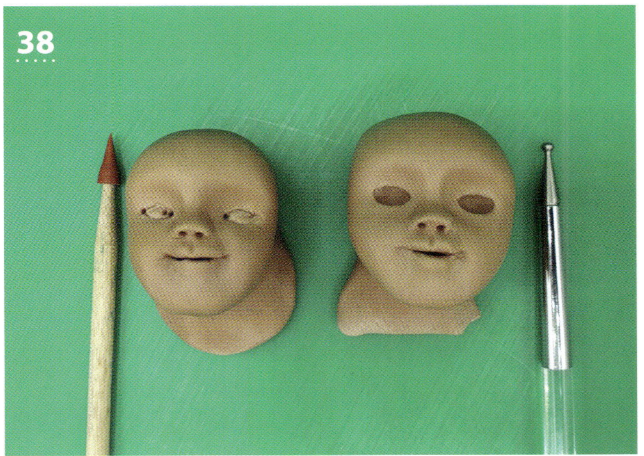

Drawing the shape for the eyes, and creating the cavity to infill.

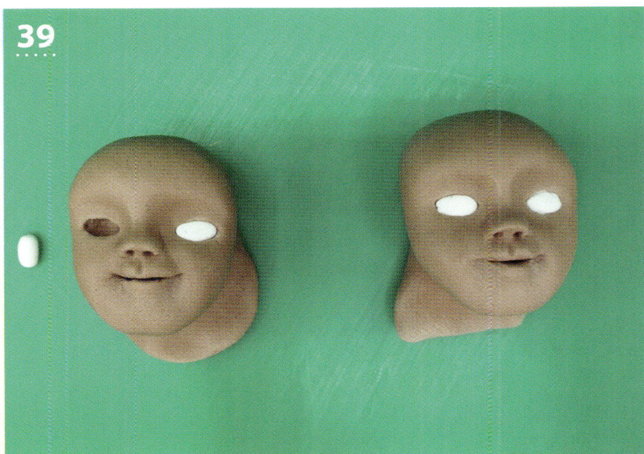

Adding the white paste for eyeballs.

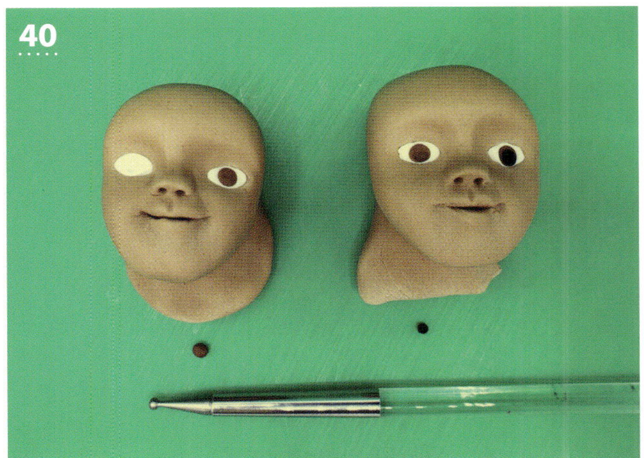

Adding the iris and pupil details to the eyes.

Creating the upper eyelids for the eyes.

Use the soft-tipped silicone tool to push the paste up under the eyes slightly, following the curve of the eye, to shape the lower eyelid and under-eye area. Roll two tiny balls of white modelling paste to add as highlights for the eyes.

Paint a fine line of edible glue or water above each eye, ready to add the eyebrows. To make the eyebrows, roll a small piece of black modelling paste until it is very fine at one end. Hold the wider end of the paste over the top of the eye socket, sticking the finer end above the outer edge of the eye and trimming it to size with a sharp scalpel above the inner edge of the eye.

Using a sharp knife, carefully cut away the excess paste from the back of the head, using a 'sawing' motion to avoid distorting the shape of the head. Smooth the cut area with your fingers to remove any rough edges.

Roll a small ball of skin-tone paste (approximately 1g) into a ball, then cut in half. Shape into two ovals for the ears. Attach to each side of the head, positioning so that the bottom of the ear is in line with the bottom of the nose. Use both ends of your Dresden tool in turn to add detail to the ears.

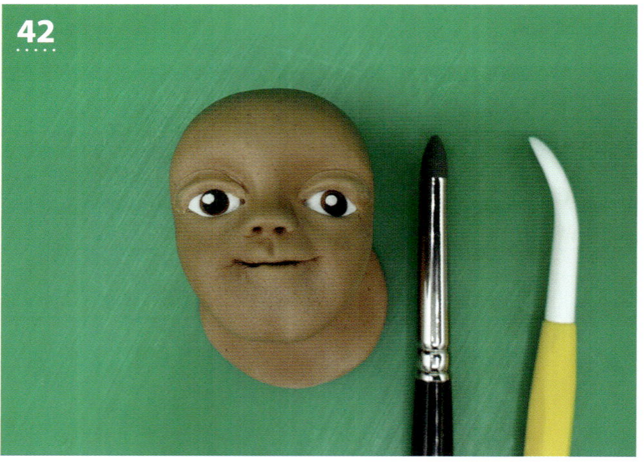

Creating under-eye details and highlights to finish the eyes.

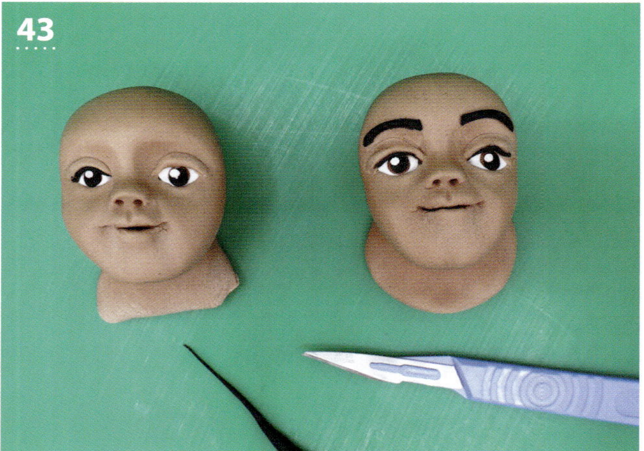

Making and positioning the eyebrows.

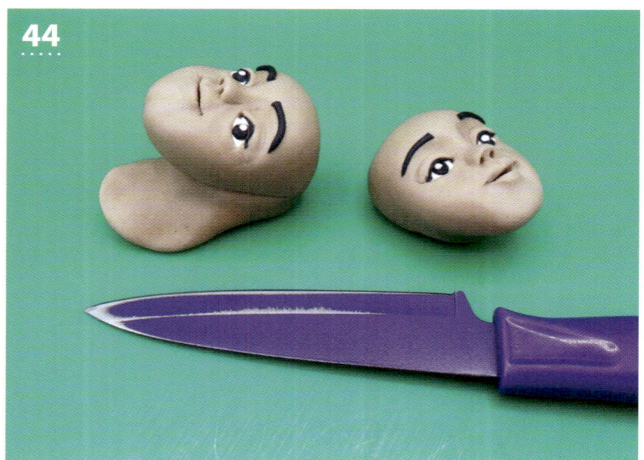

Shaping the head by removing the excess paste from the back.

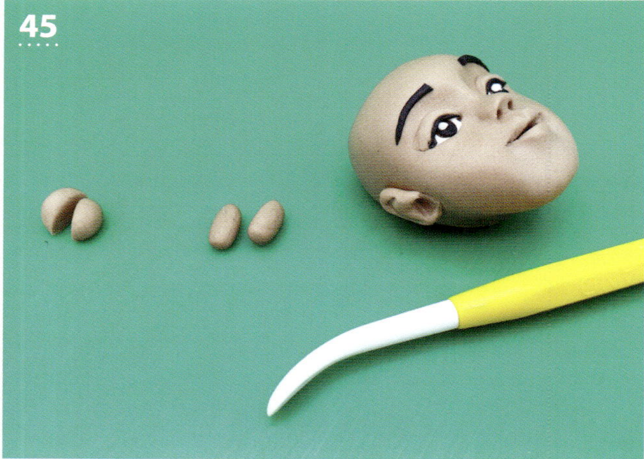

Creating simple ears and attaching them to the head in the correct position.

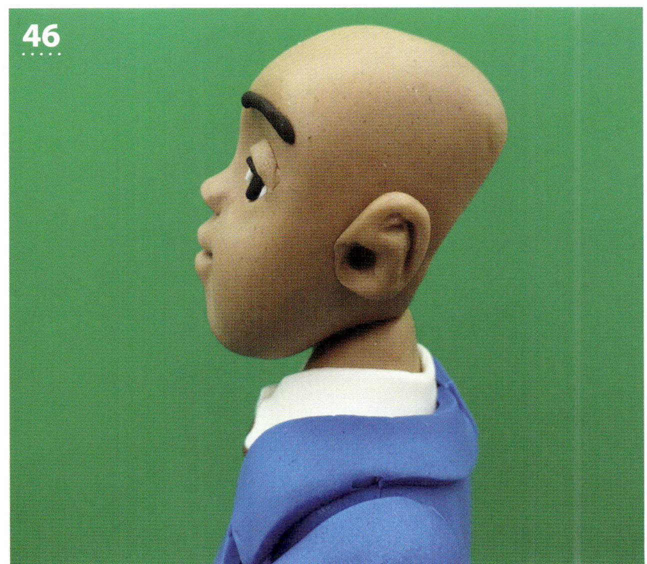
Attaching the head to your figure, being careful not to distort the shape.

Attach the head to your figure, using a little edible glue or water on top of the neck and on the wooden skewer to stick it in place. Twist the head from side to side as you gently push it down on to the wooden skewer.

Making the Hair

Roll 10g of black modelling paste into a ball, then flatten it with your fingers and thumb until it is quite thin and large enough to cover the back and top of the head: this is the base layer for the hair.

Attach the base layer to the head with a little edible glue, trimming away any excess paste with small, sharp scissors so that it fits close to the head like a shower cap. If there are any gaps when you create the hairstyle, this base layer will hide the scalp below.

Creating the base layer for the hair.

Adding the base layer of hair to cover the top and back of the head.

Shape 5g of black modelling paste into a cone, then flatten this cone into a triangular shape and texture it by drawing lines with the narrow end of your Dresden tool.

Wrap the paste round the back of the head, trimming the excess paste where it meets at the top with small, sharp scissors.

Use 5g of black modelling paste to shape two additional cones, one larger than the other. Flatten and texture with the narrow end of your Dresden tool as before.

Attach the two pieces of hair to the front of the head to finish. You may also wish to style the hair in a different way, or use a different colour.

Starting to create the top layer of the hairstyle and adding texture.

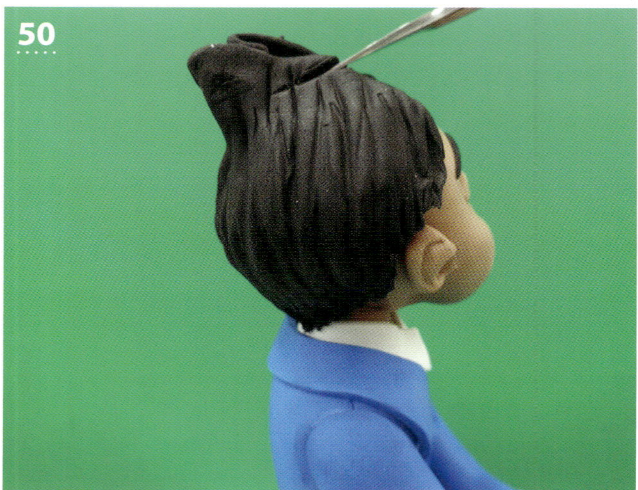

Adding the top layer of hair to the back of the head.

Creating the two front parts of the hairstyle.

Finishing off the hairstyle.

Alternative Design Elements for the Male Wedding Figure

Alternative Hairstyle

Roll 20g black modelling paste into a ball and then flatten it, thinning the edges between your finger and thumb. Texture with the narrow end of your Dresden tool, then stick to the head with edible glue, continuing to texture as required, paying attention to the direction in which the hair would be growing/styled.

An alternative way of creating hair for the male figure.

Using Silicone Moulds

Applying a thin layer of white vegetable fat (Trex) or cornflour will stop your paste from sticking to the mould, making it easier to release. Flex the edges of the mould to loosen the paste ready to turn it out. If you still have problems releasing the paste from your mould, place it in the freezer for five minutes and it should then be easier to remove.

Bow-Tie Detail

Using a silicone mould, press coloured modelling paste into the small bow-shaped cavity. Turn the bow out and attach to the figure instead of a tie.

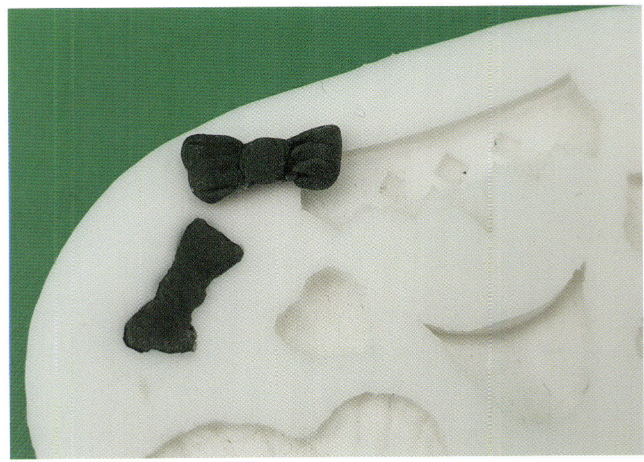

Using a mould to make a bow tie to use instead of a tie.

Buttonhole Flower Detail

Using a silicone mould, start by adding white modelling paste into the flower part of the mould, then fill with green for the leaves. Turn out of the mould and attach to the top jacket pocket, instead of the handkerchief detail. You could also use a small blossom plunger cutter to make a flower to add for the buttonhole.

Using a mould to make a buttonhole flower to add to the figure.

CHAPTER 9

Female Standing Figure

Using simple internal support and introducing some more advanced techniques, this figure is a great way to develop your modelling skills even further. With this model you will learn how to add clothing to a figure and create a more detailed face.

STANDING BRIDE FIGURE

For this standing figure, we will start by making the shape of the dress/body first, before adding the dress details; we will then move on to the arms and the head. At the end, some alternative decorative details are included, that you can use to personalize your figure.

Making the Dress/Body Shape

Roll 100g ivory-coloured modelling paste into a ball and then into a long sausage shape. Use the edge of your hand to indent the waist, in a rocking motion, approximately one third of the way down the shape.

Using your fingers and thumb to push the paste, gently manipulate it into a dress shape by widening the top and bottom, whilst continuing to narrow the waist area.

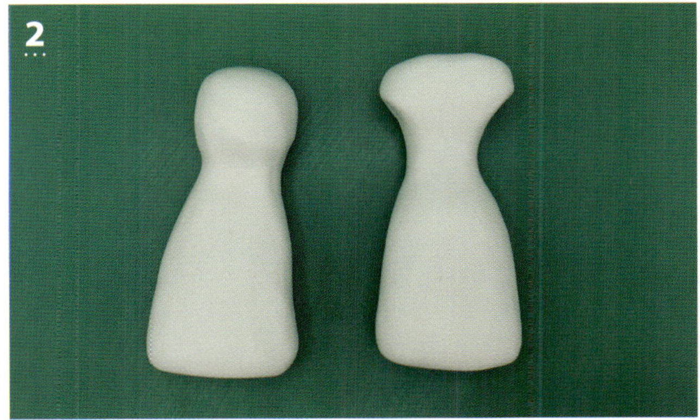

Making a start on creating the dress/body shape.

Giving more definition and detail to the shape of the body/dress.

◀ This standing female figure, featuring a wedding-style dress, uses a simple internal support to enable her to stand on top of your cake. She can be personalized by changing the colour and style of her dress as well as her hair/eye colour and hairstyle. The flowers in her bouquet can also be adapted to compliment the wedding flowers.

Equipment

- small rolling pin
- sharp knife
- scalpel
- ball tools (variety of sizes)
- Dresden tool
- small, sharp scissors
- small pliers
- 1 wooden skewer
- dried spaghetti strands
- soft silicone rounded tipped modelling tool
- hard silicone pointed tipped modelling tool
- 12mm circle cutter
- paintbrushes for water and for dusting cheeks/applying make-up to the face

Materials

- 160g white modelling paste
- 5g blue modelling paste
- 10g black modelling paste
- 40g skin-tone modelling paste
- 65g brown modelling paste

40g skin-tone and 35g brown pre-coloured modelling paste were mixed to achieve the desired skin tone for this figure. Also 150g of the white modelling paste was coloured with a tiny amount of cream gel colour to make an ivory tone for the dress. For the hair colour, 10g black and 30g of brown modelling pastes were mixed together.

You may find the following additional equipment/materials useful for adding decorative elements to the figure

- textured rolling pin or embossing mat to pattern the dress
- Katy Sue Designs 'Blossoms and Birds' silicone mould
- blossom flower plunger cutter
- various shades of petal/lustre dust for adding make-up
- white vegetable fat (Trex)

Or you may have something similar that you can use instead to achieve a similar result.

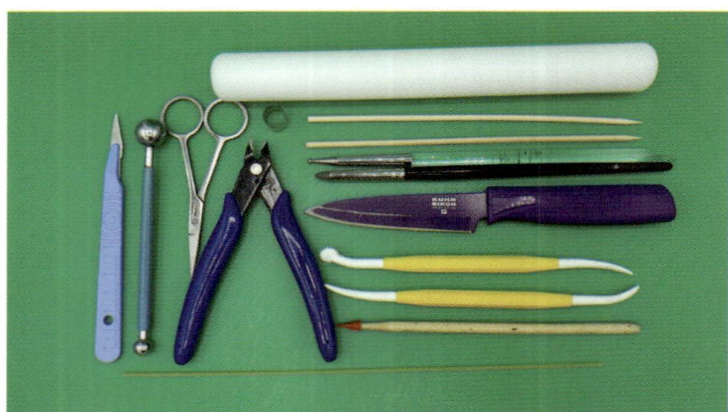

There are a few extra tools that will be useful for achieving the more detailed facial features on this model, in addition to the basic modelling tool set and general cake-decorating equipment that have been used previously.

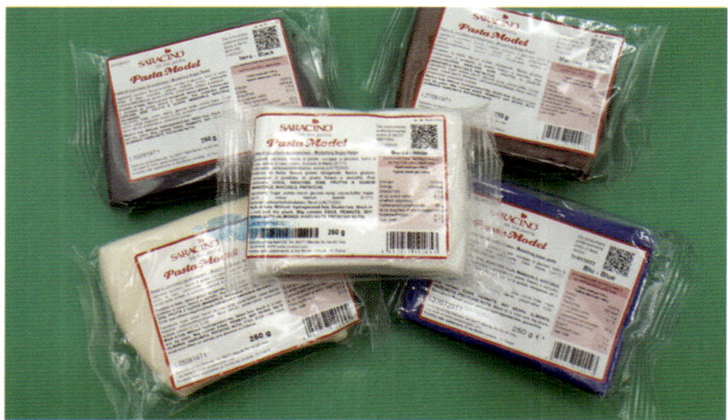

Ready-coloured Saracino modelling paste in white, blue, black, skin tone and brown is used to create this model. You can substitute different colours for the clothing, hair and other details if you wish, when creating your figure.

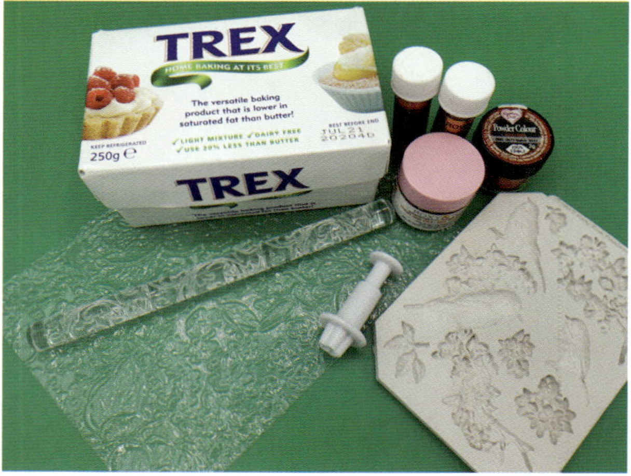

Silicone moulds and textured rolling pins/embossing mats like these can be useful for adding decorative details to your figures without having to create them by hand. A range of different coloured petal and lustre dusts are perfect for adding make-up to your model.

Create the bust area at the top of the body, using your Dresden tool, softening any lines with your finger. This only needs to be a basic shape as the dress will cover this area, but it gives the impression of the figure's shape.

Helpful Tip

When you are adding separate clothing to a figure, make the body size slightly narrower than you normally would, as the extra layer of paste from the clothing will add more bulk to the shape.

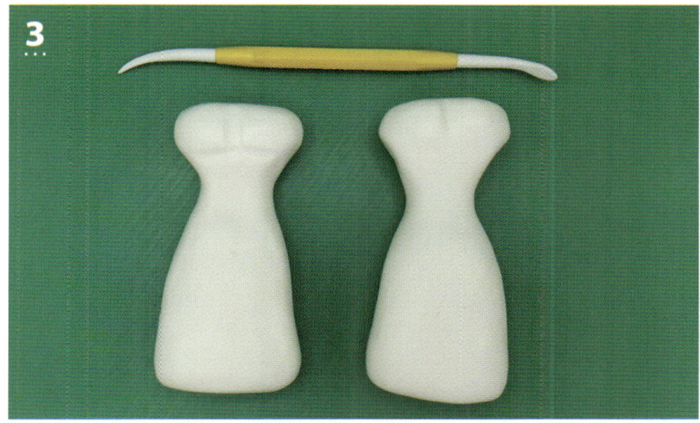

Creating the bust definition, which will sit underneath the dress.

Adding the Shoulders and Neck

Take 15g of the skin-tone modelling paste and roll it into a smooth ball; then narrow one side by rolling it between your finger and thumb to create the neck shape. Smooth out any edges or marks with your finger.

Widen the bottom area until it is the same size as the top of the dress, and attach it to the body using a little edible glue or water. Use your Dresden tool to continue the shape of the bust area upwards slightly, then cut the top of the neck at an angle with a sharp knife. This will enable the neck to fit to the contour of the head later.

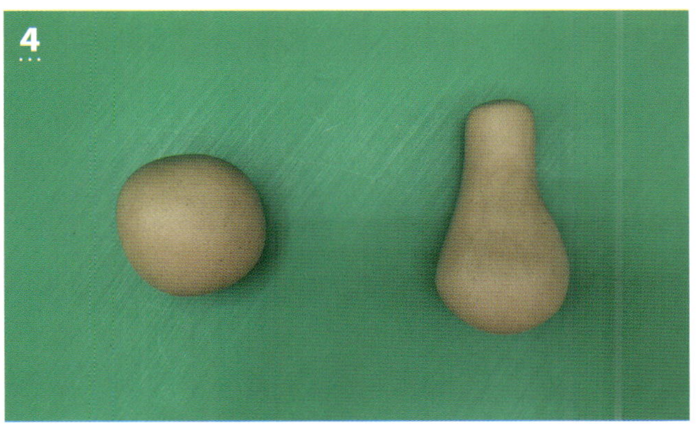

Shaping the figure's neck with skin-tone modelling paste.

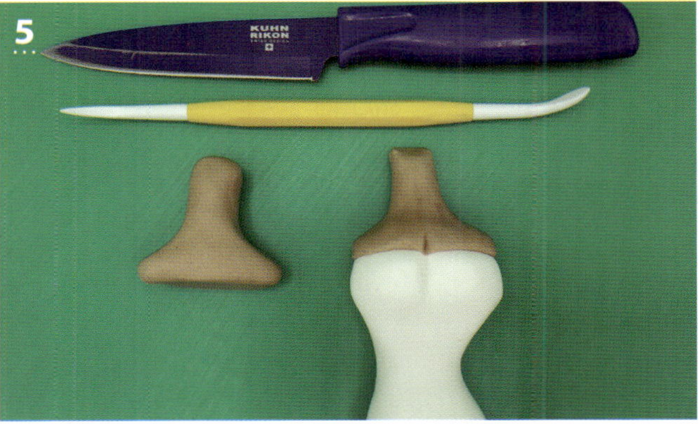

Adding the shoulder shape and attaching it to the body.

Dressing the Figure

Roll out the remaining 50g of ivory paste into a rectangle shape, approximately 1–2mm thick. If you want to add texture or pattern detail to the dress, use either a textured rolling pin or an impression mat at this stage, making sure that you roll or press evenly over the paste in order to achieve a consistent depth to the pattern.

Trim the paste so that it measures from the bottom of the body to just over the bottom edge of the shoulder join.

Wrap the paste around the body, trimming at the back where it joins. Make sure you smooth the paste to fit the contours of the body (especially the waist area). Rub your finger lightly along the joined edge to blend.

Make a belt by cutting a long, thin strip of the textured paste, securing it around the waist with a little edible glue, and trimming where it meets at the back.

Insert a wooden skewer from the top of the neck, through the body and out of the bottom, twisting the skewer as you push it through to avoid distorting the shape. You will need to push the skewer through into a polystyrene cake dummy to give it support. This piece of the skewer will then be inserted into your cake when finished, helping the figure to stay in place.

Creating and texturing the dress 'fabric'.

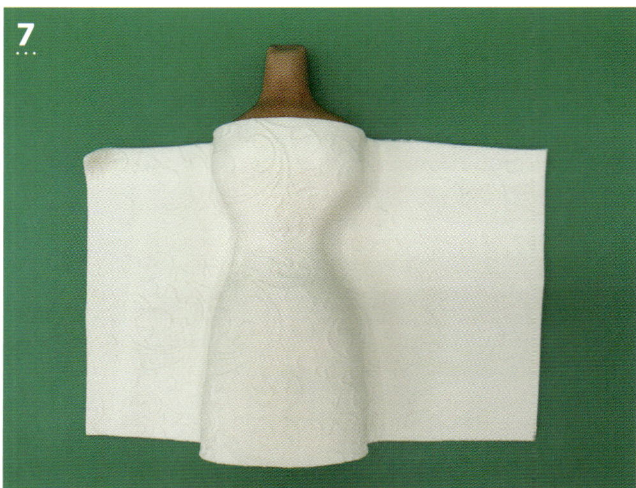
Measuring the height of the dress 'fabric' for size against your figure.

Adding the dress to the body, concentrating on fitting it to the contours of the shape you have created.

Adding a belt, and the internal structure that will keep the figure supported as it stands.

Roll a piece of the remaining ivory paste to a thickness of 1–2mm, texture it in the same way as the dress, then trim to shape (like a triangle with the top cut off). You can adjust the size, depending on the length you wish this part to trail behind the figure.

Make gathers/pleats in the paste with your fingers, and tuck under the paste at each side to neaten.

Attach to the lower half of the back of the dress with edible glue or water, smoothing the join into the dress with the wider end of your Dresden tool.

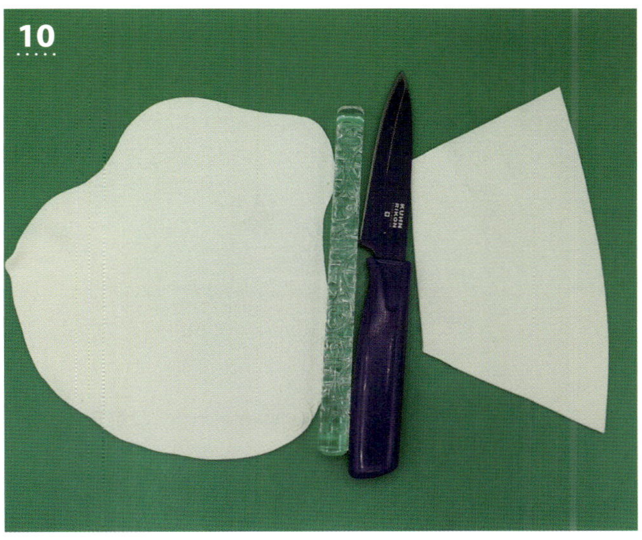

Making extra detail for the dress: a ruffled effect for the back.

Making a gathered/pleated effect with the paste.

Adding the extra fabric detail to the back of the dress.

Making the Arms

Roll 20g of skin-tone modelling paste into a long, thin sausage, cutting in half diagonally with a sharp knife. Bend halfway along to form an elbow, defining by pinching gently with your finger and thumb at the top and bottom of the bend. Thin the lower end of the arm by rolling gently between your finger and thumb, then narrow further at the wrist. Flatten the hand area with your fingers. There is no need to make the fingers and thumb, as the hands will be covered by the flower bouquet. However, if you are not making the bouquet, then follow the instructions showing how to make the hands from the male standing figure (*see* previous chapter page 100).

Insert small pieces of dried spaghetti into the body at a 45-degree angle, leaving a small amount sticking out for the arms to attach to. Use a little edible glue or water to secure the arms in place, joining the hands in front and adhering them to the front of the body.

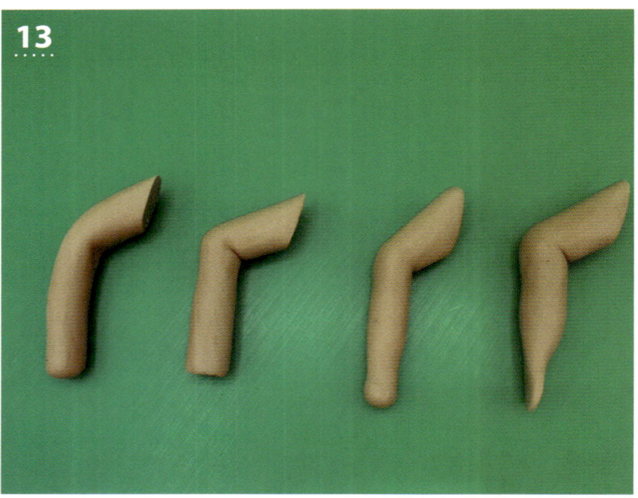

Making the arms and adding the elbow and wrist definition.

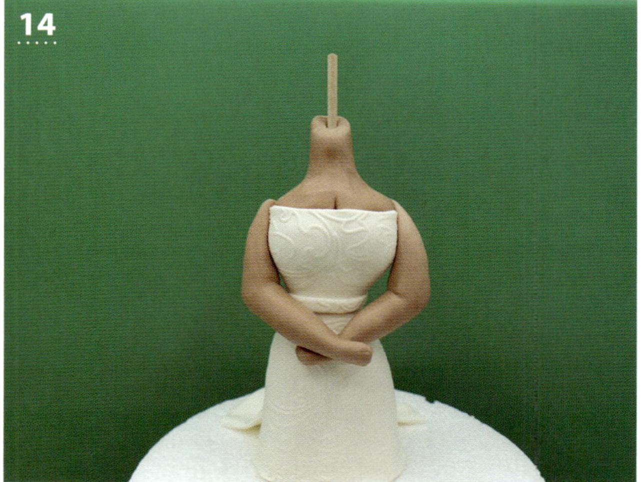

Securing the arms to the body and positioning them ready to 'hold' the flower bouquet.

Finishing the Top of the Dress

Roll out a rectangle of ivory modelling paste and trim the edges. Texture as for the dress, then fold over the long edges of the paste slightly towards the back of the paste.

Attach the strip to the body with edible glue or water, covering the join at the shoulders and top of arms, and trimming it with a sharp knife to fit at the back of the figure.

Making the 'fabric' piece of paste for the top of the dress.

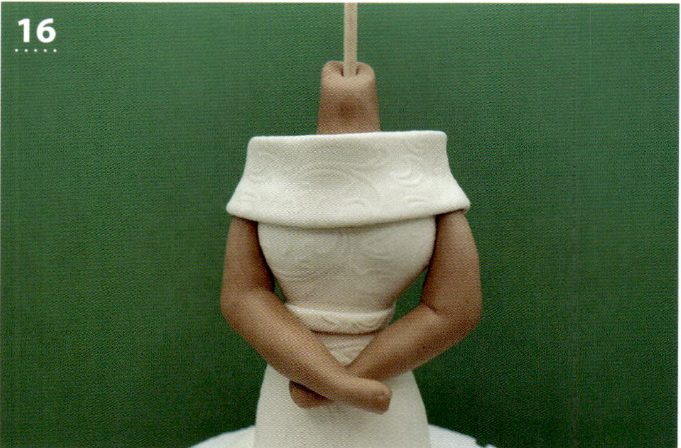

Attaching it to the dress, covering the tops of the arms and shoulder joins to finish off.

Roll out small pieces of blue and white modelling paste, to a thickness of 1–2mm. Using a small blossom flower plunger cutter (or something similar), cut out a mixture of the different coloured flowers.

Shape a small piece of white modelling paste to fit over the hands, secure in place with edible glue or water, then attach the flowers randomly, starting from the top edge, working downwards.

Continue to add flowers until the white paste is completely covered and you are happy with the size and shape of the bouquet.

Cutting out the blossom flowers for the bouquet.

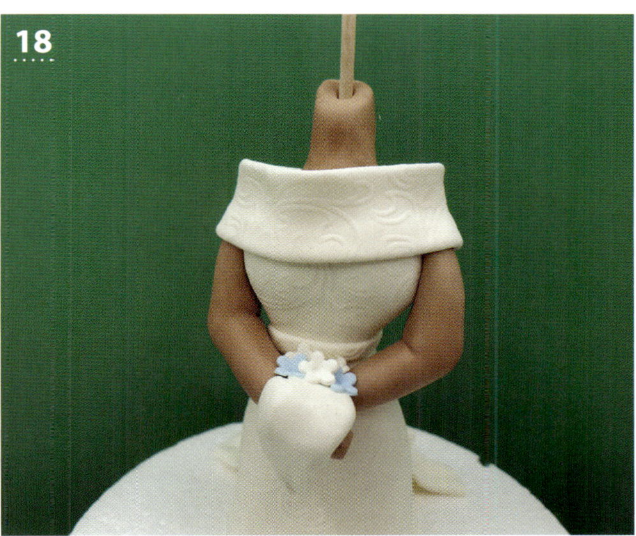
Creating the shape of the bouquet and starting to add flowers.

Finishing the flower bouquet with your choice of flowers and colours to cover the hands of the model.

Making the Head

Roll 40g of skin-tone modelling paste into a smooth ball with your hands, then form into an oval/egg shape. Squeeze the paste at the back of the head downwards gently to make a 'foot' to stick to the board as you work (it will look like an old-fashioned loaf of bread from the side).

Use the side of your hand to create an indent across the middle of the face area – rock your hand backwards and forwards gently across the paste. You could also use your finger, or the handle of a ball tool, making sure you smooth any lines left by the tool with your finger. Use a ball tool to create two eye sockets, moving in an L-shaped motion, but upwards then outwards.

Use the wider end of your Dresden tool to define the nose, stroking down the sides and underneath the nose area, gently pushing the paste away to leave the nose shape. Gently soften and smooth away any tool marks with your fingers. Use the sharp-pointed silicone-tipped tool to create the two nostrils. Smooth the paste downwards from under the nose with your finger to flatten the area slightly. Continue to define the edges of the nose gently with your Dresden tool.

Draw a line for the mouth with the sharp-pointed silicone-tipped tool, then cut into the paste with a sharp scalpel. Move the scalpel backwards and forwards along the cut, to clean the cut edge. Open slightly by lifting the scalpel blade a little whilst still inside the cut, to lift the paste under the nose.

Use the wide end of your Dresden tool to gently press the paste above the cut, to form and shape the top lip area, marking a line up to the nose with the narrow end of the Dresden tool.

Making the head shape and securing it to your workboard.

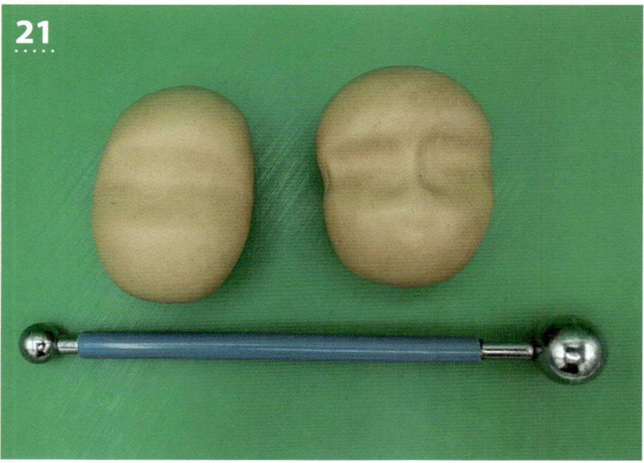

Forming the eye sockets with a ball tool.

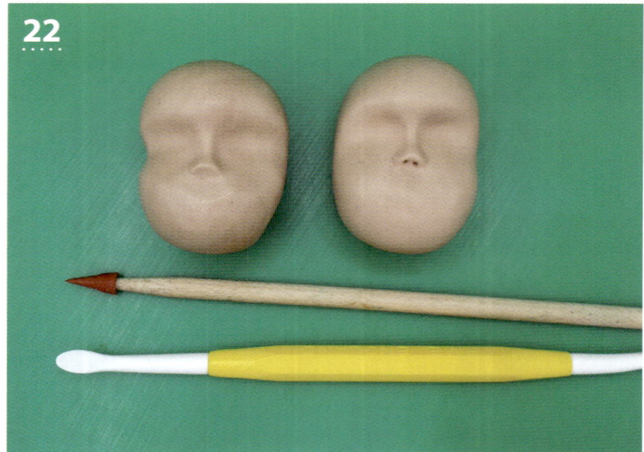

Creating and refining the nose by smoothing paste gently away from the area with a Dresden tool.

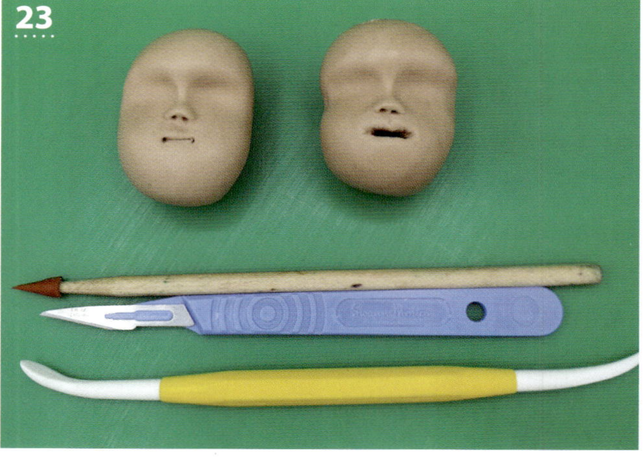

Making a cut for the mouth and creating an upper lip.

Use the wider end of your Dresden tool to draw lines down from the outer corners of the nose and from underneath each side of the mouth. Push the paste up gently to form the bottom lip. When creating female faces, the bottom lip tends to be fuller than for male faces.

Remove any tool marks by rubbing gently with your finger to soften and blend them. Use the handle of the small ball tool (or any other tool with a smooth, rounded handle) to shape the lower half of the face, pushing the excess paste downwards and under the chin area. Continue to soften and refine the facial details and shape of the head, using your Dresden tool and your fingers. You can also use a soft-tipped silicone tool to help soften lines and edges. You want to keep everything soft and rounded for a female face, unlike for a male face, which is more angular.

Use the hard, pointed-end silicone tool to draw the outline for the eyes, then push the paste inwards with a small ball tool to open up the cavities.

Roll two tiny balls of white modelling paste, and use them to fill the eye cavities. Make sure that the balls of white paste are not too big: they need to fit comfortably inside the space without going over the edges. Make an indent in each ball of white paste with your small ball tool, and fill with a small ball of brown modelling paste for the iris. Smooth with your finger so that they are flush with the white paste. You can use a different colour for the iris to personalize it to the eye colour of the person you are making.

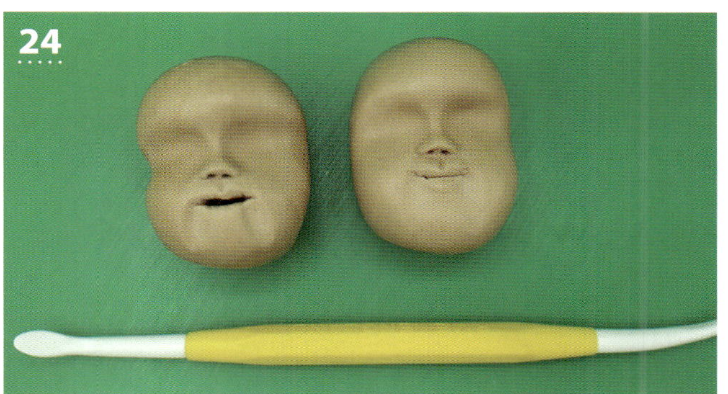

Forming the bottom lip, which tends to be fuller for a female figure.

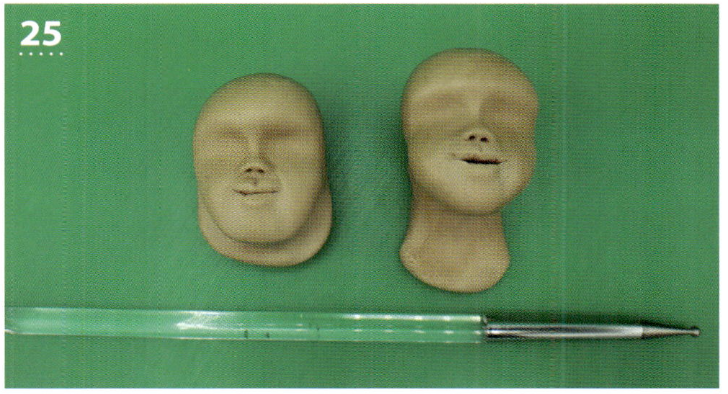

Shaping the face and chin, whilst continuing to refine the shape and details of the face.

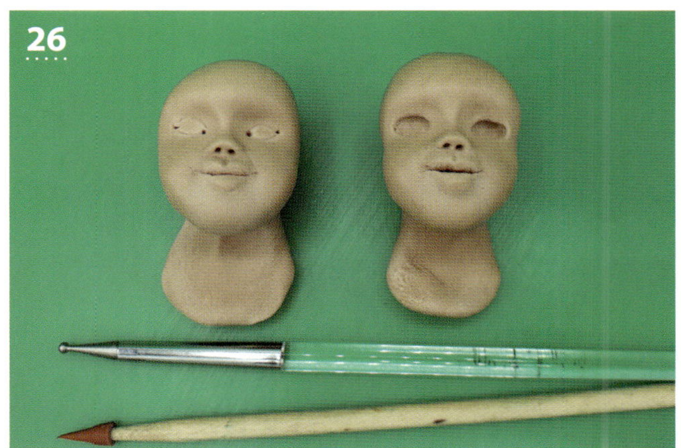

Creating the eye shape and cavity.

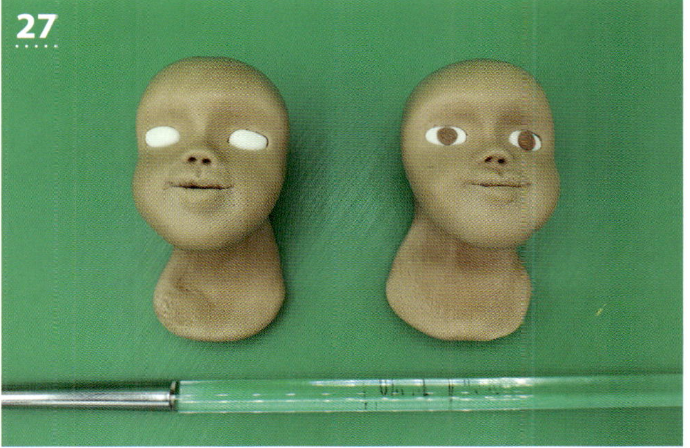

Adding the eye whites and irises. You can, of course, use your own preferred colour for making the iris.

Make a small indent and add the pupil, using a smaller amount of black modelling paste. Roll two tiny balls of white modelling paste to add highlights to the eyes. If you prefer, you can use a white edible marker pen or paint and draw the highlights on to each iris: you are better to wait for the paste to harden before adding these.

To create the upper eyelids, roll a small piece of skin-tone paste to approximately 3mm thickness. Cut out two 12mm circles, then use the same circle cutter to cut away the lower area.

Use a tiny amount of water to attach the upper eyelid in place, trimming away the excess with a sharp scalpel. Use the wider end of your Dresden tool to smooth the paste into the face, and soften any lines.

To shape the lower eyelid and under-eye contours, use the soft-tipped silicone tool to push up the paste under the eyes slightly, following the curve of the eye.

For the eyelashes, roll a small piece of black modelling paste until it is very fine at one end. Paint a fine line of edible glue on the underneath edge of the upper eyelids. Starting with the finer end of the paste at the inner corner of the eye, press gently into place and trim at the outer edge with a scalpel. Flick the black paste upwards slightly at the end.

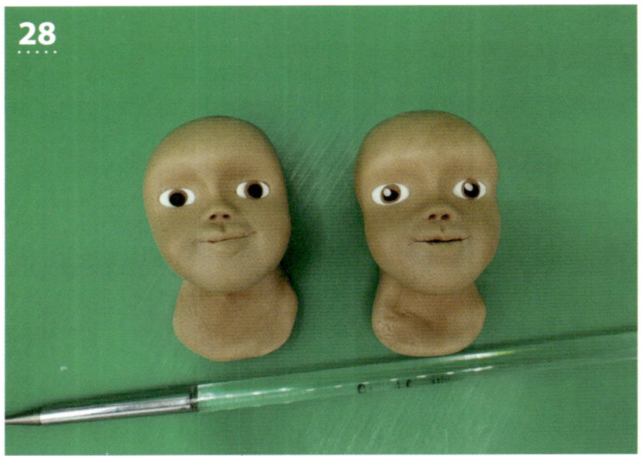

Adding the pupils and highlights.

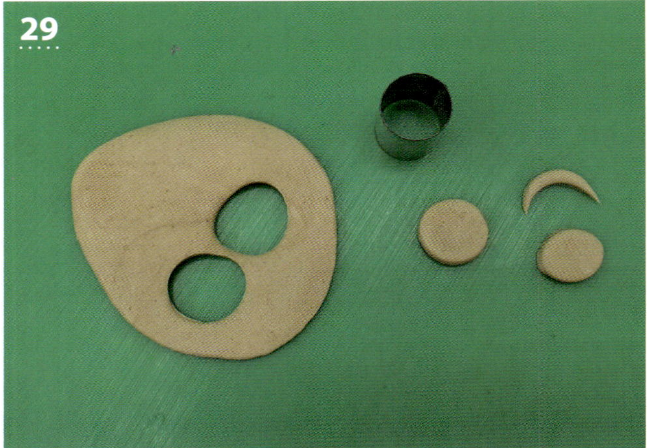

Creating the upper eyelids from skin-tone paste.

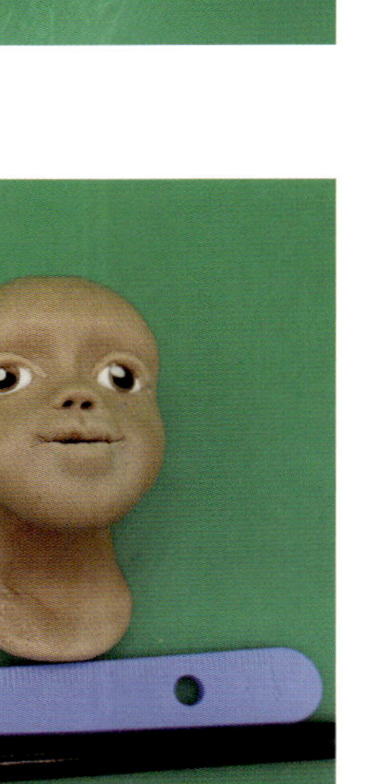

Adding eyelids to the face, blending to remove any joins, then creating the lower eyelids and under-eye contours.

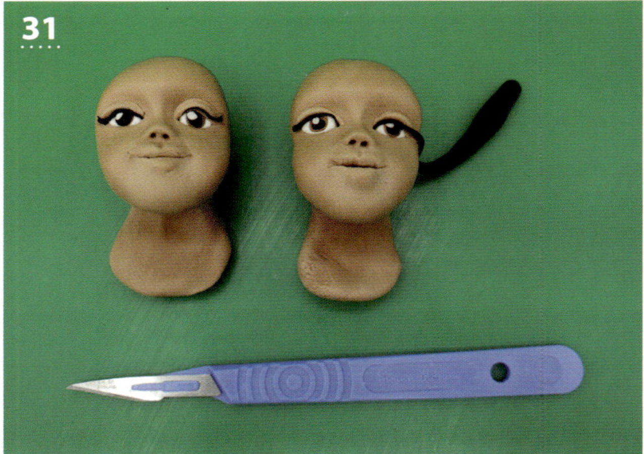

Creating and adding the eyelashes to the upper eyelids.

Applying the Make-up

Use clean brushes to apply petal or lustre-dust powders for the make-up. Apply eyeshadow to the eyelid in the colour of your choice. A lustre-type dust works well for eyeshadow, giving it a bit of sparkle and shine. Add blusher for the cheeks, using a matt pink colour (or shade of your choice). For the lips, mix a little coloured petal dust with white vegetable fat (Trex) to make a thick paste to resemble lipstick, then apply to the lips with a clean, dry brush.

Finishing the Head

Push the excess paste away from the back of the head with your fingers, whilst keeping the rounded shape to the back of the head. Trim off the excess paste with small, sharp scissors and smooth the cut area with your fingers.

Attach the head to your figure, using a little edible glue on top of the neck and on the wooden skewer to stick it in place. Twist the head from side to side as you gently push it down on to the wooden skewer, to avoid distorting the shape.

Roll a small ball of skin-tone paste (approximately 1g) into a ball, then cut in half. Shape into two ovals for ears. Attach to each side of the head, positioning them so that the bottom of each ear is in line with the bottom of the nose. Use both ends of your Dresden tool to add detail to the ears.

Helpful Tip

When adding colour to a model's face, make sure you remove excess dust from your brush before applying it, by tapping it on to a piece of kitchen paper or tissue. It is better to keep adding a little at a time and to build up the colour gradually, rather than putting on too much to start with. However, if you do add too much colour, it can easily be removed with a damp cloth. You will need to wait until the area dries completely before reapplying.

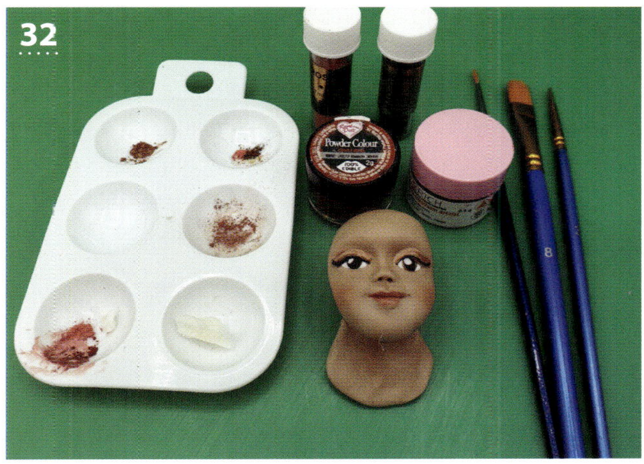

Applying make-up to the face using edible petal and lustre dusts.

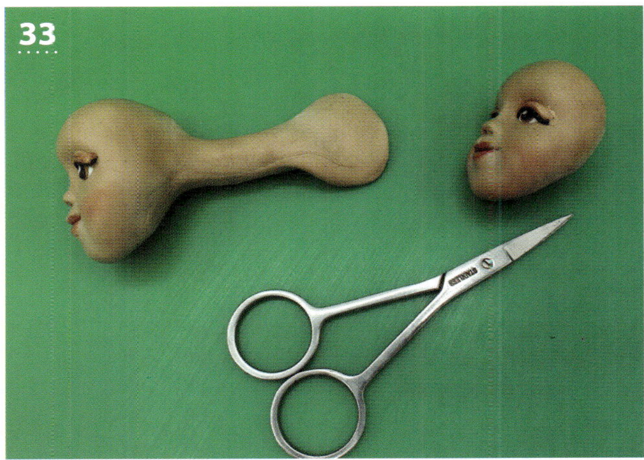

Finishing off the head by removing excess paste and shaping the back of the head.

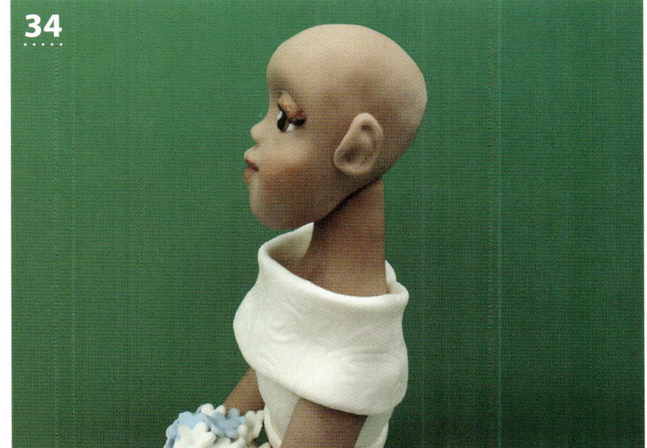

Adding the head to the body and creating ears. It is important to align the ears in the correct position when attaching them to the head.

Adding the Eyebrows and Hair

For the eyebrows, roll a small piece of dark brown modelling paste until it is very fine at one end. Apply a fine line of edible glue or water to the face ready to add the eyebrows. Holding the wider end of the paste, position it over the top of the eye socket, starting with the finer, pointed end at the outer edge of the eye. Trim to size with a sharp scalpel above the inner edge of the eye. The shape of the eyebrows can be used to give expression to your figure.

For the base layer of the hair, roll 10g of dark brown modelling paste into a ball, then thin with your fingers and thumb until it is quite thin and large enough to cover the back and top of the head. Attach this base layer to the head with a little edible glue, trimming away any excess paste with small, sharp scissors so that it fits close to the head like a shower cap.

Shape the remaining dark brown modelling paste into four cone shapes. Flatten and texture each piece of paste with the narrow end of your Dresden tool, to look like strands of hair.

Starting at the back, position one piece of hair in the centre, adding two more (one at each side), shaping them to the sides of the head, making sure that you cover as much as possible of the base layer of coloured paste.

Add the last piece of hair to the front of the head, shaping it into a wave, then flicking the paste outwards at the bottom of each piece to create a sense of movement.

To finish the figure, make three additional blue flowers to match the bouquet, adding them across the hair join on top of the head.

Creating eyebrows, and adding the base layer of the hair.

Making textured pieces of paste to form the top layer of the hair.

Adding the top layer of the hair in three separate pieces.

Completing the hair and adding the finishing touches.

Making a Sugar Bow for the Back of the Dress

Roll ivory modelling paste (or the same colour as the dress, if different) into a rectangle, approximately 2mm in thickness. Texture it in the same way as the dress, and cut out three strips of equal size.

Form the bow loops using two of the strips – fold each one in half and pinch the ends together.

On the remaining strip, fold the edges of the paste inwards on the long edges. Put the two bow loops together and wrap the remaining strip round the middle, securing in place with edible glue.

Make two extra strips for the bow tails, trimming with a diagonal cut. Attach to the back of the dress with edible glue. If the bow is quite large, you may find it better to attach it with royal icing instead.

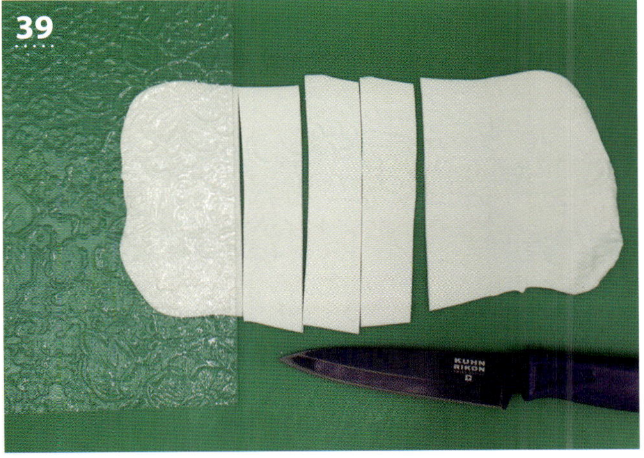

Cutting out the pieces of paste to make a matching bow for the back of the dress.

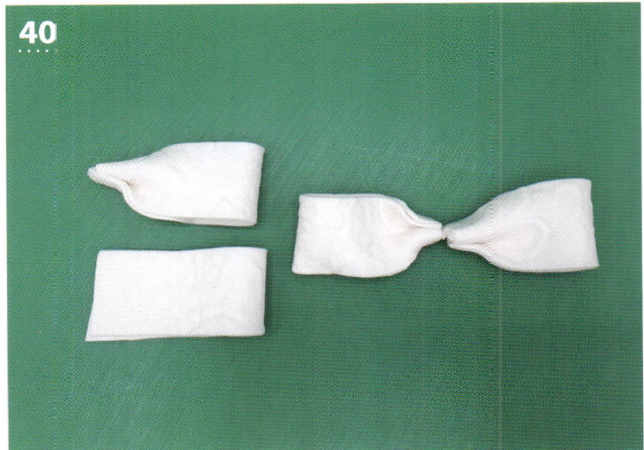

Forming the two bow loops.

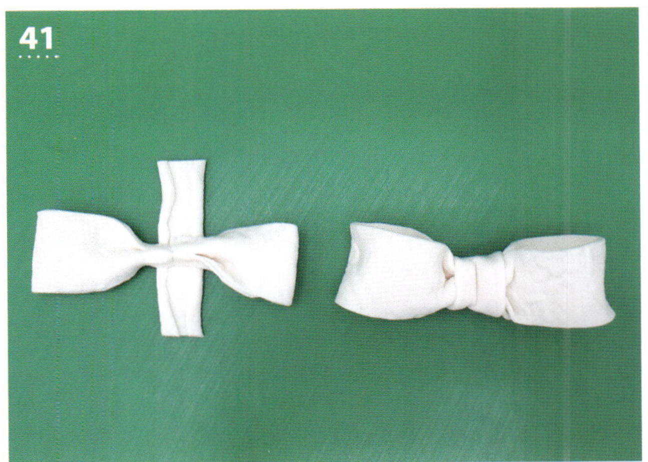

Finishing off the bow using a strip of paste around the middle.

Attaching the bow to the dress, complete with ribbon tails to finish.

Alternative Flower Bouquet

Use the silicone mould to make flowers. First add the red modelling paste for the flowers, then fill in the rest of the mould with green for the leaves. Make several pieces to create the whole bouquet.

Arrange the moulded pieces over the hands to make the bouquet, securing them with edible glue.

Using a silicone mould to make flowers.

Finishing off the moulded flower bouquet.

Alternative Hairstyle

Roll 10g dark brown modelling paste into a ball, then flatten into a circle, thinning the edges with your finger and thumb until it covers the top, sides and back of the head. Keep the middle part of the shape thicker, ready for texturing.

Texture the hair with the narrow end of your Dresden tool, from the outside edge to the centre, then adhere to the head with edible glue.

Roll a small ball of dark brown modelling paste, flatten it slightly, and indent the top with a ball tool. Texture the edges of the paste with the narrow end of your Dresden tool to resemble hair tied into a bun.

Attach the bun in place with edible glue, positioning it towards the back of the top of the head.

Roll a thin sausage of red modelling paste, attaching it around the bun, where it joins to the head.

The beginning of this alternative hairstyle starts off in a very similar way to the previous one, except hair texture is added to this piece of paste, instead of making additional pieces.

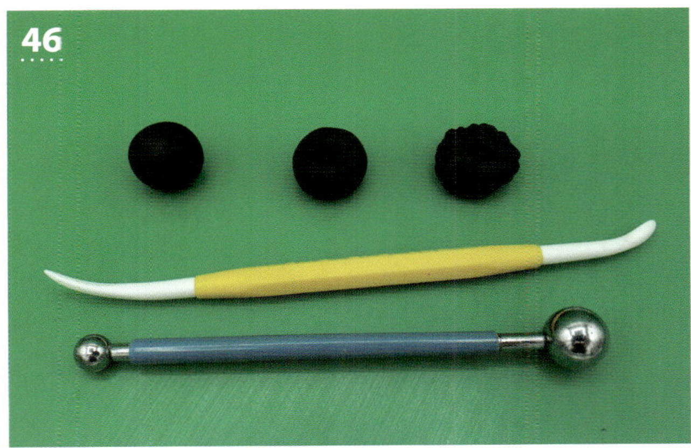

Making the bun part of the hair and texturing.

Attaching the bun to the head.

Finishing off with a red hair bobble.

Three different wedding cake designs have been created here, all of which have the modelled wedding couple figures as the main focus. You may wish to add other decorations, such as flowers, but just be careful not to overshadow the figures, which should be the main design feature. The cake designs are all based on a three-tier cake, with a 25cm (10in) round bottom tier, a 20cm (8in) round middle tier, and a 15cm (6in) round top tier. The tiers are all covered with white sugar paste, and are stacked on to a 30cm (12in) round cake drum, also covered with white sugar paste.

To attach the figures to the top tier of the cake, add a small amount of royal icing under the feet/dress before pushing the skewer into the cake. As the wooden skewer is food safe, no barrier is required when inserting it into the cake.

The addition of a rustic ribbon adds a simple yet effective decorative element to the wedding cake, together with a coloured ribbon to co-ordinate with the colour scheme.

Design One

This design features a simple rustic ribbon, teamed with green ribbons to compliment the colour scheme of the wedding couple.

Preparing the Ribbons

I have used a rustic-looking jute/hessian-style ribbon, but since this is not suitable for being in close contact with the cake, you will need to add a barrier to protect the sugar paste from the fibres. Food-safe acetate on a roll is a great choice, although it is wider than needed; cut it to the correct length to fit round the bottom of each tier, then cut to slightly more than the width of the ribbon, just to be sure that the cake is totally protected.

Attach the acetate using a small amount of royal icing at the back of the cake.

Add the rustic ribbon over the top of the acetate, securing with royal icing; then finish with a 15mm green ribbon over the top (or use a different colour of your choice).

Cutting acetate roll to size, to provide a food-safe barrier for the jute/hessian ribbon.

Securing the acetate to the cake tiers with royal icing.

Adding the two ribbons to finish the design.

Design Two

For this design, I have used artificial foliage to create thin wreaths around the bottom of each tier.

Artificial foliage can be purchased in long lengths, and easily trimmed to size with a pair of small pliers. Measure and cut to the length required to wrap round the bottom of each tier. If you cut two lengths per tier, this will give a thicker coverage.

Add a green ribbon round the bottom of each tier to keep the leaves away from the sugar paste (you could also use acetate, as in the first design), then wrap the leaves round the tier, twisting the wires together at the back of the cake.

Cutting the artificial foliage to the correct length for each cake tier.

Adding the artificial foliage wreaths to the cake, securing them at the back.

This simple design incorporates artificial foliage to give a minimalist look to the wedding cake, ensuring that the wedding couple figures are the main feature of the cake.

Design Three

For the final design I have replaced the bottom white tier with a striking purple colour, to give a real pop of colour to the cake, which also coordinates with the colour scheme of the wedding couple figures.

Mix white sugar paste (fondant) with purple gel colour to achieve the desired colour. For darker colours, it is better to colour in advance and let the colour develop more overnight to darken. Cover the bottom tier with the purple paste, stack, and then finish off with a 15mm purple ribbon round the bottom of each tier, securing these at the back of the cake with a little royal icing. Add the same ribbon to the edge of the cake drum, using either a non-toxic glue stick or double-sided tape.

Colouring white sugar paste (fondant) to a deep purple shade, using gel colours.

A striking purple-coloured tier gives a bold pop of colour, with a modern look. You could change the colour to co-ordinate with the colour scheme of the wedding.

CHAPTER 10

Figures with More Complex Internal Armatures

To allow for more freedom when modelling figures, an internal armature support can be used, to enable the figure to be positioned in a wide variety of gravity-defying or complex poses. These are particularly useful for 'action poses' to be used as cake toppers for cakes with a sporting or dance theme.

THE INTERNAL ARMATURE SUPPORT

Different materials can be used for the internal structure, the most commonly used being armature wire or thick florist wire. As mentioned in the equipment section at the beginning of the book, I generally use florist wire taped together, which is strong enough to hold the figure in position, yet pliable enough to be bent to shape without too much effort. In this chapter you will see how to design and build the internal armature frame, as well as how to apply paste to the armature, and how to make it food safe when using it as a cake topper.

The ballerina figure is pictured on a 15cm (6in) round cake.

Designing Your Internal Armature

You can find inspiration for your figure in many places, for example from a photograph, drawing or a search of images online.

When designing the internal armature, first you need to draw a simple sketch, showing the outline of your figure in the desired position, and at the actual size you want it to be.

Draw internal lines, which fit inside the outline of your sketch, to determine where the armature will need to be positioned.

Either transfer the internal armature lines on to a separate piece of paper, or use the previous drawing to use as a guide whilst you build the internal support.

◀ This ballerina figure, dressed in a tutu and standing 'en pointe', has an internal armature so she can be posed in position and stand securely on top of your cake.

Outline sketch of the figure you are making, in the pose and actual size you want to make. Enlarge this template by 200%.

Draw straight lines inside the sketch to indicate where your armature will sit. Enlarge this template by 200%.

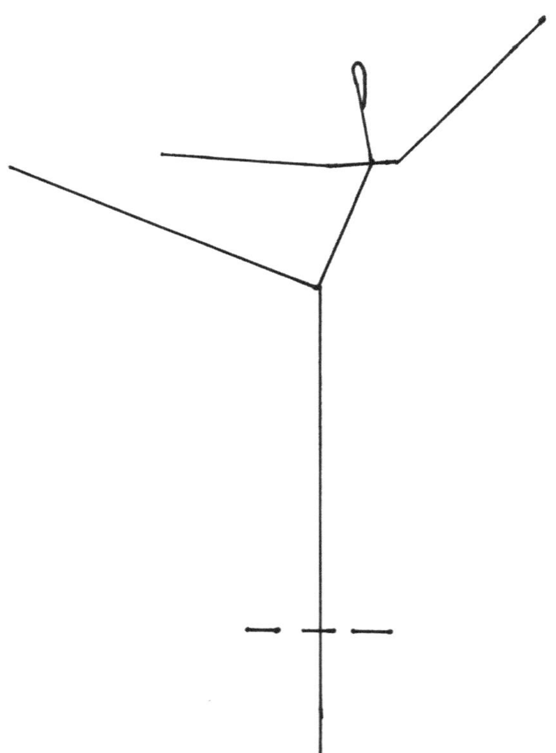

Transfer the internal armature plan on to a separate piece of paper (optional). Enlarge this template by 200%.

Internal armature frame

Equipment

- 2 strands of 16-gauge florist wire
- 2 strands of 18-gauge florist wire
- florist tape on a roll
- pliers to cut the wire
- a small polystyrene cake dummy to hold your armature in place whilst working on your model

Equipment needed to build your internal armature.

Building Your Internal Armature

Now you have designed your internal armature for your model, it is time to start constructing it. For this example, two different gauges of thick florist wire are used taped together with florist tape, as these are readily available materials, commonly used by cake decorators.

Separate the florist wires into two sets, each containing one of each sized wire (16-gauge and 18-gauge). Take one set and tape the two wires together with florist tape, starting from the middle and working your way along to one end. Repeat with the other set of two wires. Taping the wires together will give additional strength, as well as allowing the 'stick figure'-shaped armature to be created as one piece.

Place both sets of wires together, on top of your armature diagram, to work out the positioning of the body/torso area. You need to measure the length of the legs, allowing an additional piece at the ends which will be inserted into your cake later, to give support to the figure. Tape the two sets of wires together along the torso line, between the tops of the legs and the arms.

Again, using your diagram to help, you can now bend the wires that will hold the arms and legs into position. You should be able to do this with your hands, but if you find it difficult, use pliers to bend the wire into place. Keep referring to your diagram as you work, as it is easy to alter the shape accidentally as you bend the separate limbs into position. For the arms you need to bend the thinner of the two wires outwards – that is, the 18-gauge wires – leaving the two 16-gauge wires upright.

The remaining two 16-gauge wires will be used to form the neck and the head support. Trim one wire to the length of the neck on your diagram, and cut the other wire to double the length of the head loop, as shown on the diagram.

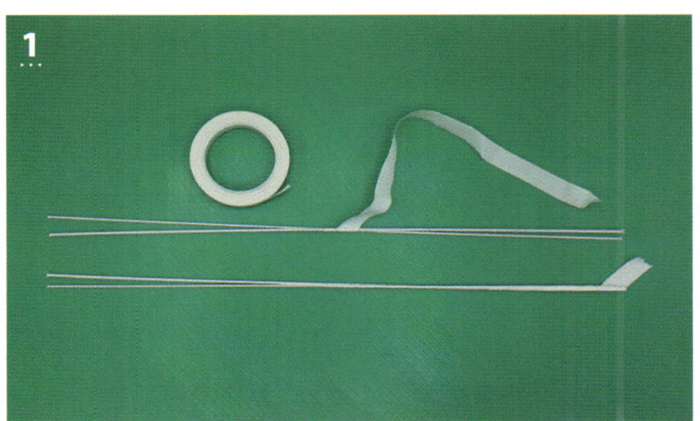

Preparing the wires to start creating the internal armature.

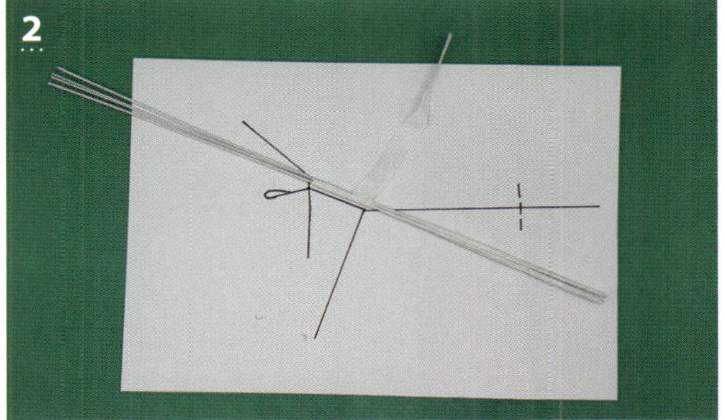

Using your guide for measuring and creating the body area of the armature.

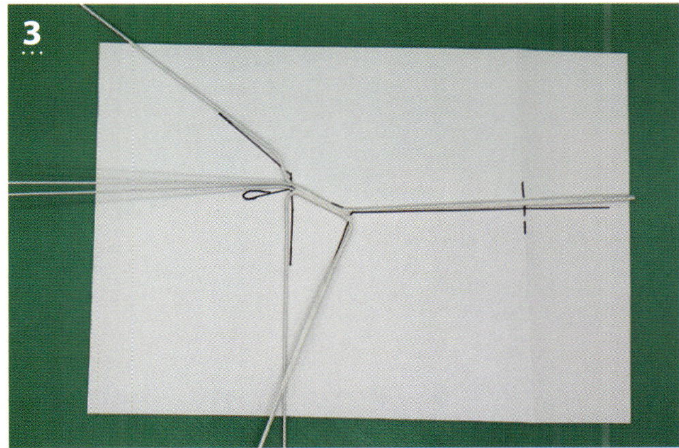

Positioning the wires that will hold the paste for the limbs in the correct positions, using your armature plan as a guide.

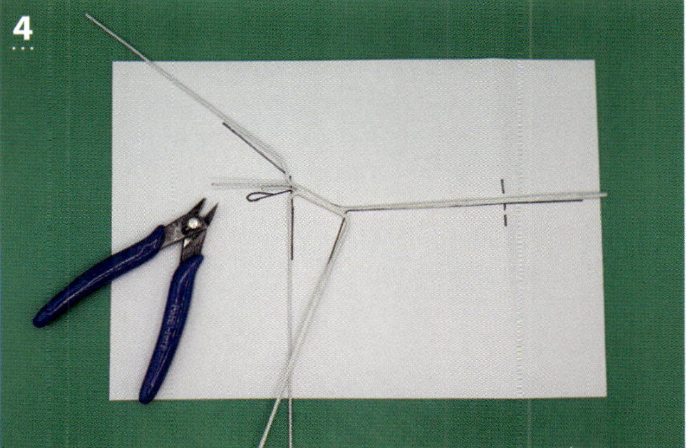

Trimming the wire to create the neck and head supports of the armature.

Use the pliers to help you to bend the head-support wire into the loop shape. This will provide additional support for the weight of the head, as well as holding the paste securely in place, due to the shape of the loop, rather than having a single, straight piece of wire. Cut the wires for the limbs to the sizes according to your diagram with pliers, although these may need to be adjusted further as you work on your model.

Push the wire armature into the top of the polystyrene dummy, using your diagram as a guide as to how far to insert the supporting wire (up to the bottom of the toes, as the ballerina figure is standing en pointe).

Your internal armature is now complete, ready for the paste to be added.

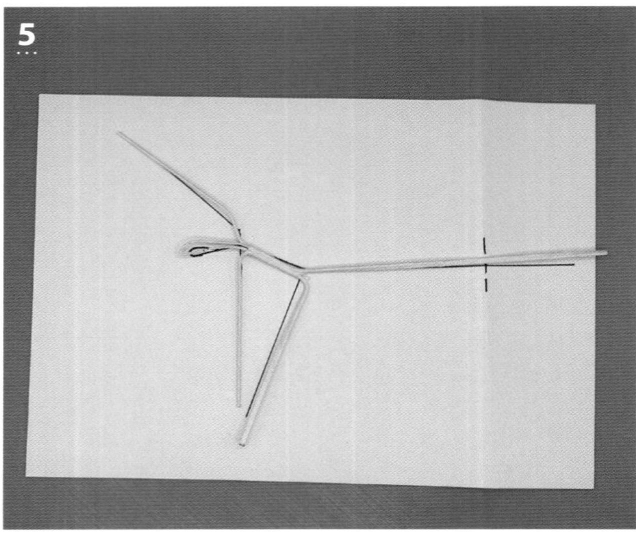

Making a loop with the wire, to create extra support for holding the head.

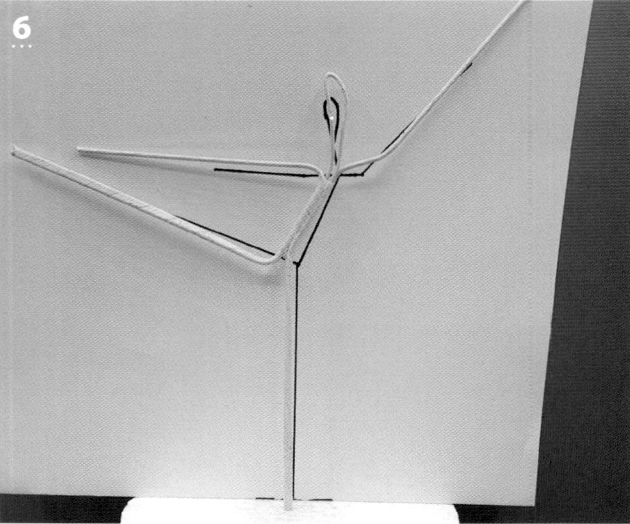

Use a polystyrene dummy to hold your armature whilst you work.

Using Florist Tape

Florist tape is available in many different shades and colours. I tend to use white florist tape when taping the wires together for an internal armature so that it doesn't show through the paste, especially when using light colours for your figure. You need to pull the florist tape with your hands to stretch it, which releases the adhesive for it to stick to the wires.

To create the ballerina figure, we will be adding paste to the internal armature for the body, and then adding the clothes separately. This needs to be taken into account, as you will need to make the torso area slightly thinner than you would normally, to allow for an additional layer of paste for the clothing. It is easy to end up with a figure that is larger than you wanted when you use this method of modelling, so pay close attention to the size as you work.

The Ballerina Figure

Equipment

- small rolling pin
- sharp knife
- scalpel
- ball tools (variety of sizes)
- soft-tipped silicone modelling tool
- Drescen tool
- hard-tipped, pointy silicone modelling tool
- frilling tool or cocktail stick
- kitchen scissors
- small, sharp scissors
- pliers
- foam pad
- set of circle cutters (I used 45mm, 60mm, 75mm, 95mm and 110mm circle cutters.)
- 3 small oval cutters (I used 15mm, 20mm and 30mm oval cutters.)
- paintbrushes for water and for dusting cheeks/eyes/ lips
- kitchen paper towel (or tissue paper) for making templates for clothing

Materials

- 140g skin-tone modelling paste
- 10g purple modelling paste*
- 20g white modelling paste*
- 15g brown modelling paste
- 1g black modelling paste
- 90g white flower paste
- paprika gel or paste colour
- petal dusts of your choice for cheeks, lipstick and eyeshadow (I used Fractal Kitty Nose Pink and Roxy & Rich Soft Rose Gold)
- White vegetable fat (to mix with dust for lipstick)

* I mixed the 10g purple and 20g white modelling paste to make a lilac shade for the leotard.

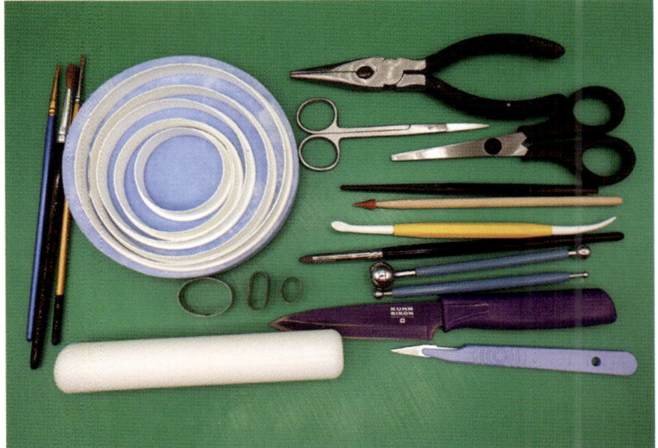

The equipment needed to make this ballerina figure, which is very similar to the tools required for the standing figures in the previous chapter, along with a few optional extras for details.

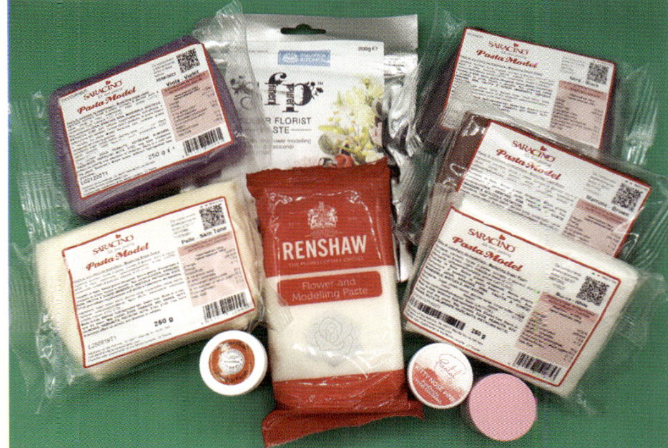

Ready-coloured Saracino modelling paste in skin tone, purple, white, brown and black was used to create this model. You can substitute different colours for the clothing, hair and other details if you wish, when creating your figure. White florist paste and a selection of petal dusts for colouring was also used.

Modelling and Adding the Legs to the Armature

Roll 30g of skin-tone modelling paste into a long sausage shape, then cut it in half with a knife. Each half needs to be approximately the length of the wire leg supports, though they can be adjusted if they become too long whilst shaping.

Roll your smallest finger back and forth over the centre of each leg, to create an indentation to form the knee area. Underneath the calf muscle area, use your finger again to roll and slim the lower part of the leg.

Create the ankle indentation in the same way as the knee, then manipulate the bottom of the leg into a simple foot shape. We will be adding paste for the ballet slipper on top of the foot, so avoid making this too large.

Use the wider end of the Dresden tool to define the kneecap area, smoothing away the paste above and below. Use soft, gentle movements, smoothing any lines left by the tool with your finger.

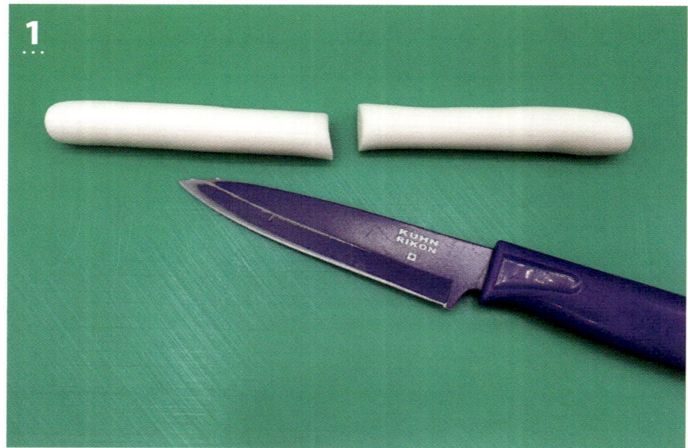

Rolling the paste to create the legs.

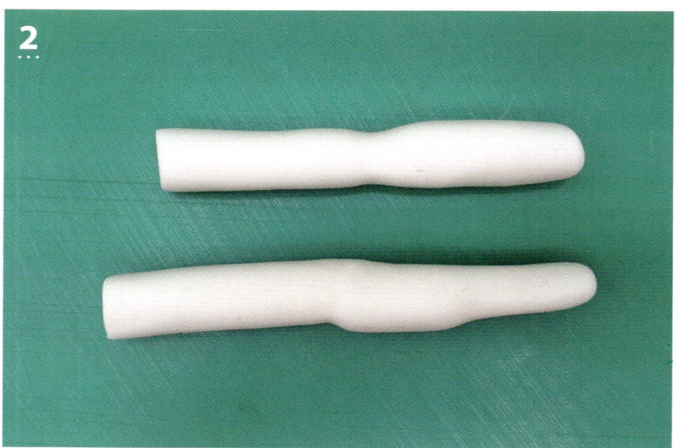

Defining knee and calf details on the legs.

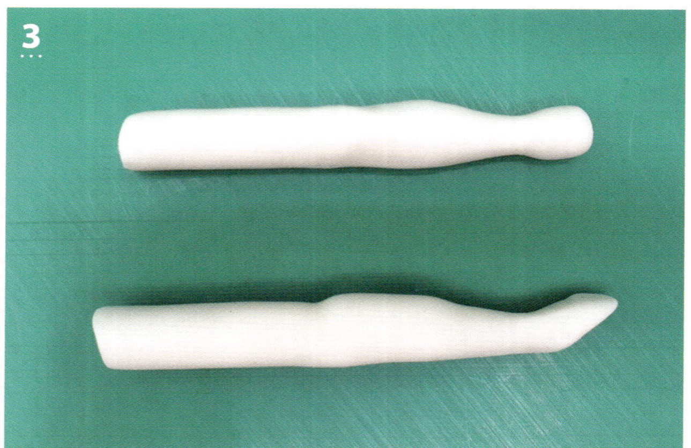

Creating ankle and foot areas for the legs.

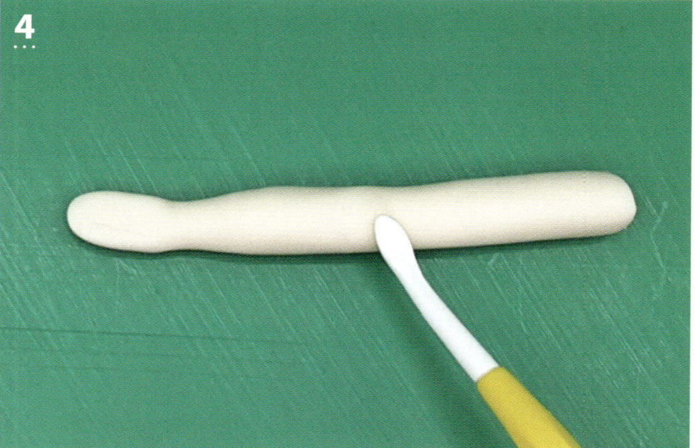

Making further refinements to the legs to create kneecaps.

Lay the two legs into position on top of your diagram, to make sure you are happy with the size and shape. Paste can be trimmed from the top when you add them to the armature, but make sure the bottom half of each leg is correct, so they stay in proportion.

To enable you to add the legs to the armature, you need to cut a long slit down the side of the leg, which will be at the back of the model. For the standing leg, this will be on the side of the leg that is facing away from the front of the model. Use a scalpel to cut the slit, which then needs to be opened up with the narrow end of your Dresden tool, to allow space for the wire to fit inside. Do not cut completely to the end of the foot.

Use a small paintbrush to brush a thin layer of water inside the cut area, so it can stick to the wire. Be careful not to add too much water: it just needs to make the paste a bit tacky, rather than wet.

Place the leg in front of the wire, then press it over gently, so that the wire fits into the opening and is covered by the paste. Gently close the cut by pinching the edges of the paste together with your fingers.

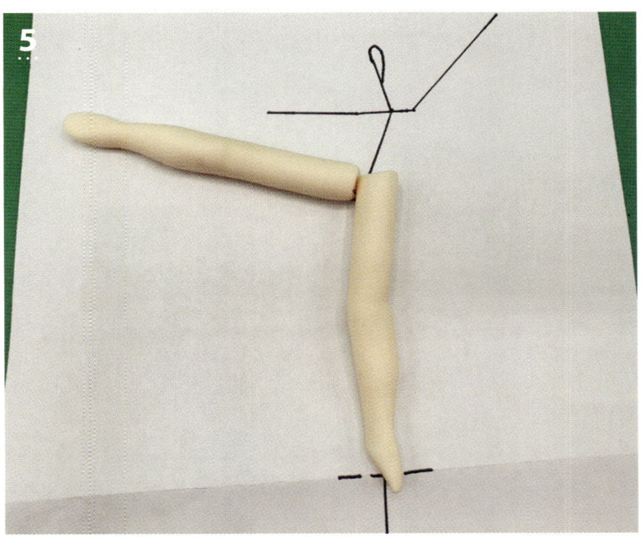

Measuring the correct size for the legs using your diagram.

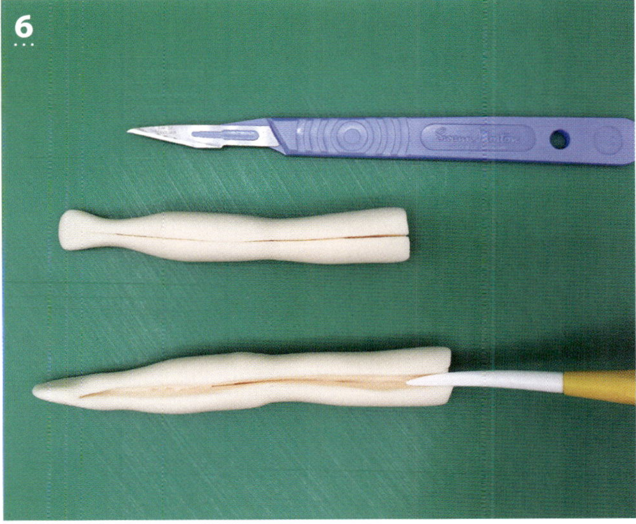

Creating a channel in the back of the leg to fit round the wire armature.

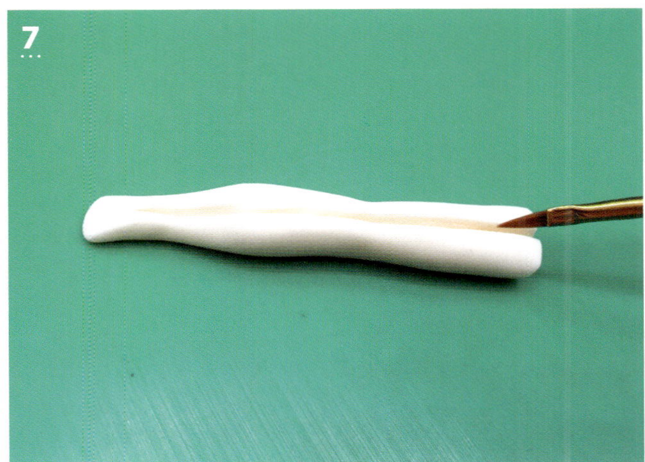

Use water sparingly so the paste can stick to the armature and itself for closing the seam.

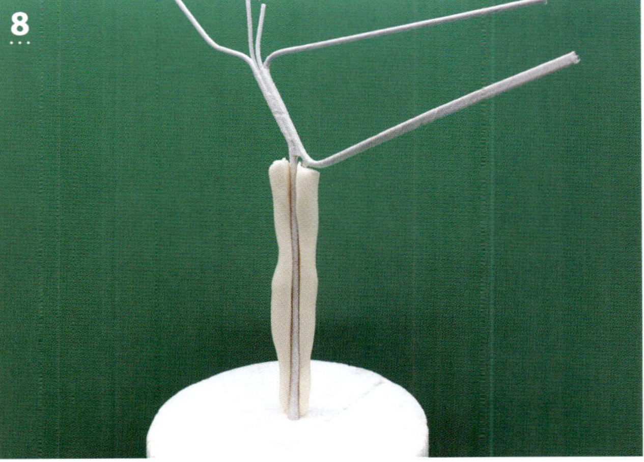

Positioning the first leg on to the armature.

Re-shape the leg if it has become flattened or squashed whilst cutting and attaching to the wire, redefining the knee and lower leg, down to the ankle and foot. Make sure that the wire is entirely covered by the paste, particularly at the bottom where it will sit on the cake.

Blend the join at the back of the leg together, by rubbing with your fingers and/or the wider end of your Dresden tool.

Add the other leg in the same way, by cutting a slit with a scalpel and then opening it up with the narrow end of your Dresden tool. Because of the positioning of this leg, you will have to make the slit at the back of the leg. Add a little water with a paintbrush to help it stick and position around the wire, closing the join with your fingers and blending the closed edges together. Check the positioning of your legs against the diagram, adjusting if necessary.

Before continuing with the model, create a template of the skirt to determine the sizing (this is easier done at this point, rather than later). Cut a rough circle from kitchen paper or tissue paper, then cut a slit into the middle.

Position the skirt template over the armature, and trim it (or make a larger one if you have cut this one too small) until you are happy with the size of the skirt. Check that you are happy with how much of the legs are showing from underneath the skirt. You can refer to any inspiration photographs or images you may be using, or just go with what you think looks best. Keep the template (or take a measurement), as this will determine the sizes of the circle cutters that you will need for making the skirt later.

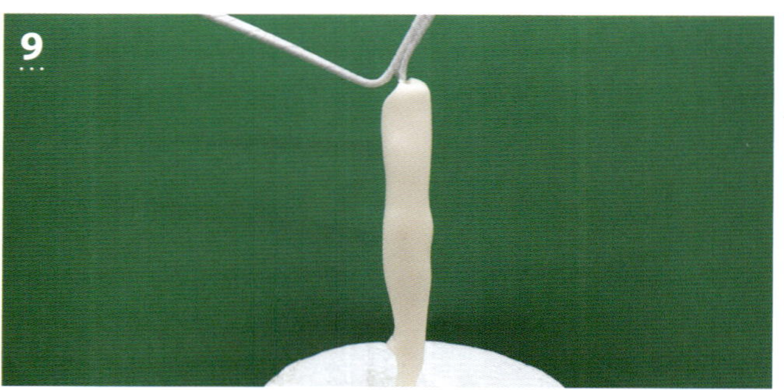

Reshape the leg if it becomes misshapen whilst attaching it to the armature.

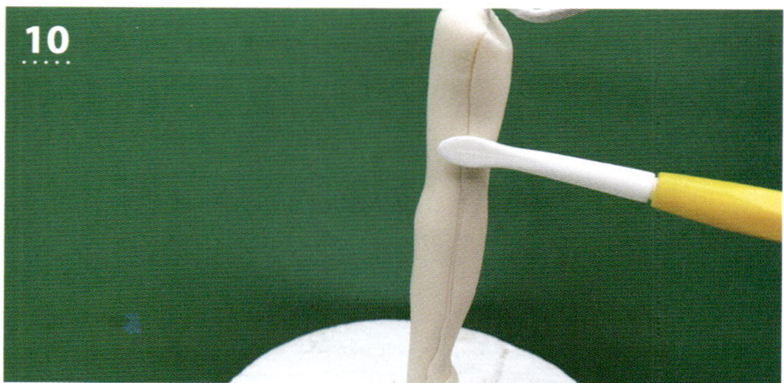

Blending together the join in the paste to hide the seam as much as possible.

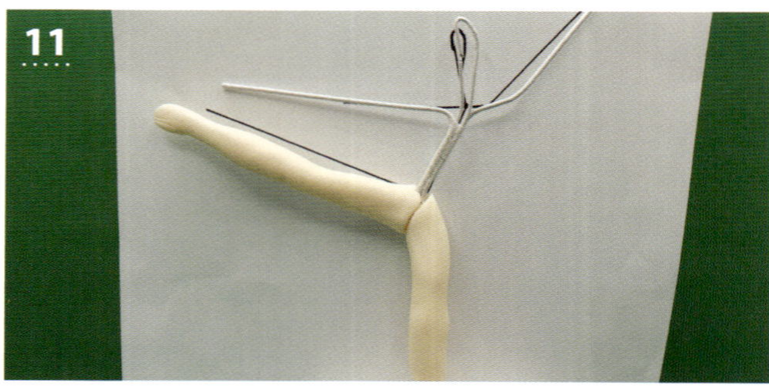

Add the second leg to the armature, paying close attention to where to make the opening for the armature to fit.

Making a template for the skirt using kitchen paper or tissue.

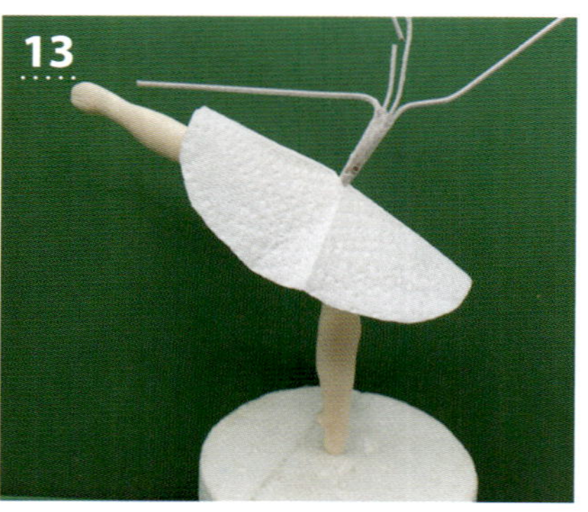

Checking and adjusting the sizing of the template.

Shaping and Adding the Torso to the Armature

Before starting on the torso, use a piece of white florist tape to tape together the bottom of the head and neck supports, as well as the wires over the tops of the arm. Do not tape over the top half of the loop, as this open loop structure helps to grip on to the paste and secure the head firmly in place.

Roll 20g of skin-tone paste into a ball and then an oval, flattening it slightly with your hand. Squeeze the paste at the top upwards, into a neck, rounding and smoothing the edges with your fingers. Narrow the paste towards the bottom of the body to form the waist area. Remember that you will be adding more layers of paste later for the leotard and skirt, so make the waist smaller to account for this.

Use a smooth-handled tool, such as the silicone smoother tool, to gently push the paste upwards from the bottom of the body and downwards from just under the neck, using a rolling motion. This excess paste will form the bust area, so depending on how big you would like the bust to be, you may want to press harder or lighter, to move more or less paste into this area. Use your Dresden tool to divide the paste into two halves, then gently smooth around each side of the paste to remove any harsh lines and edges.

To add the body to the armature, slice it in half using a gentle sawing action, so as not to distort the shape too much. You can easily reshape it once it is in place, so don't worry too much if it doesn't stay exactly the same shape.

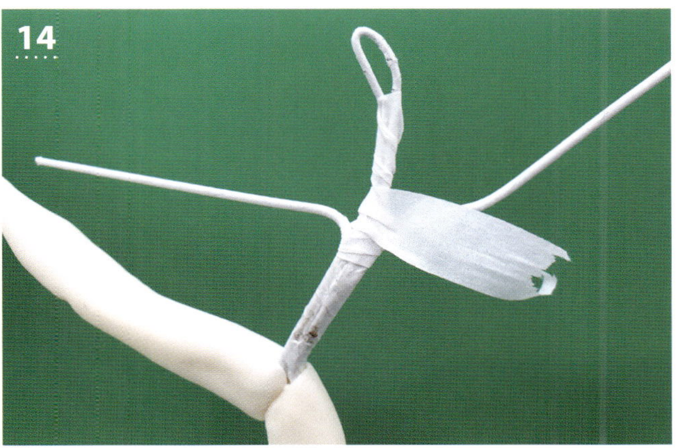

Tape together the head and neck support.

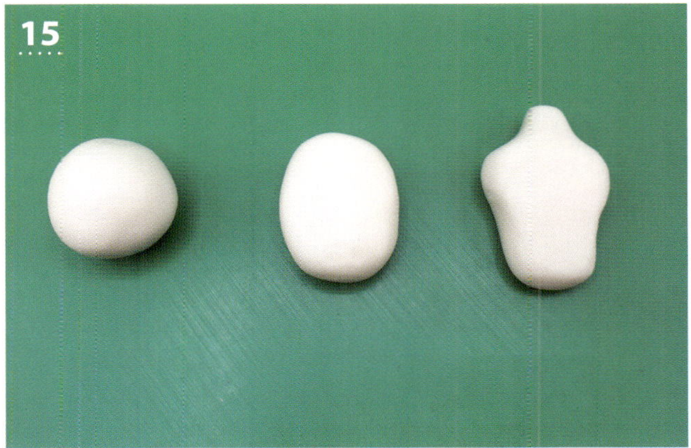

Starting to create a simple body shape.

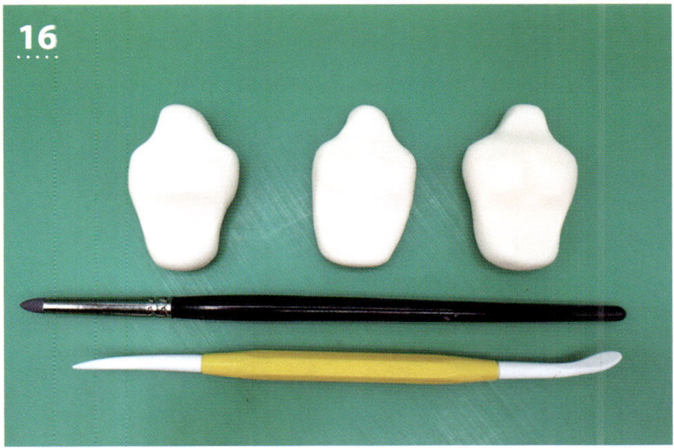

Shape the bust area of the body.

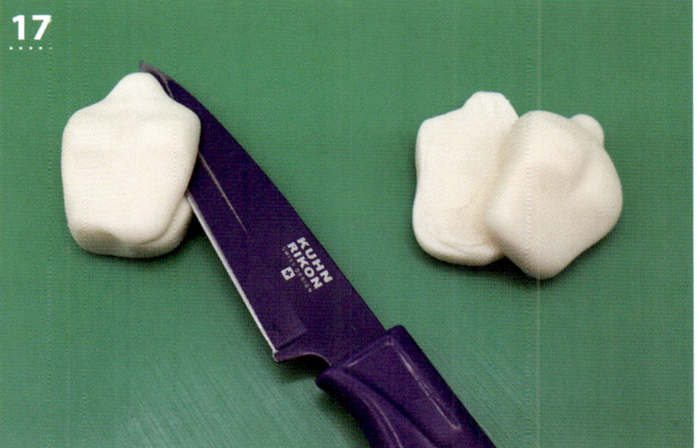

Prepare the body for attaching to the armature.

Add a thin layer of water to the inside of the back half of the body and position it behind the armature, pressing it forwards to adhere to the wires. You may have to bend the paste into position slightly to follow the lines of the armature, as the body is not completely upright for this model.

Add the front half of the body, pressing together carefully to attach to the back. Smooth the joins with your fingers and gently blend the bottom of the body over the tops of the legs. Reshape where necessary, refining any detail with your fingers or Dresden tool.

It is a good idea to cover the body in a thin layer of skin-tone paste, to give a smooth finish to any areas of the skin that will be exposed from underneath the clothing. Roll 15g of skin-tone modelling paste to approximately 1mm in thickness, then drape over the top of the body, pushing it over the wire at the top to create a small hole.

Smooth the layer of paste over the body, pressing together where it joins along the edges. Trim the edges with a scalpel or pair of small, sharp scissors, then blend the seams out with your finger.

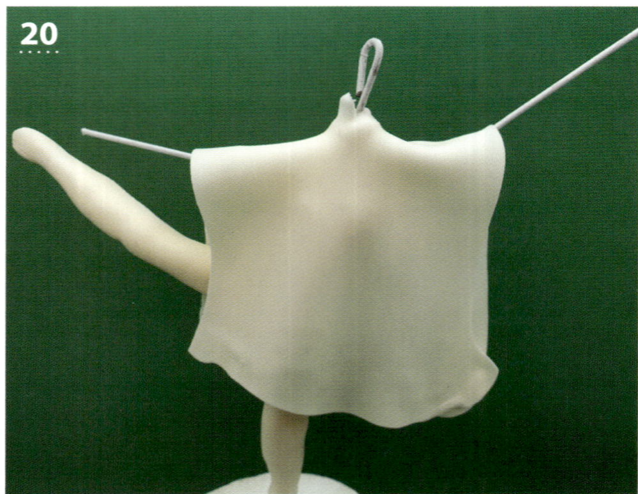

Positioning the back of the body in place, and adjusting the shape to follow the armature.

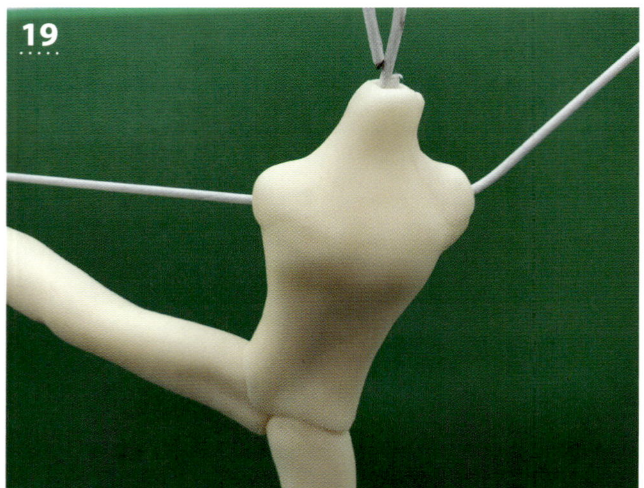

Adding the front section of the body to match to the back.

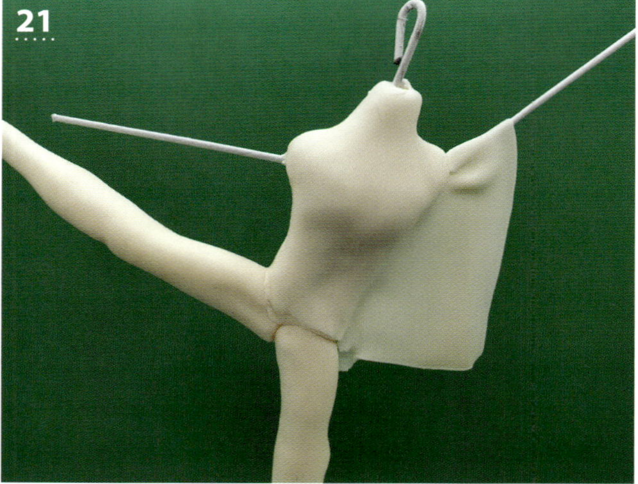

Covering the body shape with a layer of 'skin' to give a smooth finish.

Trimming the skin layer to fit the body.

Using a soft silicone-tipped modelling tool, create indents and marks on the neck where the hollow and clavicles are found. These are slightly more pronounced on this figure, due to the positioning of the head stretching upwards. Refer to your inspiration pictures or photographs if you need to, depending on the positioning of your figure.

Making and Adding the Arms to the Armature

For each arm, roll 10g of skin tone modelling paste into a ball and then into a sausage. These need to be slightly thinner than the legs. Don't worry too much about the length, as they can be trimmed to fit if too long. Concentrating on the hand end of the arms first, roll your little finger across the paste to create an indentation for the wrist. You can also create this shape by rolling the paste between your thumb and finger.

Gently flatten the paste below the wrist into a hand. Cut out a triangle of paste to separate the thumb, then cut the remaining part into four fingers. Cut a slim triangle from the centre, then split the paste on each side of it into two pieces.

Repeat for the other hand, making sure that you mirror the cuts to create a pair of hands, rather than two the same.

Very carefully, separate the fingers as much as you can. Use your finger and thumb to gently roll each finger

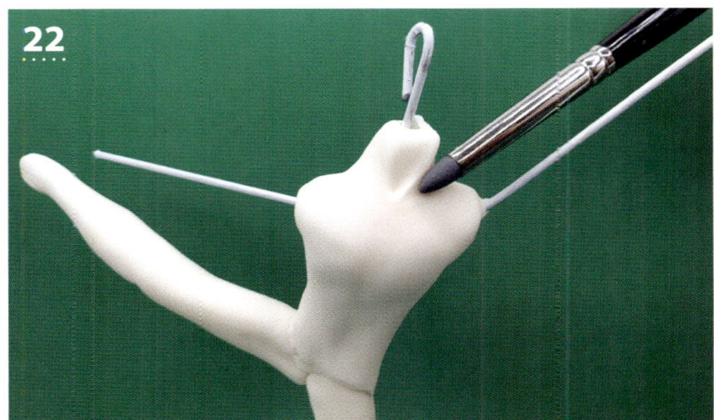

Adding details to the neck.

back and forth to make them slightly thinner and longer. Remember that they are not supposed to be the same length as each other. You can look at your own hands for help with this, although with the figure's there will not be much difference because they are so small. It just helps to give more realism to your work. I would recommend working on both hands together, to ensure you make a pair of identical hands (or as near as you can).

Trim the arms to the correct length, then roll your finger back and forth along the middle, to create an indentation for the elbow.

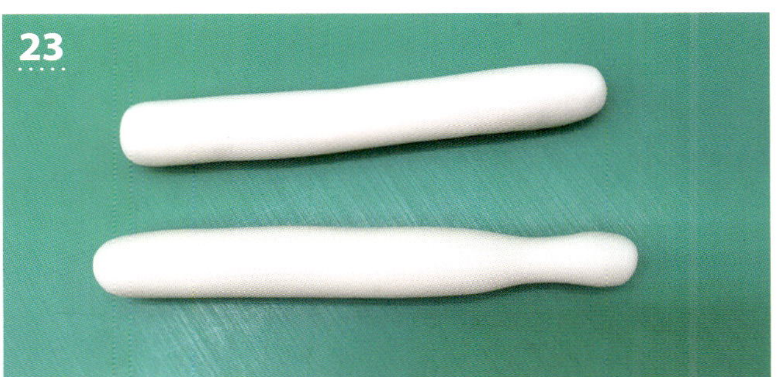

Creating the arms and forming the wrist area.

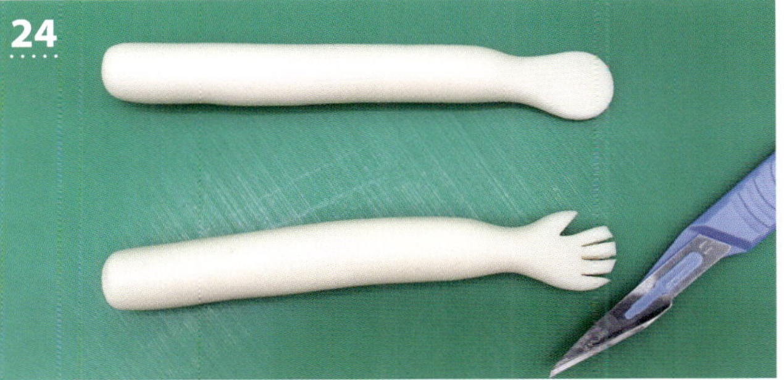

Making the hands.

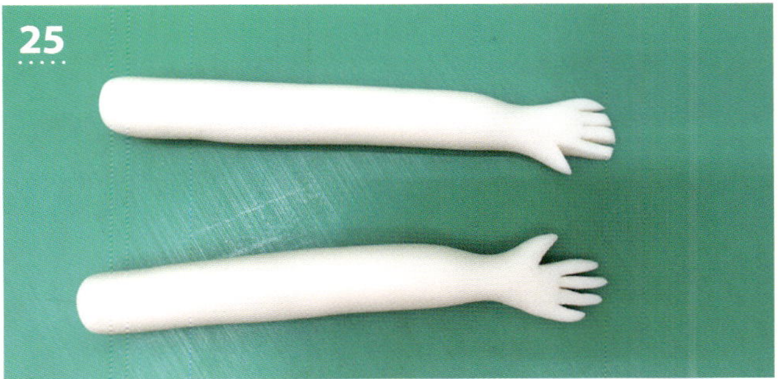

Refining the fingers and thumbs.

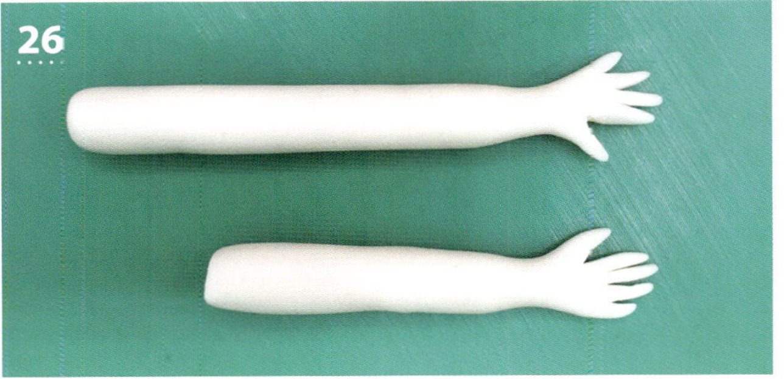

Sizing the arms to the correct length and creating elbows.

Add the arms to the wire armature, using the same method as used for the legs. Only cut the slit up to the wrist, as the hands will be too thin to hold the wire without it showing through. Measure the arm against the wire first, then trim shorter if needed with pliers, so the wire does not go too far down.

As the arms on this model are fairly straight, you can also carefully slot the arm on to the wire if you prefer, being careful to ensure that the wire does not poke through the end or out of the sides. You will need to twist the arm gently from side to side as you slot it on to the wire, so as not to distort the shape as you push. Add a little water where the arms and body meet to secure in place.

Whichever method you choose, you will need to redefine the shape of the arms afterwards, and gently rub away any finger marks with your fingertip.

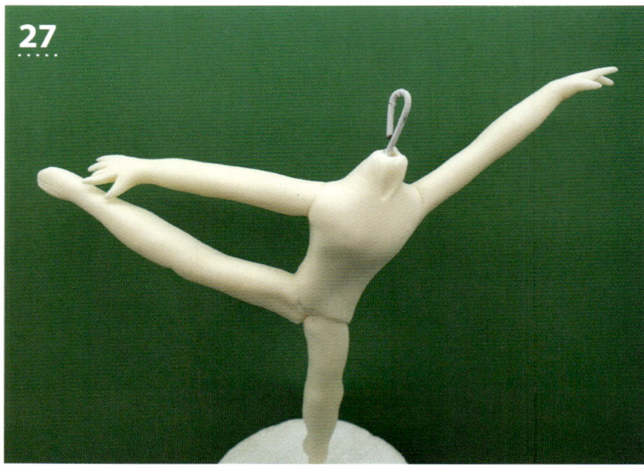
Add arms to the armature frame using the method you prefer.

Dressing Your Figure

Now that the basic body shape of your figure is complete, we will start to dress it with clothing. Remember that adding extra layers of paste to your figure can cause it to become quite bulky, so make sure that you roll the paste as thinly as you can. It is advisable to roll it to between 1 and 2mm in thickness for clothing.

For some items of clothing, especially if they need to fit to the size and shape of the body (in this instance the leotard), it is advisable to make a template for cutting out the paste. Kitchen paper towels can be used for this as they are flexible and soft, so will bend to the shape of your figure without leaving marks. You could also use tissue paper.

For looser fitting or smaller items of clothing, you can either use shaped cutters (as for the skirt and slippers), or cut freehand.

Dressing Your Figure – Socks and Ballet Slippers

The ballet slippers and socks are a peachy colour, so for this figure a tiny amount of paprika paste colour has been added to 10g of skin-tone modelling paste to achieve this shade. You could also add a peach paste/gel colour to white modelling paste if you prefer.

For the socks, roll out the peach modelling paste to approximately 1mm in thickness, and cut out a rough rectangle shape for each sock.

Colouring the paste for the ballet socks/slippers.

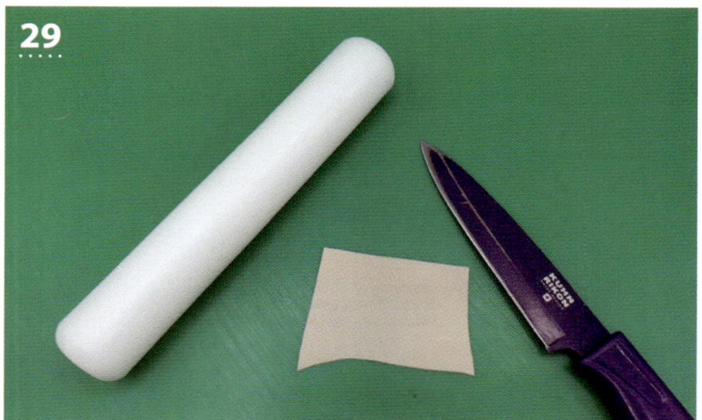
Creating the shape for the ballet socks.

Wrap the paste around the bottom of the leg, ensuring that the top of the sock is just above the ankle area, and that it covers the whole of the foot, with the join at the back. Smooth the paste, trimming away any excess with a scalpel or small sharp scissors.

For the ballet slippers, roll out the peach modelling paste to approximately 2mm in thickness, and cut out two oval shapes for soles. These need to fit on the bottom of the foot – here a 15mm cutter is used. Cut out two larger ovals, and remove the inner part with a smaller cutter. This will form the top and sides of the slipper. Here a 30mm cutter is used for the outside, and a 20mm to cut out the inside area. You may need to use different sized cutters depending on the size of your model's feet, although you can stretch the paste slightly to fit if required.

Attach the sole of the slipper with a little water, ensuring that it reaches right to the underneath edges of the foot. Paint a thin line of water around the edge of the foot and position the front of the slipper in place, wrapping the rest of the paste around the sides, trimming where it joins at the back. Smooth any excess paste underneath the slipper, or trim with a scalpel, smoothing any joins with your finger to blend the paste together.

To add straps for the slippers, cut out two tiny strips of peach-coloured modelling paste, attaching it in position with water. Trim any excess with a scalpel.

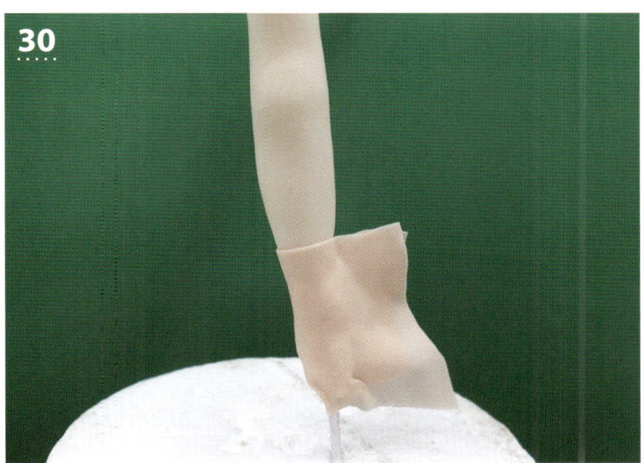

Adding the ballet socks to the figure.

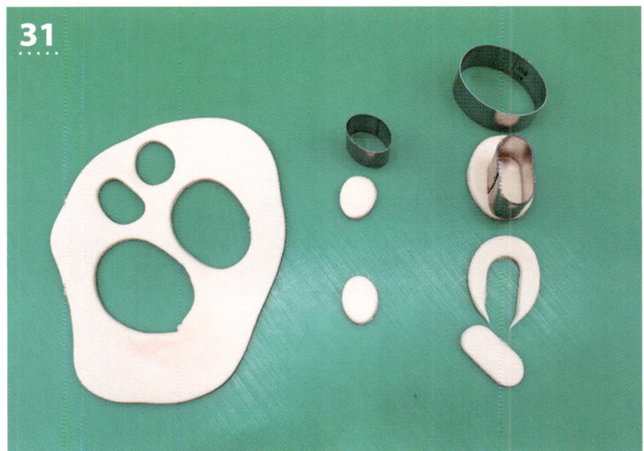

Cutting the shapes to make the ballet slippers.

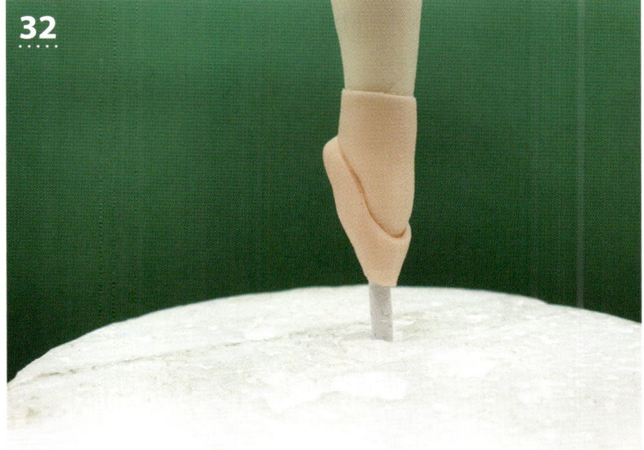

Add the cut-out shapes to the feet to create the ballet slippers.

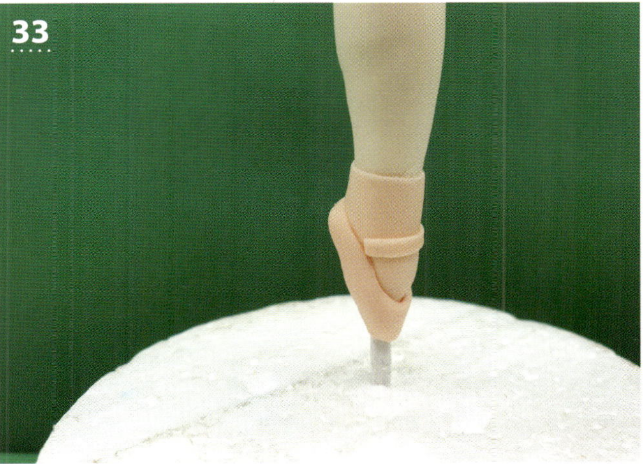

Adding straps to the ballet slippers.

Using kitchen paper towel, make a template for the leotard. You can use the same template for the front and back. Make sure it is wide enough to fit round the sides of the body too. You can keep holding it against the body to check for size and trimming where necessary, until it is the correct size and shape. It is better to make it slightly too big than too small, as you can trim the paste with a scalpel once it is fitted to the body.

To make this shade of lilac-coloured modelling paste for the leotard, mix 10g of purple and 20g of white modelling paste together. Roll the lilac paste out to approximately 1–2mm in thickness, and using the template you have made, cut out two leotard pieces with a scalpel to make the front and back.

Position one piece of the leotard on the back of the model, using a little water to hold it in place whilst you adjust it to fit. Arrange the leotard in place, ensuring that the straps fit at least halfway over the shoulders, and that the sides reach at least halfway round each side of the body. Cut slits in the side of the paste, either with a scalpel or small sharp scissors, so it will fit underneath the arms and over the legs.

Remove any excess paste from the sides and shoulders with a scalpel, smoothing the edges of any seams, ready for the front of the leotard to be added.

Creating a template for the leotard.

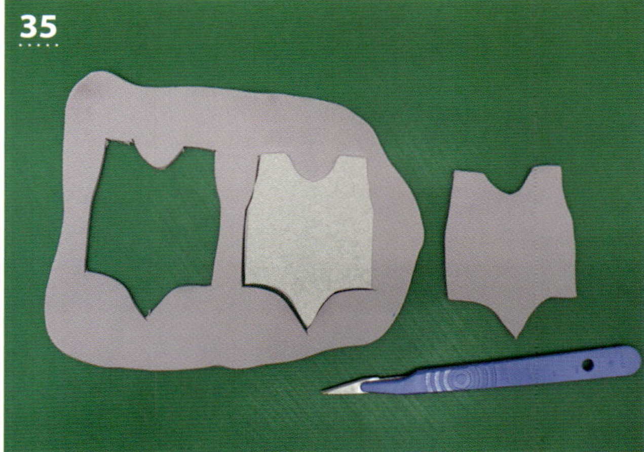

Cutting out the front and back pieces of the leotard.

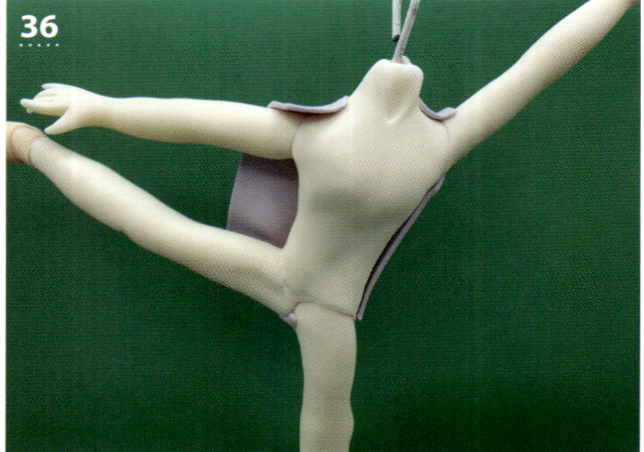

Fitting the back of the leotard to the figure.

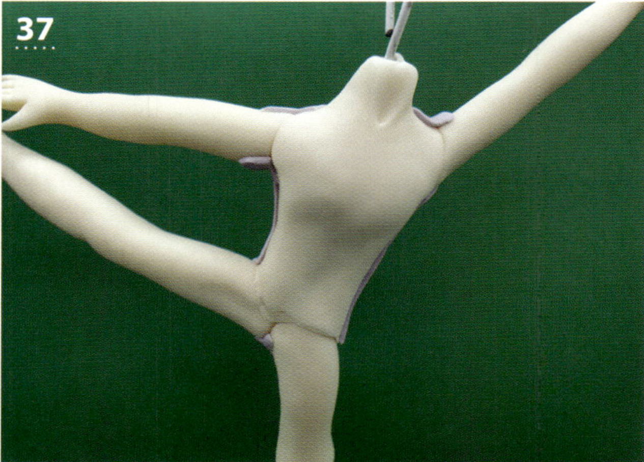

Trimming the paste to fit.

Add the front piece of the leotard, securing it to the body with a little water to hold it in position. Trim the excess paste with a scalpel, so that the seams join up neatly. Make small adjustments at a time, as it is easier to trim a little more off if required, rather than having to stretch the paste to fit if you have any gaps.

Smooth all the seams with your finger, ensuring that you have no rough or cut edges showing, and that everything fits well together.

Add crease marks with the narrow end of your Dresden tool around the arms and waist areas of the leotard. This adds more realism to the movement you are trying to capture with this style of figure. Use your inspiration picture or photo as a guide if necessary.

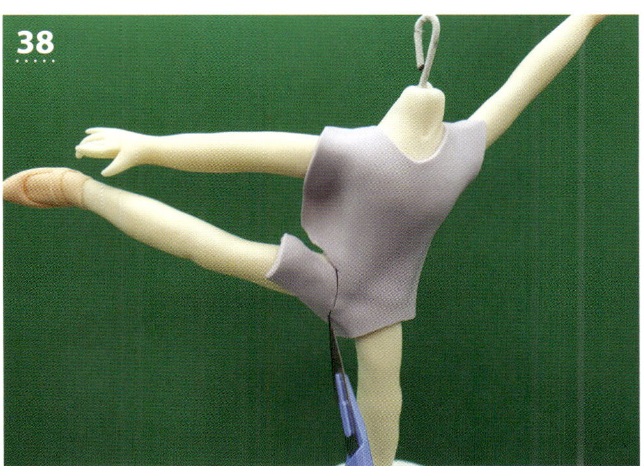

Adding the front of the leotard.

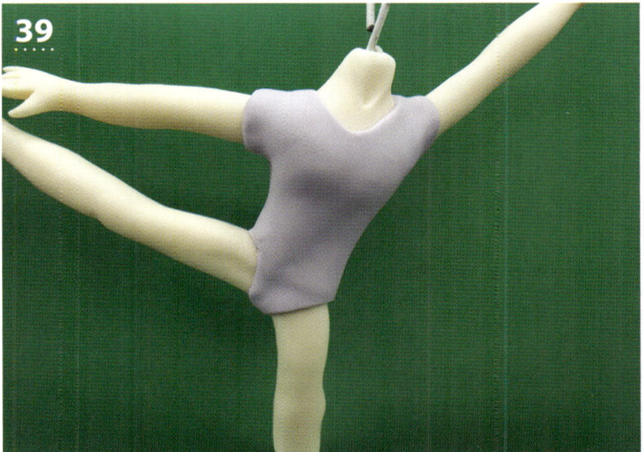

Smoothing the paste and joining up the seams of the leotard.

Adding crease marks to the leotard to give more realism and movement to the figure.

Dressing your Figure – the Tutu Skirt

If you refer back to the template you made earlier for the skirt this will help you to determine what size circle cutters to use. The largest circle cutter will be approximately the same size as the template, then you will need four smaller circle cutters. 45mm, 60mm, 75mm, 95mm and 110mm cutters were used for this figure. If you don't have circle cutters that are big enough, you can make templates to cut around instead.

Flower paste is used here to make the skirt, as it dries and holds its shape more quickly than modelling paste does, which is perfect for this, as it will help to convey the movement of the figure. However, it does mean that you must work more quickly, and I would recommend working on a maximum of two layers of the skirt at a time. I allowed 90g for the skirt, but only rolled out a third of this amount at a time to prevent it drying out.

Roll out the white flower paste to a thickness of approximately 1mm, and cut out the smallest two sizes using the smallest of your circle cutters.

Place the smallest circle on to a foam pad, and thin the edges of the paste by rolling a ball tool backwards and forwards across it. You need to position the ball tool half on the paste and half on the foam pad. This will also frill the edges slightly, to give movement to the shape. If the ball tool drags or sticks to the paste, dab it with a cornflour pouch to help it move along the paste more smoothly.

Remove the centre of the circle with an oval-shaped cutter (here, the 25mm cutter has been used) and make a cut at the back with a sharp knife to enable you to fit it to the body.

Paint a thin line of water just below the waist of your figure and add the first layer of skirt, trimming any excess paste where it joins at the back. Prepare the next circle in the same way, adding it to the figure as the second layer of skirt on top of the first.

Work on the next largest two sizes of circle, adding these in layers to the figure. Be careful to ensure that you do not position them higher up, past the waistline, as they need to cover the layer before, thus making a longer, fuller tutu effect.

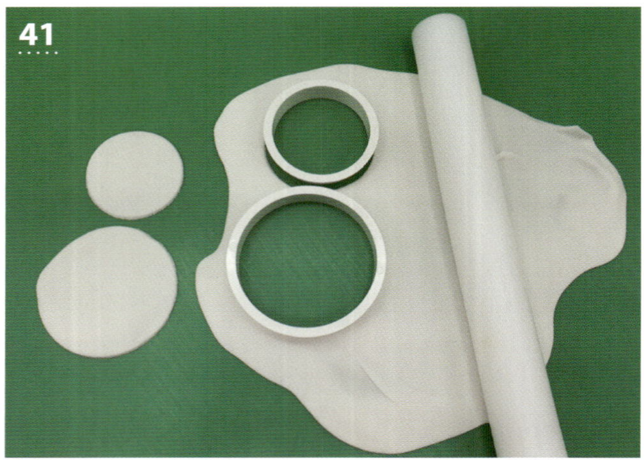

Cutting out the inner circles for the skirt.

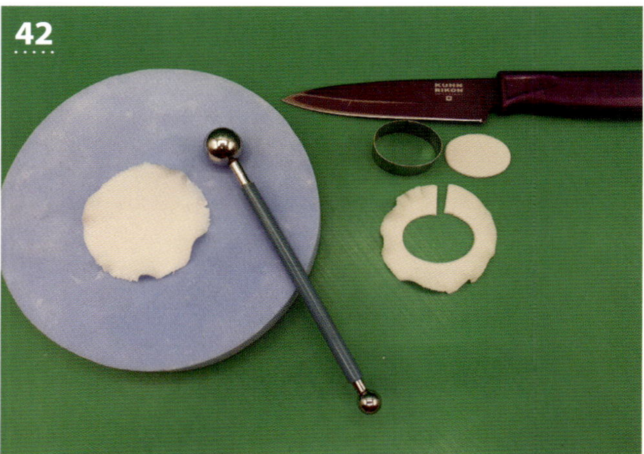

Thinning the edges of the circle, and frilling them to create movement for the skirt layers.

Adding the first two layers of the skirt to the figure.

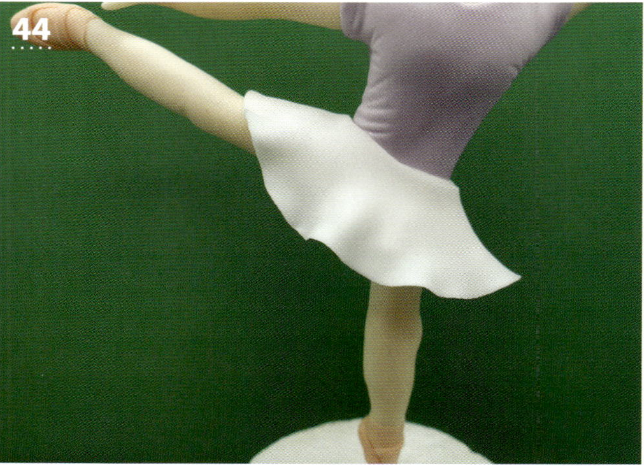

Adding a further two layers to give fullness to the skirt.

For the fifth and final circle you can use a frilling tool to add texture to the top layer of the skirt if you wish. Place the paste on the workboard and roll the frilling tool back and forth from the middle of the paste, working on small areas of the paste, then turning. If you do not have a frilling tool, you can use a cocktail stick or small wooden skewer instead.

After texturing the circle, turn it upside down (textured side down) on to the foam pad, then thin and frill the edges with the ball tool as before.

Remove the centre from the final layer, cut it at the back and position it in place, trimming at the back where it joins. You can adjust this layer by pinching the edges of the skirt slightly to give more shape and movement. If you wish, you can also place small pieces of foam or tissue underneath this layer until it dries, to add to the feeling of movement.

Finish off the skirt with a thin strip of white flower paste around the waist.

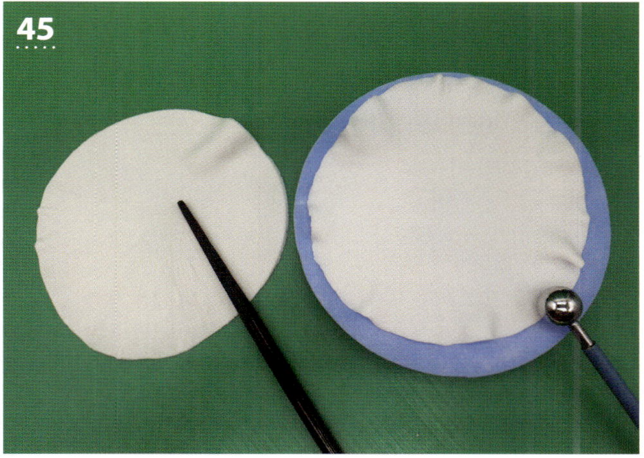
Creating texture for the top layer of the skirt.

Adding the final layer of the skirt to the figure.

Modelling the Head

Deep in concentration, or perhaps lost in the music and the dance, this ballerina figure has her eyes closed; you can achieve this look with the simple yet effective method described below.

Roll 45g of skin-tone modelling paste into a smooth ball, then into an oval shape. Use your thumb to stroke the paste at the back downwards a little, so that it sits up away from the workboard. When viewed from the side, the shape looks a little like a traditional loaf of bread.

Make an indentation halfway down the face with your finger or a rounded handle from a modelling tool; this will form the eye sockets and brow bone. Use a ball tool to make two further indents in the paste for the eye sockets, leaving a space between them where the nose will be created.

Making the shape for the head.

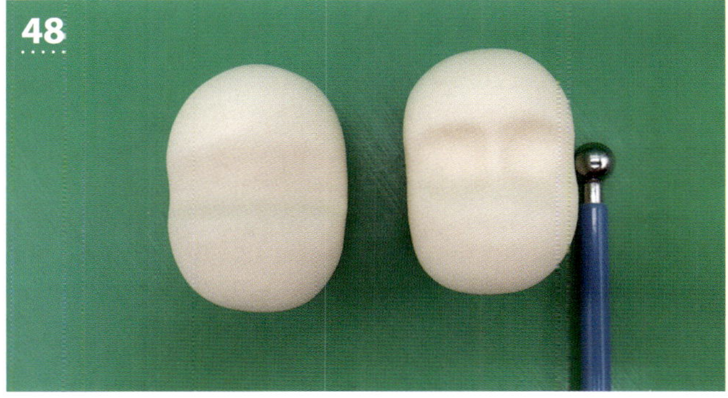
Creating the eye sockets.

With the wider end of your Dresden tool, gently push the paste downwards and outwards to form the nose shape. Soften any lines by rubbing lightly with your finger to remove tool marks, keeping all the features rounded and soft.

Use a sharp-pointed, hard silicone tool to mark the nostrils; alternatively you could use a pointed cocktail stick or tiny ball tool. With the narrow end of your Dresden tool, mark lines down from each side of the nose to help with positioning the mouth. Again, remove any hard lines left by the tool by gently rubbing with your finger.

Use a scalpel to cut a straight line for the mouth, cutting to a depth of at least 5mm. Whilst the blade is still in the cut, wiggle it from side to side to clean the cut. Then lift the scalpel blade gently upwards under the paste to form the upper lip.

With the narrow end of your Dresden tool, make a small indent for the philtrum, the groove that runs from under the nose to the middle of the upper lip. Gently press upwards at either side with your finger or the wider end of your Dresden tool to create the 'Cupid's bow' effect of the top lip.

Use the wider end of your Dresden tool to draw lines down from the outside corners of the mouth, then mark out the outline of the bottom lip. Push the paste gently downwards with your Dresden tool to form the bottom lip, which tends to be fuller than the top lip.

Use your fingers, the wider end of the Dresden tool and the soft silicone-tipped modelling tool to softy define the areas around the mouth and chin. Form the cheeks by gently stroking paste upwards and outwards, then in soft circular motions to create the fleshy areas around the cheekbone.

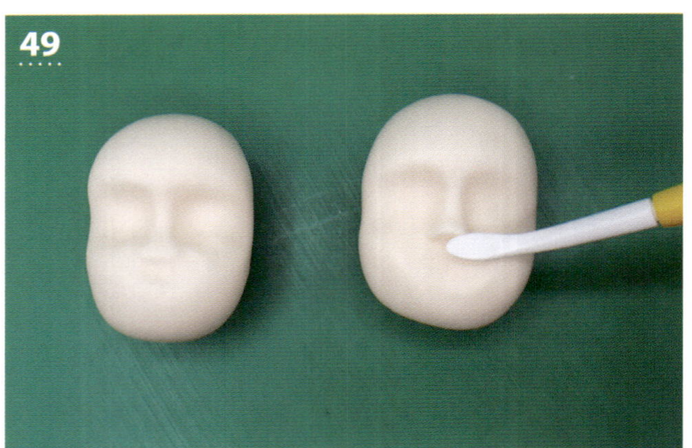

Forming the nose with gentle movements of your Dresden tool.

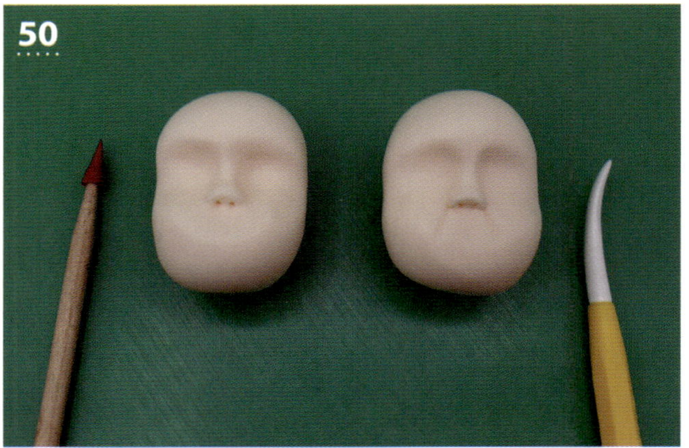

Marking in the nostrils.

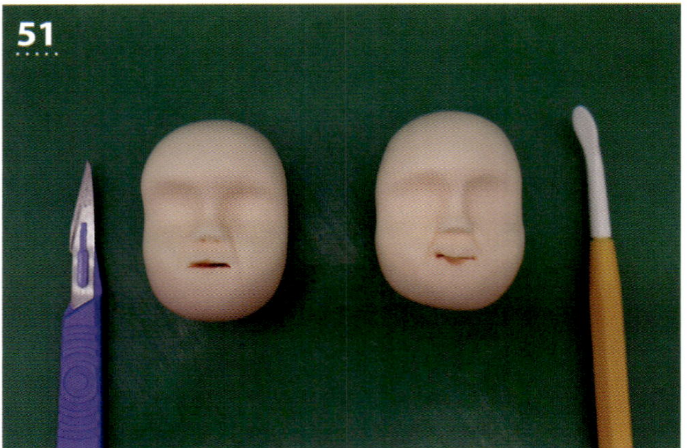

Cutting the mouth opening and forming the upper lip.

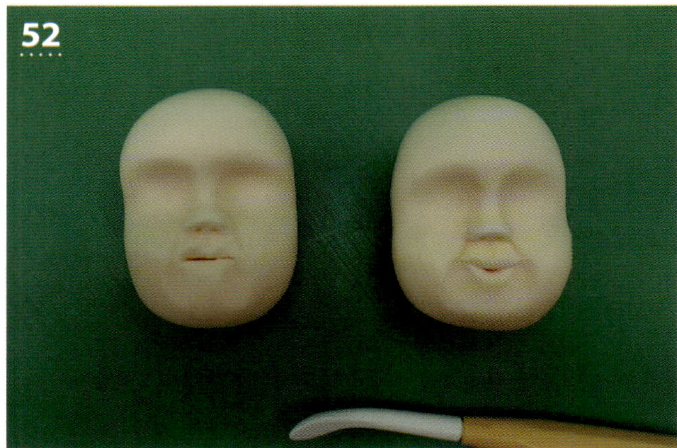

Forming the lower lip and cheeks.

To resize and reshape the face so it is in proportion to your figure model, use the rounded end of a modelling tool to mark round the chin area. For a female face, the chin tends to be thinner and more pointed as compared to the angular chin of a male face. Continue to push the paste downwards, away from the face, until you are happy with the shape.

To create the appearance of closed eyes, you first need to fill the eye-socket area with skin-tone modelling paste. Roll a small piece of paste into a ball, then elongate it slightly. Flatten it a little with your finger, and use the wider end of your Dresden tool to blend the edges of the paste into the eye-socket area. Approximately two thirds of the way down the newly added paste, draw a line with the narrow end of your Dresden tool to form the bottom of the upper eyelid. Soften the lower eyelid area with your finger.

With a small, soft brush, apply petal dust to the upper eyelid area. A metallic lustre dust works well for eyeshadow.

A Rose Gold shade has been used for this figure. To create the eyelash line, roll a tiny ball of black modelling paste into a very fine strand. Add a thin line of water under the top eyelid and position the paste with the finest point at the inner corner; trim at the outer edge with a scalpel.

Apply pink petal dust to the cheeks for blusher, using a larger brush. Before applying, remove any excess dust from the brush by tapping it on to a piece of kitchen paper. Apply the dust in thin layers, to build up the colour gradually. It is very easy to end up with too much colour on the face. If this does happen, remove some by blotting with a clean, damp tissue. Wait for the paste to dry completely before reapplying the colour.

For the lipstick, add a little white vegetable fat (Trex) to the petal dust to make a creamy consistency, and apply to the lips with a thinner brush. This helps to give a more realistic lipstick effect.

Sizing and shaping the head, to be in proportion to your figure.

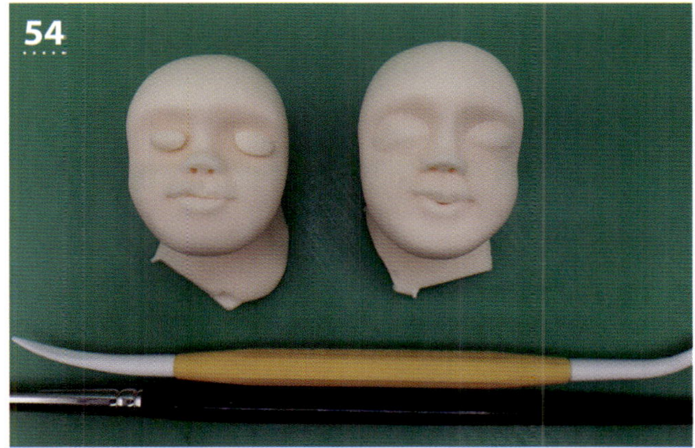

Creating the closed eyelids.

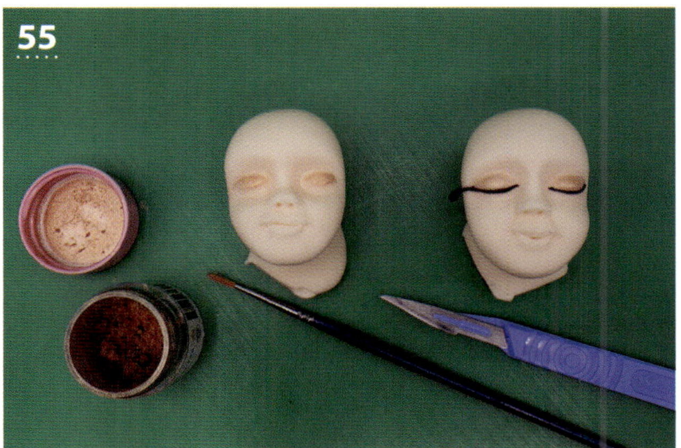

Applying colour to the eyelids and adding a simple eyelash line.

Applying colour to the cheeks and lips.

Roll a small ball of brown modelling paste into thin strands to create the eyebrows, in the same way as for the eyelash line. This time, however, the thinner part of the eyebrow goes to the outside edge of the face, in line with the outer corner of the eyelid. Trim above the inner part of the eyelid.

Eyebrows can be used very effectively when creating different expressions for faces, as their shape helps us to illustrate how faces change with a range of emotions. For example, very arched eyebrows can convey surprise, whereas one raised eyebrow suggests confusion or curiosity.

Remove the excess paste at the back of the head with scissors (or a sharp knife), and smooth round the edges with your finger, ready for adding to the armature.

Consider the positioning of the head before attaching it to the armature. Hold it in front of your model and adjust the angles until you are happy with how you want it to look. To attach it, brush a little water on top of the neck and the armature. Holding the head gently, push it down on to the armature wire, twisting from side to side as you push carefully downwards.

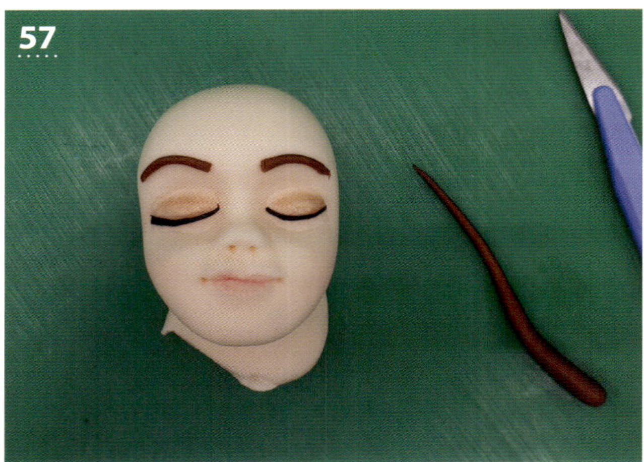

Creating and adding the eyebrows.

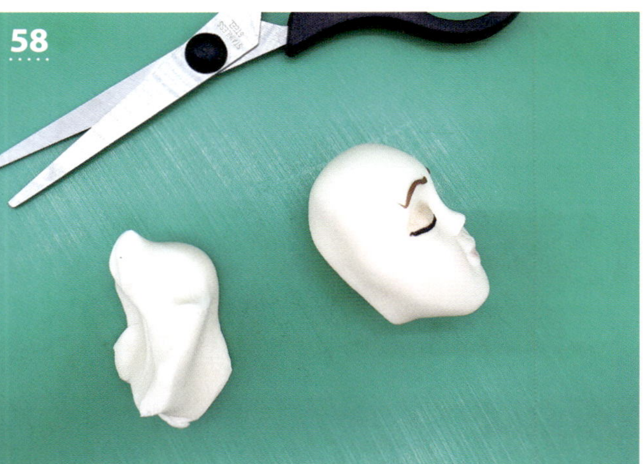

Trimming excess paste from the back of the head.

Adding the head to the armature, being careful not to misshape it.

Roll 10g of brown modelling paste into a ball, flattening it out into a circle with your fingers. This helps to give it a more natural look, rather than rolling out the paste and cutting a circle from the flat paste. The circle-shaped paste needs to cover the part of the head where the hair will sit; hold it up to the back of the head to check it for fit, adjusting it until it is the correct size. Use the narrow end of your Dresden tool to apply texture from the middle of the circle to the outer edge for the hair.

The ears will be positioned over the edge of the hair, as it has been scraped back into a bun. Roll two tiny balls of skin-tone coloured paste, then roll them into ovals. Flatten slightly and add an indentation with a small ball tool.

Brush a little water on to the back of the head to hold the hair in place, then smooth the brown paste on to the head. Once you are happy with the positioning, add the ears, so that the bottom of each ear is in line with the bottom of the nose.

For the bun section of the hair, roll a ball of paste, approximately 4g, and then flatten it slightly with your finger. Mark the centre of the shape on the top, then texture the hair with the narrow end of your Dresden tool with upward strokes, into the middle of the top.

Creating and texturing the hair.

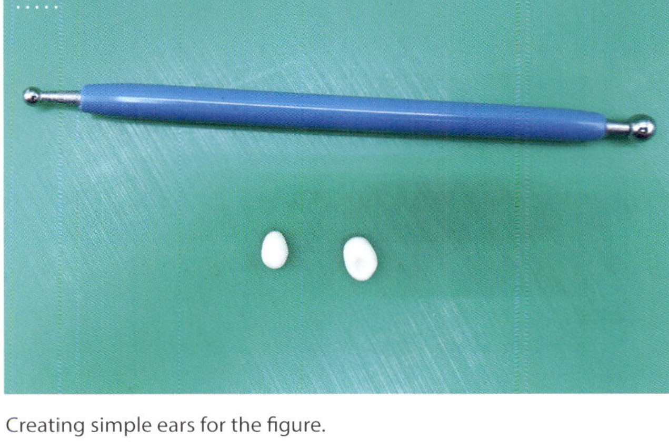

Creating simple ears for the figure.

Adding the hair and ears to the head, paying attention to the positioning.

Creating the bun section of the hair.

Attach the bun to the back of the head with a little water. Roll out a thin strand of lilac paste and wrap it round the join, trimming any excess at the back with a scalpel.

Your ballerina model is now complete. It is advisable to leave it to dry and harden for at least a few hours before attaching it to your cake, to ensure that you don't accidentally make any marks or indents in the paste whilst handling it.

Attaching the bun to complete the hairstyle.

The finished model needs time to dry and harden before adding it to your cake, to prevent any accidental damage whilst handling it.

ATTACHING THE CAKE TOPPER TO YOUR CAKE

Because the internal armature inside your figure is not food safe, this is not considered to be an 'edible cake topper'. Likewise, for supporting the figure in a gravity-defying position such as this one, the portion of the armature below the foot – which has been inserted into the polystyrene dummy whilst creating the figure – is not suitable for inserting directly into your cake.

To insert this portion of the armature into your cake, it needs to be made food safe, using the following equipment:

- a thin hollow cake dowel (it needs to fit over the taped wires of the armature)
- kitchen scissors
- royal icing (in a piping bag with a small-holed nozzle)
- dimpled foam flower pad (or similar soft support)

The method used here to do this also helps to give further support to the figure, which enables you to transport the figure and cake together more confidently.

Trim the hollow dowel with scissors to the same height as your covered cake. This will form a complete barrier for the armature, as well as added support.

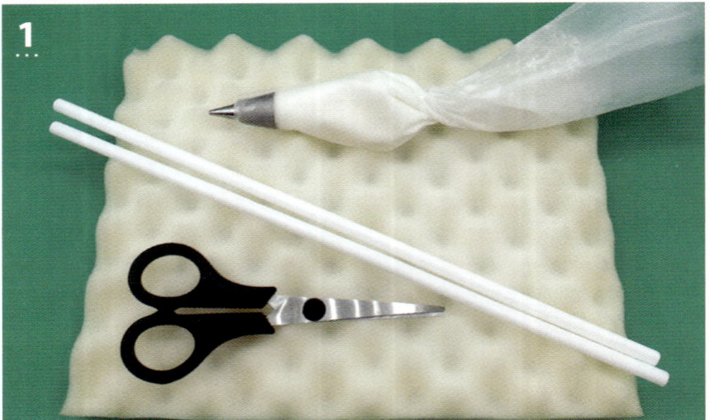

The equipment needed to add your figure to your cake in a food-safe way.

Trimming the dowel to the same height as the cake will prevent the armature from touching the inside of the cake.

Pipe royal icing into the hollow dowel until it is full. You can use a piping bag with a fine nozzle attached, or a strong food-safe bag with a corner snipped off (just make sure to cut only the very tip of the corner off, as the hole needs to be very small to fit inside the hollow dowel). You can also make small piping bags with greaseproof paper.

Gently remove your figure from the polystyrene dummy and lay it on a dimpled foam pad for support. Do not place it on a flat surface, as you risk damaging the back of the skirt. Slot the royal icing-filled dowel over the wire below the standing foot.

Insert the dowel into your cake and allow the royal icing to set before transporting the cake, thus providing maximum stability for the figure.

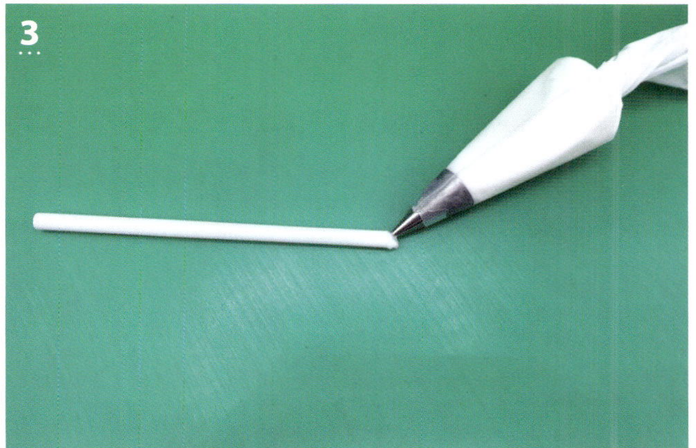

Add royal icing into the dowel as added support for holding the figure in place.

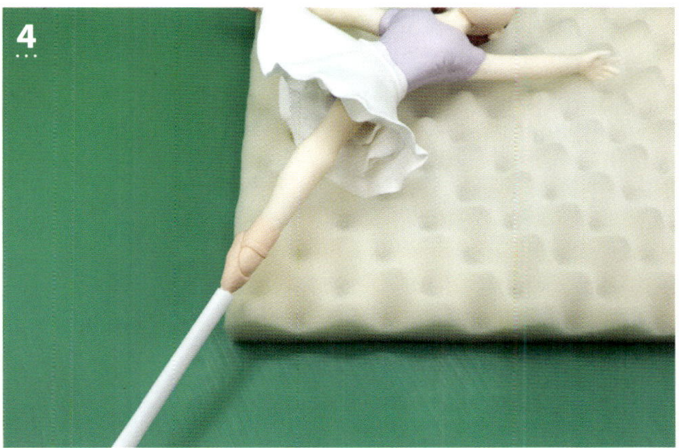

Attaching the dowel to the armature under the figure, being careful not to damage the model.

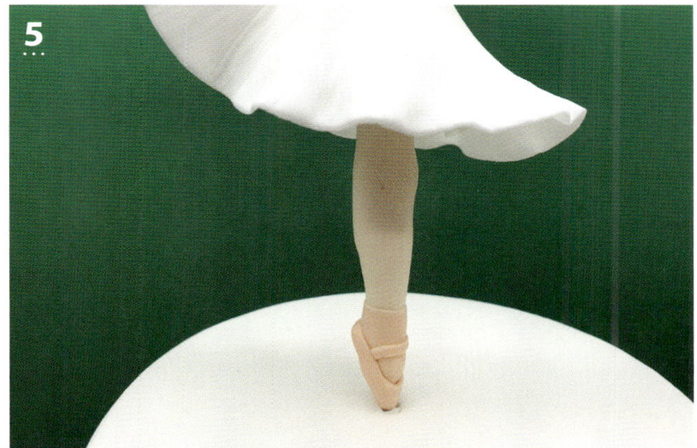

Adding the figure securely in position on the cake.

CAKE DESIGN IDEA

The purple-coloured delicate ruffle effect coordinates beautifully with the colour of the ballerina's leotard for this cake design, suitable for a wide range of ages. The addition of a personalized plaque with the recipient's name adds the finishing touch, perfect for any budding ballerina. You can, of course, change the colouring to suit, or add the name to the front of the cake board instead of using a plaque if you prefer.

The delicate purple ruffles compliment this ballerina-themed cake beautifully, whilst the addition of the personalized plaque makes it perfect for a birthday celebration.

Start by covering a 15cm (6in) round cake with white sugar paste, and attach to a 25cm (10in) round cake drum, which has also been covered in white sugar paste.

Making the Personalized Plaque

Roll out a piece of white sugar paste to a thickness of approximately 2–3mm. Embossing letters were used here to emboss the name into the paste; these are widely available from cake-decorating equipment suppliers, under many different brands. Use a large oval-shaped cutter to cut the paste, leaving plenty of space around the outside of the embossed name. You could also use a plaque-shaped cutter if you have one.

Paint the inside of the embossed name carefully with a thin paintbrush. For the edible paint, mix gold lustre dust with rejuvenator fluid. The rejuvenator fluid evaporates quite quickly, so if you find that the paint is thickening as you are working, add a few more drops of the fluid to thin it to the correct consistency again.

Once painted, place the finished plaque over a polystyrene dummy, the same diameter as your cake, to dry. If you try to attach it to the cake whilst it is still soft, you risk misshaping it.

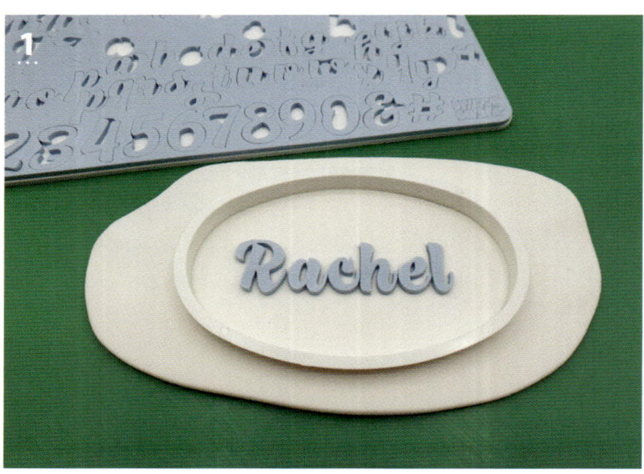

Use embossing letters and an oval cutter to create this simple personalized plaque.

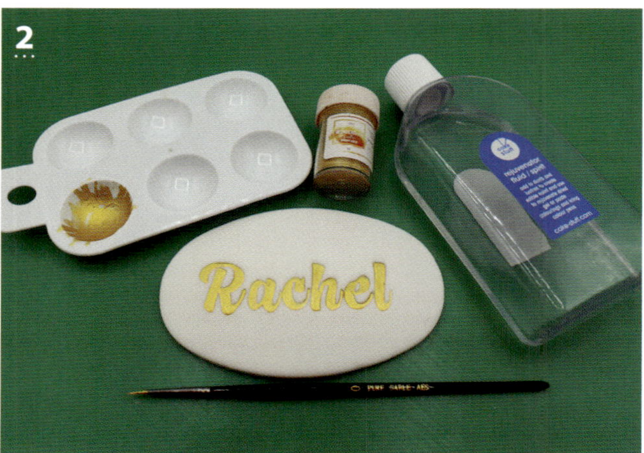

Add colour to the inside of the letters, using a fine paintbrush and edible paint.

Leave the finished plaque aside to dry slightly, before adding it to the cake.

Creating the Ruffles

Mix together 400g (14oz) of white sugar paste (fondant) and 100g (3.5oz) of white flower paste (gum paste). This paste will be stronger than the sugar paste and you will be able to roll it out thinly, but it won't dry as brittle as the flower paste would be on its own. Colour the paste using a purple gel colour. Add a small amount at a time, as you don't want the colour to be too dark.

To make the ruffles, roll out a small piece of paste to approximately 1–2mm in thickness. Cut out a few circles at a time, using a 45mm round cutter. Place the circles on a foam pad, and thin round the edge with a ball tool (as for the ballerina's skirt). Fold each circle in half gently, holding it in the centre, then fold again into quarters. Pinch the paste at the centre bottom and leave it to firm up slightly on a dimpled foam pad.

Create several ruffles before adding them to the cake, working in batches.

Prepare a mixture of sugar paste and flower paste, coloured with purple gel colour for making the ruffles.

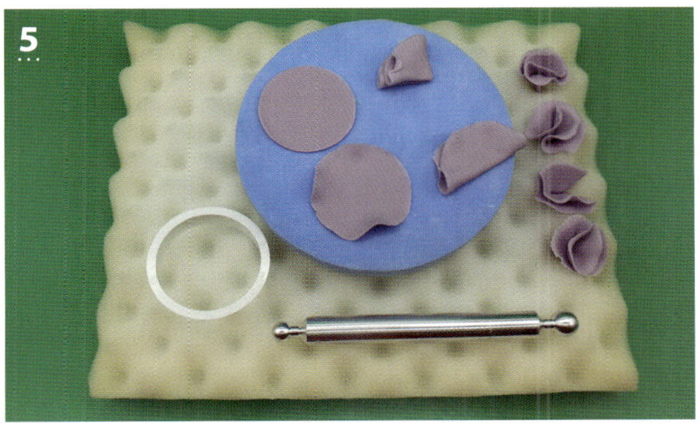

Creating simple ruffles, with a circle cutter and simple tools/equipment.

Adding the Ruffles and the Plaque to the Cake

Paint a thin layer of water or edible glue round the bottom of the cake to hold the ruffles securely in place. Attach one at a time, pressing it on to the cake with the Dresden tool if needed. Work your way round the bottom of the cake, until you get back to where you started.

By now the plaque should have firmed up enough to be handled, so attach it to the front of the cake with a few small dabs of royal icing. Continue to make more ruffles, attaching them round the edges of the plaque, up to the top of the cake, and working to the back of the cake until it is completely covered.

Add your ballerina figure, using the food-safe method as shown. Add a purple ribbon to the edge of your cake drum, using a non-toxic glue stick or double-sided tape, to finish.

Start adding the ruffles in a layer round the bottom of the cake.

Attach the plaque to the front of the cake, and continue to add ruffles until the cake is completely covered.

Recipes

· · · · ·

n this section you will find some of my favourite recipes for sponge cakes and fillings. They are mostly simple sponge cakes with a butter cream filling, with a chocolate ganache crumb coat applied before the sugar paste covering, ready for adding the final decorations and models/figures. The reason for using chocolate ganache to crumb coat is that it gives a much smoother finish, which sets hard. This helps with achieving a perfect finish to the sugar-paste layer. You can of course use buttercream to crumb coat your cake – just be sure to allow it to firm up before covering. You may need to chill it briefly in the refrigerator before covering in warmer conditions.

VANILLA SPONGE CAKE

This recipe makes a soft, light sponge cake, yet it is still strong enough for covering with sugar paste, and can be stacked as part of a multi-tiered cake when using dowels for support. It is baked in two tins, each producing a cake approximately 5–7cm (2–3in) deep. For the larger sizes – 25 to 30cm (10 to 12in) – it is best to divide the ingredients into two halves and mix as two separate batches before adding to the tins and baking.

When filling, cut each sponge in half, giving you four layers of sponge.

Ingredients for the Vanilla Sponge Cake

Round tin size	15cm (6in)	18cm (7in)	20cm (8in)	22cm (9in)	25cm (10in)	28cm (11in)	30cm (12in)
Square tin size	12cm (5in)	15cm (6in)	18cm (7in)	20cm (8in)	22cm (9in)	25cm (10in)	28cm (11in)
Margarine (or butter)	300g (10oz)	300g (10oz)	400g (14oz)	500g (1lb 2oz)	700g (1lb 8oz)	900g (2lb)	1,100g (2lb 4oz)
Caster sugar	300g (10oz)	300g (10oz)	400g (14oz)	500g (1lb 2oz)	700g (1lb 8oz)	900g (2lb)	1100g (2lb 4oz)
Self-raising flour	300g (10oz)	300g (10oz)	400g (14oz)	500g (1lb 2oz)	700g (1lb 8oz)	900g (2lb)	1100g (2lb 4oz)
Eggs	6	6	8	10	14	18	22
Vanilla extract	½tsp	½tsp	¾tsp	1tsp	1¼tsp	1½tsp	2tsp
Baking time	50min	50min	50min	1hr	1hr 15min	1hr 30min	1hr 30min

Method

1. Pre-heat your oven to 160°C (315°F/gas mark 2–3).
2. Grease and line the base and sides of both tins with greaseproof paper.
3. Whisk together the margarine and caster sugar until pale and fluffy, to incorporate lots of air into the mixture (this will take around five minutes with an electric whisk or with a stand mixer).
4. Add the eggs gradually, one at a time, whilst mixing on the slowest setting. Beat well after each addition. You may also wish to add a tablespoon of flour after each egg to help prevent the mixture from splitting. If it does split, don't worry – it will come back together when the remainder of the flour is added at the end.
5. Add vanilla extract (or you can substitute this with a different flavour if required, such as lemon extract).
6. Add the flour: mix slowly until the flour starts to be incorporated into the mixture, then stop and continue to fold in gently by hand. You do not want to overmix the cake batter at this stage, as you risk knocking out the air.

7. Split the mixture evenly between the two tins, levelling with the back of a spoon. For extra accuracy you may wish to weigh the mixture in each tin to ensure an even bake.

8. Bake in the middle of the oven for the time indicated for your size of tin.

9. Test with a skewer or sharp knife. It should come out clean when inserted into the centre of the cake. If not, return the cakes to the oven for an additional five minutes, and recheck.

10. Once removed from the oven, leave to cool for 5 to 10 minutes in the tin first, then turn out on to a cooling rack.

11. Allow to cool completely before filling/covering.

To convert this vanilla sponge cake recipe into a chocolate cake, replace 20 per cent of the self-raising flour with cocoa powder.

For other flavour choices, simply replace the vanilla extract with a different flavoured extract, such as lemon, orange or almond.

VANILLA MADEIRA CAKE

A Madeira cake is a stronger, more densely crumbed sponge cake, which makes it ideal for using for shaped or carved cakes. It also has a slightly longer shelf life than the vanilla sponge cake. This recipe is baked in one tin, producing a sponge measuring approximately 7cm (3in) deep.

Ingredients for the Vanilla Madeira Cake

Round tin size	15cm (6in)	18cm (7in)	20cm (8in)	22cm (9in)	25cm (10in)	28cm (11in)	30cm (12in)
Square tin size	12cm (5in)	15cm (6in)	18cm (7in)	20cm (8in)	22cm (9in)	25cm (10in)	28cm (11in)
Margarine (or butter)	175g (6oz)	225g (8oz)	350g (12oz)	450g (1lb)	550g (1lb 2oz)	700g (1lb 8oz)	850g (1lb 14oz)
Caster sugar	175g (6oz)	225g (8oz)	350g (12oz)	450g (1lb)	550g (1lb 2oz)	700g (1lb 8oz)	850g (1lb 14oz)
Self-raising flour	175g (6oz)	225g (8oz)	350g (12oz)	450g (1lb)	550g (1lb 2oz)	700g (1lb 8oz)	850g (1lb 14oz)
Plain flour	75g (3oz)	125g (4½oz)	175g (6oz)	225g (8oz)	275g (10oz)	350g (12oz)	425g (15oz)
Eggs	3	4	6	8	10	12	15
Vanilla extract	½tsp	¾tsp	1tsp	1¼tsp	1½tsp	2tsp	2½tsp
Baking time	1hr	1hr	1hr 15min	1hr 30min	1hr 30min	1hr 45min	2hr

Method

1. Pre-heat your oven to 160°C (315°F/gas mark 2–3).

2. Grease and line the base and sides of your tin with greaseproof paper.

3. Whisk together the margarine and caster sugar until pale and fluffy, to incorporate lots of air into the mixture (this will take around five minutes with an electric whisk or with a stand mixer).

4. Add the eggs gradually, one at a time, whilst mixing on the slowest setting. Beat well after each addition. You may also wish to add a tablespoon of flour after each egg to help prevent the mixture from splitting. If it does split, don't worry, it will come back together when the remainder of the flour is added.

5. Add vanilla extract (or you can substitute this with a different flavour if required, such as lemon extract).

6. Add the flour, mixing slowly until the flour starts to be incorporated into the mixture, then stop and continue to fold in gently by hand. You do not want to overmix the cake batter at this stage, as you risk knocking out the air.

7. Pour the cake batter into the prepared tin, levelling it with the back of a spoon.

8. Bake in the middle of the oven for the time indicated for your size of tin.

9. Test with a skewer or sharp knife. It should come out clean when inserted into the centre of the cake. If not, return the cakes to the oven for an additional five minutes and recheck, repeating until cooked.

10. Once removed from the oven, leave to cool in the tin, placed on a cooling rack.
11. Allow to cool completely before filling/covering.

To convert this vanilla Madeira cake recipe into a chocolate cake, replace 20 per cent of the self-raising flour with cocoa powder.

For other flavour choices, simply replace the vanilla extract with a different flavoured extract, such as lemon, orange or almond.

. . . .

CHOCOLATE FUDGE/MUD CAKE

This cake has a denser, more fudge-like crumb than the sponge cake (similar in texture to a chocolate brownie). It has a very rich, decadent chocolate flavour. This recipe is baked in one tin, producing a cake approximately 7cm (3in) deep, which can be split into two or three layers.

Ingredients for the Chocolate Fudge/Mud Cake

| Round tin size | 15cm (6in) | 18cm (7in) | 20cm (8in) | 22cm (9in) | 25cm (10in) | 28cm (11in) | 30cm (12in) |
Square tin size	12cm (5in)	15cm (6in)	18cm (7in)	20cm (8in)	22cm (9in)	25cm (10in)	28cm (11in)
Margarine (or butter)	110g (4oz)	130g (4½oz)	190g (6½oz)	220g (8oz)	250g (9oz)	400g (14oz)	440g (15½oz)
Dark chocolate	110g (4oz)	130g (4½oz)	190g (6½oz)	220g (8oz)	250g (9oz)	400g (14oz)	440g (15½oz)
Instant coffee	2tsp	3tsp	4tsp	6 tsp	8 tsp	8 tsp	2 ½ tbsp
Water	80ml (2¾fl oz)	95ml (3fl oz)	140ml (5fl oz)	160ml (5½fl oz)	180ml (6fl oz)	290ml (10fl oz)	320ml (11fl oz)
Plain flour	65g (2oz)	75g (2½oz)	110g (4oz)	125g (4½oz)	150g (5oz)	250g (9oz)	280g (10oz)
Self-raising flour	65g (2oz)	75g (2½oz)	110g (4oz)	125g (4½oz)	150g (5oz)	250g (9oz)	280g (10oz)
Cocoa powder	25g (1oz)	30g (1oz)	40g (1½oz)	50g (1¾oz)	60g (2oz)	90g (3oz)	110g (4oz)
Caster sugar	240g (8½oz)	300g (10½oz)	420g (15oz)	480g (1lb 1oz)	550g (1lb 3oz)	860g (1lb 14oz)	960g (2lb 2oz)
Bicarb. of soda	¼tsp	¼tsp	¼tsp	½tsp	½tsp	¾tsp	1tsp
Eggs	2	2	3	4	4	7	8
Vegetable oil	4tsp	5tsp	6tsp	7tsp	8tsp	2½tbsp	3tbsp
Sour cream	60ml (2fl oz)	70ml (2½fl oz)	95ml (3fl oz)	110ml (3½fl oz)	125ml (4fl oz)	200ml (6½fl oz)	220ml (7fl oz)
Baking time	1hr 5min	1hr 20min	1hr 30min	1hr 40min	1hr 45min	2hr 15min	2hr 30min

Method

1. Pre-heat your oven to 160°C (315°F/gas mark 2–3).
2. Grease and line the base and sides of your tin with greaseproof paper.
3. Place butter, chocolate, coffee and water into a pan, and gently melt over a low heat, stirring occasionally until the mixture is combined together. Remove from the heat whilst you prepare the rest of the ingredients.
4. Sieve together the flour, cocoa powder and bicarbonate of soda into a mixing bowl.
5. Put the eggs, vegetable oil and sour cream into a jug, stirring with a fork (or small hand whisk) until they combine together.
6. Add the two wet mixes to the dry ingredients, mixing thoroughly with an electric whisk or stand mixer. This cake batter is quite runny in consistency compared with sponge mixes.
7. Pour the cake batter into the prepared tin.
8. Bake in the middle of the oven for the time indicated for your size of tin.
9. Test with a skewer or sharp knife. It should come out clean when inserted into the centre of the cake. If not, return the cakes to the oven for an additional five minutes and recheck.
10. Once removed from the oven, leave to cool in the tin, then turn out.
11. Allow to cool completely, before filling/covering.

VANILLA BUTTERCREAM

Ingredients

- 250g unsalted butter (at room temperature)
- 500g icing sugar (sieved)
- ¼tsp vanilla extract

Method

1. Beat the butter until soft and pale in colour – this will take around 5–10 minutes with an electric whisk or stand mixer.
2. Add the icing sugar, a little at a time, mixing slowly until it is all incorporated, before adding more icing sugar.
3. Add vanilla extract (or extract flavour of your choice) and mix thoroughly.

Storing Buttercream

Excess buttercream can be stored in an airtight container in the refrigerator for approximately two weeks. However, if you have added any milk, this will decrease the shelf life of your buttercream considerably. If you need to keep the buttercream for more than a few days it is advisable to add cooled boiled water instead of milk.

CHOCOLATE BUTTERCREAM

Ingredients

- 250g unsalted butter (at room temperature)
- 500g icing sugar (sieved)
- ¼tsp vanilla extract
- 75g dark chocolate

Method

1. Beat the butter until soft and pale in colour – this will take around 5–10 minutes with an electric whisk or stand mixer.
2. Add the icing sugar, a little at a time, mixing slowly until it is all incorporated, before adding more icing sugar.
3. Add the vanilla extract and mix thoroughly.
4. Break the chocolate into a microwave-safe bowl, and melt in the microwave in 30-second bursts, stirring between each burst.
5. Allow the chocolate to cool slightly, then add to the buttercream, mixing until completely combined.

If your buttercream is too thick or stiff, you can add a little milk, or cooled boiled water (approximately ½–1 tablespoon at a time), and mix until you reach the desired consistency.

CHOCOLATE GANACHE

Chocolate ganache is often used to crumb coat cakes, as it sets very firm, creating a great surface for covering with sugar paste. This helps you to achieve a smooth finish and sharp edges on your cake, with fewer problems than when using buttercream. It also holds up better during hotter weather conditions, when buttercream tends to become very soft, sometimes putting the stability of your cake at risk.

Ingredients

- Dark chocolate ganache ratio – 2:1 chocolate to double cream (600g chocolate/300g cream)
- Milk chocolate ganache ratio – 3:1 chocolate to double cream (900g chocolate/300g cream)
- White chocolate ganache ratio – 3:1 chocolate to double cream (900g chocolate/300g cream)
- For a luxurious ganache, the best chocolate to use is couverture chocolate. This can be purchased as callet-shaped chips, which melt easily and consistently, making them perfect for ganache made with the hob method. You can also use block chocolate, broken into smaller pieces, which lends itself better to the microwave method of making ganache.

Troubleshooting

Sometimes, making and using chocolate ganache can be quite challenging. Below you will find the solutions to some of the more common problems encountered.

- When using the pan method, if the chocolate is not completely melted by the heated cream, return to the pan over a very low heat and stir until melted and thoroughly combined.
- If your ganache splits when you make it, add a little splash of hot water from the kettle and stir until it comes back together.
- If you overheat your ganache when reheating in the microwave, place it in the refrigerator for a few minutes, then remove and stir. Repeat until it reaches the correct consistency.

Hob Method

1. Place the chocolate into a heatproof bowl.
2. Pour the cream into a pan and heat over a low heat on the hob until just starting to boil.
3. Pour the heated cream over the chocolate, ensuring it is fully covered. Leave to stand for around 30 seconds, and then stir gently until the chocolate is melted and combined with the cream. Once combined, mix thoroughly, until it comes away clean from the sides of the bowl.
4. Pour the ganache into a container with a lid (such as a Tupperware-type tub), and chill in the refrigerator until it thickens and sets.

Microwave Method

1. Place the chocolate into a microwave-proof bowl. Heat in the microwave in bursts of 30 seconds on full power, stirring well in between, until melted. For the quantities above this will normally take four lots of 30-second bursts.
2. Pour the cream into a microwave-proof jug and heat for 1 minute at full power in the microwave.
3. Pour the heated cream over the melted chocolate, ensuring it is fully covered. Leave to stand for around 30 seconds, and then stir gently to combine the two ingredients. Once combined, mix thoroughly, until it comes away clean from the sides of the bowl.
4. Pour the ganache into a container with a lid (such as a Tupperware-type tub), and chill in the refrigerator until it thickens and sets.

Take the ganache out of the fridge a couple of hours before using (or the night before), to come to room temperature. Decant smaller quantities into a microwave-proof bowl and reheat gradually in the microwave until it reaches a spreadable consistency, similar to chocolate spread.

Note: When reheating white chocolate ganache, use the microwave at half power, as it tends to be less stable and can quite easily split.

Stockist Information

Some of the basic tools and materials can be sourced in the UK from high street shops such as Hobbycraft or Lakeland Stores. More specialist items, such as modelling pastes or modelling tools, can be purchased from cake-decorating shops or online retailers.

The following UK-based online retailers supply the products featured in this book.

Sugar and Crumbs Limited
https://www.sugarandcrumbs.co.uk/

Cake Stuff Limited
https://www.cake-stuff.com/

The Cake Decorating Company Limited
https://www.thecakedecoratingcompany.co.uk/

Squires Kitchen Limited
https://www.squires-shop.com/

Vanilla Valley Limited
https://www.thevanillavalley.co.uk/

Conversion Tables

Weight		Liquid measures		Length		Temperature	
Metric	Imperial	Quantity	Metric	Metric	Imperial	Celsius	Fahrenheit
15g	½oz	1 teaspoon	5ml	5mm	¼ inch	110°C	225°F
30g	1oz	1 tablespoon	15ml	1cm	½ inch	120°C	250°F
60g	2oz	¼ cup	60ml	2.5cm	1 inch	140°C	275°F
90g	3oz	⅓ cup	80ml	5cm	2 inches	150°C	300°F
125g	4oz	½ cup	125ml	7cm	3 inches	160°C	325°F
175g	6oz	⅔ cup	160ml	10cm	4 inches	180°C	350°F
250g	8oz	¾cup	180ml	12cm	5 inches	190°C	375°F
300g	10oz	1 cup	250ml	15cm	6 inches	200°C	400°F
375g	12oz	1¼ cups	300ml	18cm	7 inches	220°C	425°F
400g	13oz	1½ cups	375ml	20cm	8 inches	230°C	450°F
425g	14oz	1 ⅔ cups	400ml	23cm	9 inches		
500g	1lb	1 ¾ cups	450ml	25cm	10 inches		
750g	1½lb	2 cups	500ml	28cm	11 inches		
1kg	2lb	2 ½ cups	600ml	30cm	12 inches		
		3 cups	750ml				

Index